DATE DUE

JUL 0 9 2007		
SEP 1 8 2007		
JUL 1 4 2008		
AUG 0 4 2008		
MAY 1 2 2010		
OCT 0 9 2012		
NOV 0 8 2012		

Dream Backyards

Dream
Backyards

From Planters to Decks
Over 30 Projects to Create a
Beautiful Outdoor Living Space

With the Editors of

Reader's
Digest

The Reader's Digest Association, Inc.
Pleasantville, New York/Montreal

A READER'S DIGEST BOOK

FOR THE FAMILY HANDYMAN
Project Editor: Spike Carlsen
Assistant Editor: Mary Flanagan
Graphic Designer: Teresa Marrone
Copy Editor: Dinah Swain Schuster
Indexer: Harriet Hodges
Archive/Finance Manager: Alice Garrett
Design Director: Sara Koehler
Editor in Chief: Ken Collier
Editorial and Production Team: Donna Bierbach, Tom Caspar, Jean Cook, Roxie Filipkowski, Joe Gohman, Jeff Gorton, Shannon Hooge, Shelly Jacobsen, Duane Johnson, Randy Johnson, Tim Johnson, Vern Johnson, Travis Larson, Peggy McDermott, Dave Munkittrick, Lisa Pahl Knecht, Becky Pfluger, Dave Radtke, Judy Rodriguez, Bob Ungar, Gary Wentz, Marcia Wright Roepke
Photography and Illustrations: John Keely, Mike Krivit, Phil Leisenheimer, Don Mannes, Ramon Moreno, Frank Rohrbach, Eugene Thompson, Bill Zuehlke

FOR READER'S DIGEST
U.S. Project Editor: Marilyn Knowlton
Canadian Project Editor: Pamela Johnson
Associate Art Director: George McKeon
Executive Editor, Trade Publishing: Dolores York
Manufacturing Manager: John L. Cassidy
Director of Production: Michael Braunschweiger
President & Publisher, Trade Publishing: Harold Clarke

Library of Congress Cataloging-in-Publication Data

Dream backyards from planters to decks, over 30 projects to create a beautiful outdoor living space / from the editors of the Family handyman magazine.
 p. cm.
 Includes index.
 ISBN: 0-7621-0635-2 (hardcover)
 ISBN-10: 0-7621-0839-8 (paperback)
 ISBN-13: 978-0-7621-0839-8 (paperback)
  1. Garden structures—Design and construction—Amateurs' manuals.
  2. Landscape construction. I. Family handyman. II. Title.
TH4961.D73 2006
690.8—dc22
                                    2005057410

Printed in China

3 5 7 9 10 8 6 4 2 (hardcover)
1 3 5 7 9 10 8 6 4 2 (paperback)

Address any comments about
Dream Backyards to:
The Reader's Digest Association, Inc.
Adult Trade Publishing
Reader's Digest Road
Pleasantville, NY 10570-7000

For more Reader's Digest products and information, visit our website:
www.rd.com (in the United States)
www.readersdigest.ca (in Canada)
www.familyhandyman.com

A Note to Our Readers
All do-it-yourself activities involve a degree of risk. Skills, materials, tools, and site conditions vary widely. Although the editors have made every effort to ensure accuracy, the reader remains responsible for the selection and use of tools, materials, and methods. Always obey local codes and laws, follow manufacturers' operating instructions, and observe safety precautions.

Introduction

When you build an outdoor project, you get double the enjoyment: First when you build it, second when you use it. The "building part" is enjoyable because—if nothing else—you get to work in the great outdoors. The mess stays outside, nothing leaks (hopefully) and it's easier to add your own creative twist to that deck, patio or water garden.

The "using part" is enjoyable because spending time in the backyard naturally slows down the pace and makes life more casual. The computer and remote control (hopefully, even the cell phone!) are out-of-sight, out-of-mind. Something spilled? No problem.

Dream Backyards features dozens of projects—great and small—to help you double your enjoyment. Some projects, like the container water garden on page 40, can be completed in an afternoon by a novice. Others, like the maintenance-free deck on page 48, can consume a month's worth of weekends for even an advanced do-it-yourselfer. But regardless of the project, each is delivered using clear step-by-step photos, illustrations and directions.

Inside each project you'll hear the experienced voice of one of the editors from *The Family Handyman* magazine (pictured here)—each and every one, a former carpenter or tradesperson. This hands-on, real-world experience is what makes each story unique and each project truly buildable.

Even if you're not the hands-on sort, this book is full of ideas you can use while planning. So go to it; have fun, be safe and enjoy yourself.

—The Editors

From left to right: Bruce, Spike, Ken, Jeff, Gary, Dave, Travis (on sawhorse), Duane (kneeling).

Contents

1 Dream Water Gardens

2 Dream Decks

3 Dream Arbors, Trellises & Garden Accents

4 Dream Paths & Patios

5 Dream Gazebos & Sheds

6 Dream Furniture & Planters

7 Dream Fences, Walls & Lighting

CHAPTER

Dream water gardens

Backyard stream & waterfalls

This cascading stream flows into a gravel bed, not a pond, so it stays clean with little maintenance.

—*Kurt Lawton*

W e've all stopped, gazed and listened upon encountering a rippling brook or waterfall—to soak up the serenity that nature provides. But where is that spot when we need it most?

Since you probably can't drive and hike to a tranquil location after a hard day's work, you can use this project to help you re-create these all-too-fleeting moments in your backyard. And you can build your stream in two weekends.

We designed this stream to eliminate the filtering and cleaning maintenance that comes with ponds. The trick to low maintenance is to let nature (layers of gravel and stone) filter the water, using an underground sump basin at the lower end to catch the filtered water before pumping it back up to the top of the stream. All you have to do is occasionally add water to replace what evaporates—and rainfall may handle this task for you.

In this story, we'll show you how to slope the stream, lay the liner and install the pump and the catch basin as well as landscape the stream. We'll help you plan the

Project at a glance

Skill level
Intermediate

Special tools
Drill
Hand tamper
Level
2-wheel ball cart

Approximate cost
$1,200 for project shown

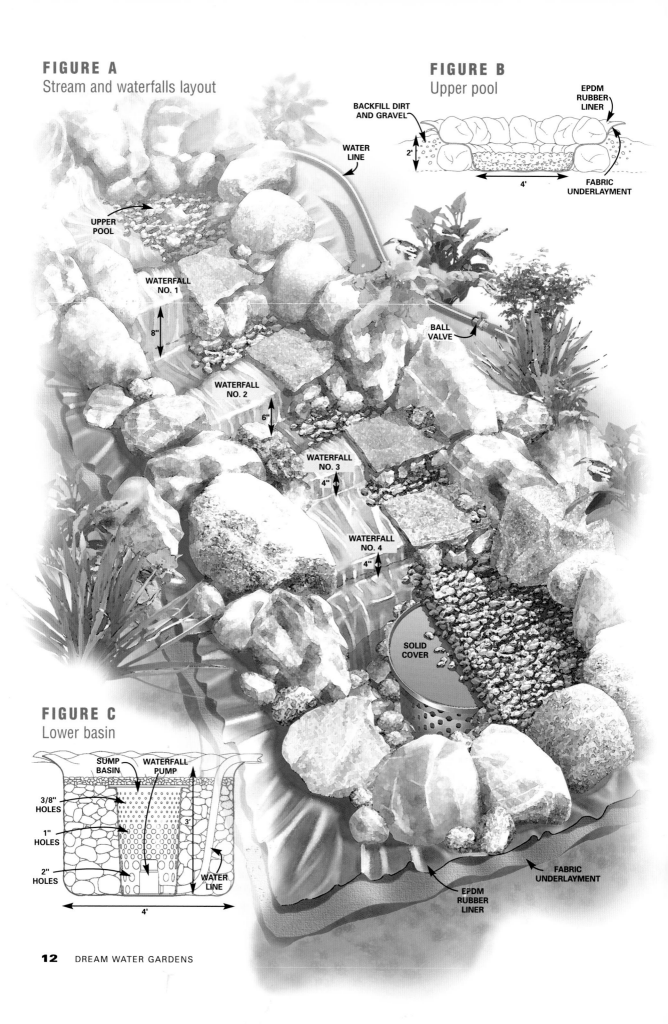

FIGURE A
Stream and waterfalls layout

UPPER
POOL

WATER
LINE

WATERFALL
NO. 1

8"

WATERFALL
NO. 2

6"

WATERFALL
NO. 3

4"

BALL
VALVE

WATERFALL
NO. 4

4"

SOLID
COVER

FABRIC
UNDERLAYMENT

EPDM
RUBBER
LINER

FIGURE B
Upper pool

BACKFILL DIRT
AND GRAVEL

EPDM
RUBBER
LINER

2'

4'

FABRIC
UNDERLAYMENT

FIGURE C
Lower basin

SUMP
BASIN

WATERFALL
PUMP

3/8"
HOLES

1"
HOLES

2"
HOLES

3'

WATER
LINE

4'

MATERIALS LIST

Large waterfall pump

Hose kit and connections

PVC primer and cement

Ball valve and clamps

Sewage basin (18" x 30") and lid

Two hole saw bits (2" and 1")

EPDM pond liner

Underlayment fabric

Waterfall foam sealant

Gravel

Field boulders

Decorative boulders

1 Haul in your boulders and stones and place them around the worksite. Outline the location of your stream with a garden hose, then paint a line around it. Also use paint to mark waterfall locations and ideal spots for large decorative boulders.

ideal location and size of your stream, and tell you how to select liners, pumps and stone. We won't get into kits that are available either on-line or at home centers. We chose to build our system with parts and components that are readily available and less expensive than kits. They'll give you more flexibility to design the stream that best fits your yard.

You can complete this project successfully even if it's your first water feature. But it's heavy work. The only special tools you'll need are a strong wheelbarrow (one with pneumatic tires is best) and a two-wheel ball cart ($18 per day to rent) for moving and placing heavy boulders.

What's my investment?

For the basic materials (pump, plumbing, tools, sealant—see the list above), plan to spend about $300, not including the liners. Add in the underlayment and

liner cost at about $1.20 per sq. ft. of stream. (We used 120 sq. ft.) We purchased all materials from a home center, except for black expanding-foam sealant made for ponds and waterfalls and the EPDM rubber liner, which we bought from a local pond supplies dealer (see Resources, p. 252). The company guarantees its liners; other suppliers may void the guarantee once you trim the liner to size.

The largest additional cost of the project is the stone. The amount of stone and gravel will depend on your stream design. Take your plan (see Figure A) to the stone and gravel retailer to get help with estimates. All told, our "deluxe" stream used 8 tons of stone and gravel, which came to $725, plus tax and delivery. One could easily reduce stone costs to $350 for this 15-ft. stream with fewer specialty boulders. You could save even more if you dig the entire stream into the ground rather than building the upper section higher.

2 Dig the hole for the lower basin so it sits below the stream bed. Place boulders to build up the sides of the upper pool and upper portion of the stream, which are above the original grade (Figure A). Pack dirt and gravel to hold stones in place.

3 Drill holes in the basin using three different size hole saw bits (see Figure C). Prime, cement and attach the hose adapter to the pump.

Plan by ear

Sit in a favorite spot and visualize where a stream with waterfalls would fit into your landscape—perhaps near a patio or deck. Planning elements to consider:

Foundation. If your soil is easy to dig, then excavate the entire project. If digging is difficult, build your stream above ground with stones for the base.

Slope. Very little slope is needed (minimum 2 in. drop per 10 ft. of stream). For faster-moving water or taller waterfalls, make the grade steeper (which also adds more sound).

Size. Plan your stream size first to determine how much water the lower basin and upper pool must hold when the pump is off. Plan on 5 gallons per linear foot of flowing stream (2-1/2 ft.

wide x 3 in. deep). Our lower basin (40 gallons) and upper pool (240 gallons) easily held our 75-gallon stream capacity.

Sound. For a babbling brook sound, use a waterfall height of 2 to 4 in. To drown out street noise, use 10-in. and greater waterfall drops. More waterfalls equals more noise.

Location. Waterfalls should be visible from your favorite deck, patio or inside-the-home chair. Consider a location near the bedroom if you like the sound of running water at night; you can always turn it off if it's too loud or distracting. Make sure your pump location (lower basin) is close to an electrical source and that you can reach the stream with a garden hose to add water as needed.

For our site, we wrapped an S-shaped stream next to a ground-

---

Buy Smart

Submersible pumps are rated by gph (gallons per hour) at a specific discharge height (known as head or lift). To calculate the gph you need, figure 150 gph for each inch of your widest waterfall. Next, to figure the head/lift you need, calculate the distance your water line travels from the pump to the upper pool (measure vertical and horizontal; 10 ft. of horizontal distance = 1 ft. of vertical rise). Look for a high-quality pump (bronze, brass or stainless steel; not a cheap sump pump) that can exceed the gph and lift you need.

4 Lay the fabric underlayment and rubber liner in the basin hole, then add the pump basin with pump. Attach the hose. Then add stone layers (Figure C) and the basin lid.

5 Carve a winding streambed 6 to 8 in. deep, 2 to 3-1/2 ft. wide. Dig the channel so it stair-steps down at waterfall No. 3, and dig 3- to 4-in. deep pools below waterfalls No. 2 and 3 (Figure A).

level deck built into an existing perennial garden. We varied the height of the four waterfalls and the width of the stream to give it a more natural look and sound. Plus we added a ball valve to the return water line so we could speed or slow the flow rate and control the sound level.

Order stone

When you start your stone search, look under "Rock," "Quarries" or "Sand & Gravel" in the Yellow Pages. Call to check prices and types of stone available. Go visit dealers to get exactly what you want, plus you can select specific colorful accent boulders and flat stones for the waterfalls—then have it all delivered (for a $100 to $200 fee). Some quarries will even bag the stone by type and size (for a fee), and these palleted bags take up less space on a driveway, as opposed to piles of gravel and boulders.

For gravel (3/4-in. to 2-in. stones), figure you'll need

Plan Smart

Although these pools are shallow, they can be a drowning hazard for small children. Check with your local building department for local regulations. And be watchful of toddlers.

1/2 ton per 10 ft. of stream, plus we used 1 to 1-1/2 tons for the upper pool and lower basin. For basic field boulders (6 in. to 24 in.) to line the stream banks, figure 3/4 ton per 10 ft. of stream. Add 1-1/2 to 2 tons more of larger 12-in. to 24-in. boulders for the upper pool and lower basin. Because we built the top half of the stream above ground, we used 3-1/2 tons of extra boulders.

If you want specialty colorful accent boulders, expect to pay premium prices—about $200 to $300 per ton. The flat waterfall stones cost about $3 per sq. ft. Avoid limestone, as it can encourage algae growth.

Map the stream and start digging

After all the stone and gravel arrive, map out your design and mark it with spray paint (Photo 1).

We built the upper half of the stream and two waterfalls above the ground, then carved the lower half of this

6 Pack dirt and gravel around the border stones to build waterfalls No. 1 and 2 above the existing grade. Level the rows. Inspect the entire streambed and remove anything sharp. Tamp down the entire stream, banks and upper pool area.

Labels in photo: UPPER POOL / RUBBER LINER / WATERFALL NO. 1 / WATERFALL NO. 2 / SHALLOW POOL / WATERFALL NO. 3 / SHALLOW POOL / BORDER STONES

15-ft. stream out of the soil (Figure A). Pick whichever technique works with your soil and go with it. Either way, keep the ibuprofen handy to soothe those sore lifting and digging muscles!

Next, dig the lower basin for the sump basin and surrounding stone and gravel. Dig a square hole at least 2 ft. wider than the basin diameter and 6 in. deeper than the height. It should be at least a foot wider than the stream.

Simultaneously, build a ring of stone for the upper pool foundation and the stream banks (Photo 2). Place 12-in. tall stones flat side up (if possible) so the next layer of stone will fit more securely on top (Figure B). Use a rubber mallet to pack dirt and gravel tightly around the stones to hold them in place.

Complete the lower basin first

Use a 2-in. hole saw bit and drill holes every 4 in. in the bottom third of the pump basin (Figure C and Photo 3). Repeat the process with a 1-in. hole saw bit for the middle third, then use a 3/8-in. bit for the top third.

Remove sharp objects from the bottom of the basin, then lay in the underlayment and liner. Calculate the size carefully and cut the underlayment first. Then cut and fit the liner so it is tucked in all corners and extends about 2 ft. out of the hole in all directions. With the pump basin in place, insert the pump, connect the water line and lay it in place to ensure it will reach the top of the upper pool. Add layers of stone around the basin and top with the lid (Figure C and Photo 4).

Plan Smart

A few days before you plan to dig for your stream, call (888) 258-0808 to have underground utilities in the area located and marked.

7 Lay the underlayment and a rubber liner into the streambed. Leave 3 to 4 in. of slack in the liner at the base of the waterfalls, extend about 2 ft. up each bank and overlap the basin liner by 2 ft. Place decorative boulders at waterfall locations.

8 Lay the underlayment and liner over the upper pool, overlapping the built-up boulder edges. Overlap the lower liner by about 2 ft. Backfill stream edging boulders for stability.

Dig out (or build) a long staircase

First, at each waterfall location, dig down to the approximate depth of the drop you desire or build up the fall if you're working above grade. This gives you a streambed depth target. Now move to the bottom of the stream and carve a 2 to 3-1/2 ft. wide streambed 6 to 8 in. deep, sloping upward as you dig upstream to meet that streambed depth target at each waterfall (Photo 5). Then dig out shallow pools below waterfalls as needed (Figure A) to slow the water flow.

Since we built above ground for the upper section of the stream, we next added a level row of stones for waterfalls No. 1 and 2 (Photo 6). Pick the height you desire. Use 6-in. tall stones to frame the banks. Also finish compacting a gravel and dirt mixture to the inside and outside of the upper pool stones. Then tamp down the upper pool area and the streambed.

Handy Hints®

Pick stones with fractures and broken edges to place under waterfalls for more water sound and movement.

Lay the liner and position waterfall stones

Position the fabric underlayment and liner to extend from the lower basin to the upper pool, with slack at the base of each waterfall, because placing boulders can stretch and rip a tight liner (Photo 7). Place decorative boulders at the side of each waterfall, and add an extra piece of rubber liner underneath each heavy stone to protect the base liner.

For stable, above-ground stream edges, backfill the edging stones with a gravel and dirt mixture and compact it (Photo 8). Next, lay the final piece of underlayment and liner in the upper pool so it tucks in at all corners and extends 2 ft. out in all directions. There's no need to tape the liners to each other; just make sure the top liner overlaps the liner underneath it by at least 1-1/2 to 2 ft. Then add the top layer of stones around the upper pool.

9 Set decorative boulders at each side of waterfalls No. 1 and 2. Then coat the bottom of the flat spill stones with foam sealant so they adhere to the liner. Wedge stones into cracks between the spill stones and the sides of the stream bank.

10 Force gravel along all sides and under spill stones, then apply foam sealant in the gaps so water flows only over the top of all spill stones.

Add spill stones and foam the gaps

Once you place the decorative boulders at the waterfall locations, place all the flat spill stones. Apply black expanding foam sealant, designed for ponds and waterfalls, to the underside to adhere them to the rubber liner. Now fill all gaps with stones to force water to go only over the waterfall (Photo 9). Then apply foam sealant to all sides and to the underneath of each spill stone to create a good seal (Photo 10).

> # Work Smart
>
> If you live in a freezing climate, make sure the pump and hose are easy to blow out or remove.

After the foam has dried for 30 minutes, take your garden hose and run water down the stream. Look for any water trails (leaks) along the spill stone edges and underneath. Fill any leaks with more foam and repeat until all water goes over the top of the spill stones.

Add gravel and clean the stream

The final construction step is to place steppingstones in the middle of the stream to make it inviting for people, birds and pets. Then carefully layer in gravel to cover any exposed liner (Photo 11).

Spray down the entire stream area with a garden hose nozzle until the water level rises above the gravel in the bottom basin. Now power up the pump and direct the pump hose away from the stream. Keep washing down the stream and rock until the water from the pump hose runs clear. Then insert the pump hose into the upper pool (make sure it is hidden), and finish your stream by trimming and covering any rubber liner that shows (Photo 12).

Now it's time to take that favorite seat, with a cold beverage in hand, and relax to the soothing sounds of your new stream.

GRAVEL FOR STREAM BED

WATERFALL NO. 3

STONES TO HIDE RUBBER LINER

11 Add a top layer of small boulders to complete the upper pool and stream bed. Place stepping-stones in the middle of the stream and the stones below the waterfalls. Cover the rest of the stream bed liner with gravel.

12 Fill the bottom basin with water and plug in the pump. Spray down all stones and the stream until the water from the pump runs clear. Place the hose from the pump into the upper pool. Trim off remaining exposed liner and adjust stream flow by moving rocks and adjusting the ball valve.

Water wicking

Soil, sand or plants that cover the edge of the liner can draw water up and over the liner. The evidence of this wicking is wet soil around the pond.

The solution is to remove plants, soil and sand from the water's edge. Be careful not to damage the liner as you dig. Rocks and gravel won't wick out water, but as a preventive measure, occasionally clean out the sand and soil that washes into the spaces between the rocks that surround the pond. If you prefer to let plants spread over the liner's edge and into the water, you'll just have to live with a pond that frequently needs water added.

SOIL DRAWS WATER FROM POND

Preformed liner-type pond

Preformed shells and ready-to-go pumps make pond building simple. Moving five tons of stone—well, that's another matter!

—*Spike Carlsen*

Whether it's a stream in the middle of the woods or a fountain in the heart of downtown, few things rival the sight and sound of moving water. It's relaxing, mesmerizing, contemplative. Well, you don't have to pack up the family and drive for hours for that experience. You can create your own water garden, complete with babbling brook, in your own backyard.

We'll show you how to create a water garden—without spending a fortune or your entire summer doing it. Preformed shells, rubber liners and off-the-shelf pumps and filters put the project's costs and skill requirements within easy reach of any do-it-yourselfer. You'll put in your share of sweat equity busting sod and hauling stone. But when you're done, you'll have a landscape feature to enjoy for years. Here's the story.

Project at a glance

Skill level
Beginner to intermediate

Special tools
Level
Shovel
Wheelbarrow

Approximate cost
$1,500 for project shown

Water gardens—no two are the same

Since every yard and homeowner is different, every water garden is unique. Yours can be large or small, simple or complex.

There are two basic ways to create a water garden. The first is to use a flexible rubber-like liner made of EPDM, the same material used for flat commercial roofs. Using this method, you dig the shape and size pond you want, then line the hole with a sheet of this heavy-duty material. Homeowners who want to "dive into" water gardening in a big way choose this flexible liner; they can create large, deep ponds that can hold many—and many varieties of—fish and plants. (For information on building this type of pond, see p. 30.)

We elected to go the other route by using preformed rigid shells or liners. (Actually, we joined two shells with a small stream made from the flexible liner mentioned above.) The shells we used are constructed of heavy-duty polyethylene, but you can also get ones made from fiberglass and other materials. Most shells have built-in ledges for plants and don't require as much planning and ground preparation as the flexible liners. Shells do limit your design to the shapes available, but linking several together increases your options. For a

water garden of small to moderate size, shells offer a lot of convenience.

Preformed shells come in a wide variety of shapes and sizes. Our garden center stocked a dozen shells ranging in size from a 4-gallon mini pond to the 210-gallon butterfly-shaped shell we used. The garden center could special-order dozens of other shells as well. You can buy shells with or without spillways, the molded lips that allow water to flow from one pond to another. You can even buy preformed streams and waterfalls for connecting a series of ponds. You can install a single pond, cascade a series of ponds down a hillside, plunk one in the middle of a patio or use one as a focus for a small retreat in a corner of your backyard.

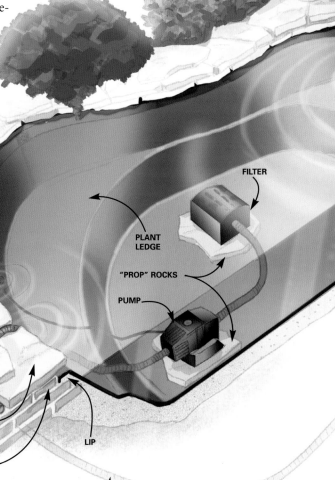

FILTER

PLANT LEDGE

"PROP" ROCKS

PUMP

TO GFCI-PROTECTED OUTLET

CAPSTONE

SUPPORT STONE

LIP

CIRCULATING HOSE

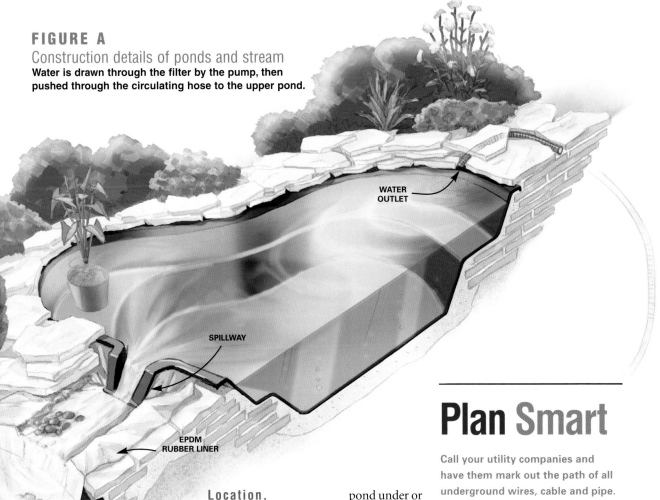

FIGURE A
Construction details of ponds and stream
Water is drawn through the filter by the pump, then
pushed through the circulating hose to the upper pond.

WATER
OUTLET

SPILLWAY

EPDM
RUBBER LINER

PREFORMED
SHELL

COARSE
SAND

Plan Smart

Location, location, location

We elected to nestle our water garden into an existing flower bed about 20 ft. from the house. But remember, a water garden is a living thing—it makes noise, attracts wildlife and requires upkeep. Locate it where you can best appreciate it. And remember that you have neighbors, too.

Our experts gave us a few helpful tips on positioning water gardens:

1. Select a location that receives four hours or more of direct sun a day if you plan on including aquatic plants.

2. Make certain the area has good drainage. Locate the pond away from the bottom of steep slopes so debris, fertilizers and pesticides don't run into your pond. If you're connecting two ponds with a stream like we did, make sure you have an adequate slope. Position your pond so runoff flows downhill and away from any houses.

3. A lot of literature warns against positioning your pond under or near trees. But if you wind up situating the pond in a treed area, expect to spend more time plucking out leaves, needles and branches before they decompose. And watch out for roots as you dig.

4. Think safety. Building codes in most areas are nebulous about water gardens. Most communities don't require barriers or fences, but ask before you dig in. Otherwise, let common sense rule. If there are free-range toddlers in the neighborhood, consider building a barrier around your yard or pond.

Remember, moving water isn't just for looks; it keeps the water filtered and aerated and helps prevent stagnation. If you install a single pond, include a pump, filter and fountain to keep the water circulating and fresh.

1 Position and adjust the preformed liners or shells until you find a design that fits the site and your tastes. Keep the shells away from steep downhill slopes where debris and lawn chemicals could run into them.

2 Dig a hole 6 in. wider and 2 in. deeper than the pre-formed liner. Mimic the shape and depth of the shell, including the ledges. Test-fit the shell frequently to ensure a solid fit.

Buy Smart

If you want a long-lasting water garden, keep these buying tips in mind:

■ Some pond shells are flimsy and more likely to flex under the pressure of heavy backfill or freezing and expanding soil. Do some comparison shopping before you buy.

■ Buy the thickest EPDM rubber liner you can find. It commonly comes in 40-mil and heavier-duty 60-mil thicknesses.

■ Invest in heavy-duty hose for circulating the water. Once it's buried, it's hard to make repairs. The corrugated version we found was quite crush resistant.

■ Pump size is based on the desired flow rate, plus the height and distance it needs to push the water. Read the manufacturer's guidelines; when in doubt, opt for the larger pump.

■ Order excess flagstone. You'll be better off finding shapes that fit than doing a lot of cutting. You can use any leftover material to build a path or a garden border.

Install the pond shells

Before making any purchases, get copies of the literature showing the size and shape of the shells your supplier has available. Select a few models, then use a garden hose to create a rough footprint of where they'd go and how they'd connect. We settled on a 210-gallon "Butterfly" pond for the lower pond and a 165-gallon pond with spillway. (See Resources, p. 252, for more information.)

Once you've obtained your shells, position them (Photo 1), then use a shovel to trench an outline 6 in. larger than the ponds. Remove the shells and dig (Photo 2) the hole for the lower pond. You need to create a hole that will support the bottom of the shell as well as the ledges. Lower the shell into the hole frequently to check the depth, shape and position of shell and ledges. Dig the hole about 2 in. deeper than the intended final elevation because the sand base you'll spread next will raise it back up (Figure A). Make certain the lip of the shell will be at least 2 in. above the surrounding soil or else dirt and muddy rainwater may flow in.

Next spread and level a 2-in. layer of coarse sand over

3 Spread a layer of coarse sand to protect the bottom of the liner and the ledges from sharp rocks. Sand also makes the leveling process easier.

COARSE SAND

4 Level the liner in every direction. Make certain the bottom and ledges are resting solidly on sand. Use a level on a long, straight 2x4 to level lengthwise.

LEDGE

RUN WATER IN POND WHILE BACKFILLING

COMPACT SAND AND SOIL AROUND LINER

5 Backfill around the liner with a 50/50 mix of sand and soil at the same rate water is filling it. Compact the soil and sand as you place it. Fully support the ledges when the backfill reaches that level.

TUCK CORRUGATED HOSE UNDER LIP ON LINER

6 Tuck the hose connecting the upper and lower ponds under the lip of the shell. Continue to extend and protect the hose from kinks and pinches as you do the stonework around both ponds.

CAPSTONES OVERHANG
LIP ON LINER

SUPPORT STONES
LEVEL WITH LIP
OF LINER

7 Position the upper liner, again first digging an oversize hole, then placing it on a layer of sand to protect it. Make sure to provide a sufficient change in elevation so there's a strong flow from upper to lower pond.

8 Install the flagstone. Set the first support layer of stone level with the lip of the liner. Overhang the second "cap" layer of stone to cover and disguise the lip of the liner.

the bottom of the hole (Photo 3). Set the shell in place and check everything out. Does the sand fully support the bottom? Is the shell level (Photo 4) in every direction? Is the lip at least 2 in. above the surrounding soil? Are the edges of any ledges supported? If the answer to all these questions is "yes," you can start backfilling the pond.

Fill the pond with 2 to 3 in. of water, then check the shell for level again. This is critical; the water in your pond will be level, so if the shell is tilted, the water line will show it! Pack a mixture of half sand and half soil around the base of the pond as you fill it with more water (Photo 5). Be sure to pack sand under the ledges before the water reaches them; they're flimsy and need support.

Once we had the lower pond backfilled within about 8 in. of the top, we tucked the corrugated hose under the lip of the shell (Photo 6). This hose is used to recirculate

Work Smart

Use the level of the water in the shell as a guide for fine-tuning the height of the ledges; the ledges are flexible enough to lift or lower an inch or so to maintain a level perimeter.

water from the pump in the lower pond to the "mouth" at the far end of the upper pond.

Dig the hole for the upper shell, then level it and line it with sand as you did the lower shell. Make sure you have an adequate height difference (Photo 7) for your falls and stream. If you're building on a slope, you may be able to bury the entire upper shell. Our site was flatter, so we used stone, sand and soil to partially build up around the shell.

Build up the edges with stone

You can disguise the lip of your liner with overhanging plants, stone or a combination of both. We primarily used stacked flagstone.

Spread a 1- to 2-in. layer of sand around the lower pond, then set a layer of flagstone so the upper surface is level with the lip of the shell (Photo 8). This allows you to cantilever the second layer of "capstones" over the lip of the pond without them weighing directly on the lip.

PLANTER

BUILD UP EDGES
OF SPILLWAY

SUPPORT
OVERHANGING
PARTS OF LINER

9 Continue to add stone to support the ledges of the upper pond. Create the walls and base of the canal leading to the lower pond at the same time. The planter area creates a stable surround as well as a more natural-looking transition between upper and lower ponds.

CANAL
WALL

ESTABLISH
DOWNHILL SLOPE
FROM SPILLWAY TO
LOWER POND

10 Spread a layer of sand in the stone canal, sloping it toward the lower pond. Continue packing and leveling the sand to create a solid "stream bed."

There's no exact science to the stonework part of this project. Use the ugliest, most irregular stones for the first support layer, since you won't see them anyway. Select and install capstones that conform to the shape of the pond edge. We built and rebuilt the stone layers around the bottom pond several times before we found a pattern we liked.

Once you have the lower pond surrounded with stone, build your way up and around the upper pond. Start with a wide stone base around the upper pond. This will allow you to lay a slightly sloped, stable wall as you build up to the lip. Solidly support the ledges of the pond with rock and soil when you reach them. We created a small rock planter (Photo 9) that stepped up to the upper pond and helped make a more natural-looking transition.

While you're doing the stonework around the upper pond, snake the free end of the corrugated hose (Photo 6) to the far end of the upper pond. Bury it and cover it within the rocks, but don't pinch it. Extend the free end of the hose so it discharges into the far end of the upper pond, then secure and disguise the hose with cap rocks.

Build a lazy river

We created a small stream from the spillway of the upper pond to the lower pond. We began by building a small canal out of stone (Photo 10), then sloped a layer of sand across the bottom. We then laid the rubber liner into the canal (Photo 11), draped the excess liner up and over the walls of the canal, then added another layer of stone to disguise it. Make sure the canal is deep enough to prevent water from escaping.

Support the liner and curve it up and behind the spillway to contain the water. Make certain the other end drapes well into the lower pond. Use water from a garden hose to test the slope and flow of your little river as you build it. Again, don't expect to get everything right the first time. Building with irregular stone isn't the same as building with flat, square wood. Use small stone chips to shim and stabilize larger stones as you work.

Once you're satisfied with the design and watertightness of your stream, use pond foam (a black, weather-resistant expanding foam available through your pond dealer) to secure thin stone to the top and face of the spillway to disguise it (Photo 12). We added smooth

60-MIL EPDM LINER

POND FOAM

FILTER

PUMP

11 Lay the rubber liner in place, draping it over the sides of the canal wall and into the lower pond. Tuck the liner up and behind the upper spillway. Use water from a garden hose to test flow and water-tightness as you work.

12 Using special pond foam, attach thin layers of stone to conceal the plastic spillway. Complete the stonework around the upper pond.

13 Connect the filter, pump and hose. Place the lower pond pump and the upper pond inlet hose as far from each other as possible. This will help ensure a more thorough water filtration and minimize stagnation. Keep a careful eye on the water level for several days to make sure there are no leaks or clogs.

stones to the bottom of the stream to hide the liner and create a more natural-looking flow.

Continue adding stone up and around the upper pond and upper pond lip.

Pumps, fountains and wildlife

If your ponds are full of sand, rock bits and other construction debris, siphon, pump or use a big wet-dry vacuum to remove the water and refill the ponds with fresh water.

Connect the filter and pump to your water circulating line so the water is drawn through the filter before it reaches the pump (Photo 13). We added a T-fitting to our pump so we could circulate water to the upper pond and to a small statue beside the lower pond.

Set the filter on a few small rocks so it doesn't rest directly on the bottom where it's more likely to become clogged with debris. Plug in your pump, then keep an eye on water levels and flow to make sure everything is functioning properly and there are no leaks. Pay attention to the pump and filter literature for maintenance information. Keep the upper end of the hose out of the upper

Work Smart

While we were photographing this project, someone stood on a sharp rock in the spillway, creating a pinhole tear in the liner. We didn't discover this slow leak until several days later. The pump in the lower pond kept circulating the water, but hour by hour, water leaked through this small cut, and less water was making its way back to the lower pond. Eventually it nearly went dry. If we hadn't caught it, we would have burned out the pump and most likely killed the flowers and fish. Water loss from even dinky leaks or splashes adds up fast.

pond to prevent a possible siphoning effect.

Maintaining clean water and establishing aquatic plants and fish are complex topics we won't even pretend to address here. Suffice it to say, understanding the dynamics of your pond and doing proper maintenance will make the difference between a pond you'll want to linger around for hours and one you'll want to fill in with dirt and plant with petunias in a few years.

Fixing pond leaks: A punctured liner

A hole in the liner is the toughest problem to locate. Begin your investigation by letting the water level drop. The draining will stop at the level of the leak. (This can take days.) This gives you only the level of the leak, not an exact location. You'll still have to move rocks and carefully inspect the liner all around the water line. If the leaking stops at the level where the water flows over a waterfall or into a stream, suspect a hole in the stream liner or waterfall basin.

Repairing a puncture is as easy as fixing a bicycle inner tube. A repair kit costs about $10 at garden centers and other pond supply dealers. Some kits are meant for all liners; others work only with specific types. If you don't know whether your liner is made from vinyl or a synthetic rubber like EPDM, cut off a small piece and take it with you to the garden center, where you can find out which patching materials to use.

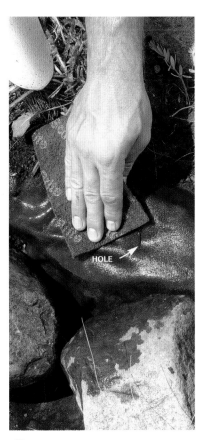

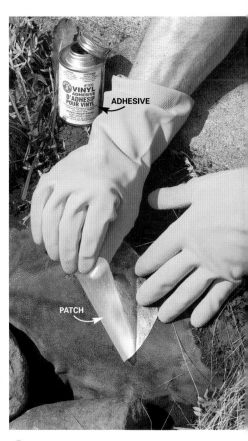

1 Let the water level stabilize, then examine the liner around the water's edge. When you find the hole, drain more water so you can make the repair.

2 Scrub the repair area with a scouring pad, then let it dry. The area has to be clean and dry for the patch to adhere well.

3 Apply repair adhesive and then the patching material. Let it set according to the repair kit directions.

Do-it-yourself water garden

Put a little piece of paradise right in your own backyard.

—*Jeff Timm*

There's something soothing about the scent, sound and sight of water, something that washes away stress and strain. While you can't stop by the French Riviera or Walden Pond after a hectic day of work, you can have a private oasis waiting for you at home, complete with gurgling water and colorful fish.

We'll walk you through the basic steps for building a backyard pond. Roll up your sleeves—it's mostly muscle work. There's no need for precise measurements, no blueprint to follow and no deadlines. Working like beavers, you and anyone else with a strong back could probably finish a large pond in a couple of weekends. But that would take the fun out of it. Give yourself plenty of time and creating a pond will be almost as relaxing as sitting beside it.

Project at a glance

Skill level
Intermediate

Special tools
Level
Shovel

Approximate cost
$1,500 for project shown

It's the hardware, not the size, that affects costs

You can install a basic 10 x 16-ft. pond with a good-quality liner and high-efficiency pump, complete with rocks and gravel, for less than $1,000. For an additional $500, you can add the convenience of a filtration system, which

1 Lay out a garden hose to establish approximate pond borders, adjusting and readjusting until you're satisfied with the shape of the pond. Then dig out the pond bed, terracing both shallow and deeper areas for plants. Exposed rocks, tree roots and anything else that might puncture the liner must be removed from the hole.

2 Establish the pond borders by setting a level on a board long enough to span the hole. Make the banks level by building up low spots or cutting down high spots.

will reduce your weekly maintenance chores. Larger ponds won't cost a whole lot more; you've already made most of your investment in pumps and filters.

Careful planning prevents a slew of trouble later on

Digging out a pond hole is grunt work, not an intellectual endeavor. Still, it requires some planning. Before you grab your shovel, roughly map out the shape, desired plant shelves (Photo 2) and the pump and waterfall locations. Here are some more key considerations:

■ Select a location where you can readily enjoy your pond, close to a patio or visible from a window. Don't stick your pond in the back corner of your yard where only the squirrels will enjoy it.

■ You can locate your pond in most any area of your yard as long as it doesn't receive runoff from rainfall. You don't want lawn and garden chemicals washing into your pond. As a rule, the more sun the better, but don't discount a shadier spot. Just stay away from the area inside the canopy of your trees, the "drip line." If you locate your pond near trees, be prepared to clean leaves from

Work Smart

Before you start digging, lay on the ground the water circulation pipe that goes from the pump to the waterfall. Throw the excavated soil on top of it. This will save you the work of digging a trench to bury the pipe.

the pond more often. Most water plants prefer sun, but some can survive in shade. Choose hardier plants and fertilize more often if you select a shaded site.

■ A toddler can drown in the smallest pond, so some building codes require fences around ponds 18 in. deep and deeper. Call your local Department of Inspections, explain that you're building a water garden (not a swimming pool) and ask what rules apply. But if you have young kids, consider installing a fence around it anyway. Be sure to choose a fence that cannot be climbed.

■ **MANDATORY:** Before you dig, call your utility company and ask to have someone come out and mark your property for buried utilities. Utility companies usually won't mark "private" lines; that is, lines added for convenience, such as a power line from a house to the garage or a gas line to an outdoor grill. Turn off the power or gas to these areas if you suspect a line is in the vicinity of your digging.

■ Oversize your pond if possible. Once you stock it with fish and plants, you'll be surprised how much smaller it'll look. Besides, a large pond is often easier to take care of than a small one. (Controlling algae is often easier with a large pond.) The additional expense is minimal. A 10 x 16-ft. size is a good starting point.

■ Water circulation is important, so position the pump as far as possible from the water inlet (waterfall, stream or fountain).

■ Digging even a small pond is a big job. Plan plenty of breaks or enlist the neighborhood teenagers to help you out for a day.

■ To power the pump, you'll need an outdoor electrical outlet (Figure A). Have a licensed electrician install a GFCI-protected outlet.

Keep it simple—choose a flexible liner

We're using a flexible liner made of a synthetic rubber called EPDM (ethylene propylene diene monomer). The liner is economical, durable and easy to install. You can create almost any shape, and it adapts well to most site conditions.

Flexible plastic liners are also available. They're made of PVC (polyvinyl chloride) and HDPE (high-density polyethylenes). These liners aren't as flexible as rubber liners. Plastic liners are often used on large holding ponds when economy is a concern and flexibility is not. The preformed liners found at many home and garden centers are less desirable. These are essentially large plastic or fiberglass tubs. At first glance, these seem easier to install, but this usually isn't the case. Preformed liners can be difficult to handle and level and, when lined with rocks and boulders, aren't as forgiving as flexible ones.

Guidelines for purchasing a liner

■ Most professionals use a 45-mil EPDM liner. (A mil is a thousandth of an inch.) It's strong, yet flexible enough to handle easily (Photo 5).

■ If you plan to have fish, make sure your liner is stamped "fish-safe." Roofers often use a type of EPDM that's been treated with chemicals that can harm fish.

■ Purchase your liner in one single sheet, large enough

FIGURE A
Pond features

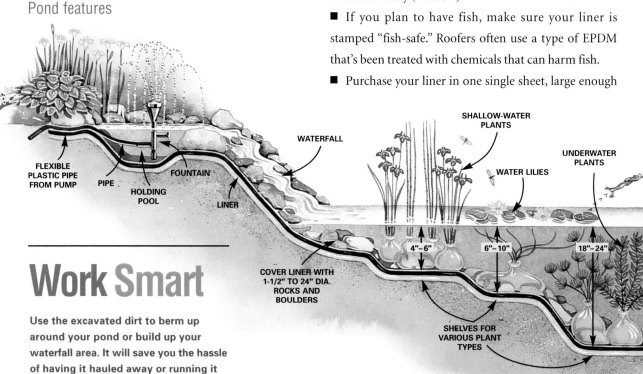

FLEXIBLE PLASTIC PIPE FROM PUMP

PIPE

HOLDING POOL

FOUNTAIN

LINER

WATERFALL

COVER LINER WITH 1-1/2" TO 24" DIA. ROCKS AND BOULDERS

SHALLOW-WATER PLANTS

WATER LILIES

UNDERWATER PLANTS

4"–6"

6"–10"

18"–24"

SHELVES FOR VARIOUS PLANT TYPES

3 Measure the depth of the hole and plant shelves, keeping in mind that the water level will be a few inches below the banks of the pond. Fish require a section at least 18 in. deep.

4 Line the pond bed with a 1/2-in. layer of newspapers. The newspaper helps prevent liner punctures and will eventually decompose and form a clay-like layer. You can also use the special pond underlayment that's available at your pond supply dealer.

to cover the entire pond bottom and sides. Liners are commonly cut and sold from 100-ft. rolls with 10- to 20-ft. widths; you can custom-order liners up to 45 ft. wide. Liners can be spliced if necessary, but it involves more work and provides an opportunity for a leak. If your waterfall or stream requires extra length, use a separate piece of liner. You don't need to glue the two liners together as long as the stream or waterfall liner is higher than the water level of the pond.

■ Calculate the dimensions of the liner by measuring the maximum length and the maximum width of your

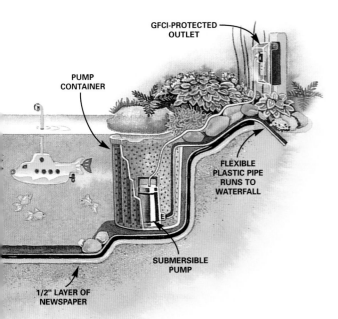

pond, then add three times the depth measurement to each dimension. Better a bit big than a bit small.

Make your pond hospitable to plants and fish

A pond is just a hole filled with water. Add plants and it becomes a water garden. Add fish and your pond comes alive. You've got an entire aquatic ecosystem right in your backyard. Here are a few things to keep in mind when planning for plants and fish.

■ Before adding plants or fish to your newly filled pond, wait a week for the chemicals in the tap water to neutralize. To accelerate the process, you can add a dechlorinator to the water. Consult your water garden supplier for more information on this chemical.

■ Anchor plants in pots or baskets designed for aquatic plants. A third option is to place the roots of each plant in "root balls," a mix of gravel and soil in nylon stockings tied with soldering wire (Figure A). Root balls are cheaper than pots or baskets and are easier to move. They also keep fish from disturbing the soil.

Mistake: Don't use standard potting soil in your pond. The high nutrient content encourages algae growth. Ordinary garden soil is just fine.

■ If you plan to stock your pond with fish, part of it must be at least 18 in. deep.

Simplify maintenance with a skimmer and filter

Keeping your pond clean isn't difficult; once you get it down, it'll be as routine as taking a bath. Your pond has two sources of pollution: debris that falls or blows into the water and algae. Pick up leaves and other wind-blown debris with a fine-mesh net. The type used for skimming swimming pools works great. Skim daily to prevent the material from sinking to the bottom, decomposing and creating sludge.

Fine-mesh net

An easier but more expensive way to clean out this debris is with an automatic skimmer system, kind of a dishwasher for your pond. Once you have one, you can't imagine pond life without it. A skimmer system works off the inflow of your pump. Water is drawn through a tub containing a mesh bag that collects leaves, paper and other debris. The system bags it for you—all you have to do is empty the bag about once a week. The frequency will depend on the time of year, the amount of wind and the number of trees in your area.

It's easiest to install a skimmer system when you build

Skimmer and filter system

- PIPE TO WATER INLET (WATERFALL)
- OVERFLOW PIPE IF WATER GETS TOO HIGH
- PUMP ASSEMBLY
- FILTER
- POND LINER
- SKIMMER INLET DRAWS WATER INTO CONTAINER
- FAKE ROCK LID HIDES SKIMMER

SKIMMER CONTAINER BURIED IN SOIL OUTSIDE POND

your pond. If you decide to add it later, you'll have to drain your pond, dig a hole and readjust the liner.

The second threat to a clean pond is algae, microscopic plants that'll turn your pond green. A small amount of algae is beneficial, but large amounts can

have your pond looking like the swamp monster scene from Scooby-Doo.

Keep algae at bay by limiting nutrients and sunlight. Here are some tips to do this:

- Shade the surface of the pond with water plants such as lilies. A good rule of thumb is to cover one-third of the surface with plants.
- Install a variety of plants. Plants consume nutrients from fish waste and decomposing matter in your pond, stealing the food algae need to live.
- Keep debris out of the water. As debris decomposes, it releases nutrients into the water.
- Don't overstock your pond with fish. Too many fish will release more nutrients than the plants and bacteria can consume, leaving food for algae.
- Don't overfeed your fish. Food not consumed by the fish provides nutrients for algae.
- As a further measure, biological and mechanical filters are available from your pond supplier. They take a lot of guesswork out of keeping a balanced, clean and clear pond.

Once you establish a biological balance in your pond, maintenance is minimal. A thorough annual cleaning (draining and rinsing out the pond) and periodic maintenance (keeping debris out) are all that's required. Your pond may still go through a "green" phase in early spring, but it won't last long if your pond is balanced. Buy your materials from a reputable source and the staff will offer lots of advice to help you overcome any obstacles you might encounter.

Filter system

- FILTER CONTAINER OUTSIDE OF POND AND BURIED IN SOIL
- WATER PASSES THROUGH ROCK INTO FILTER
- WATER PASSES THROUGH MESH FILTER
- PIPE FROM PUMP TO BOTTOM OF FILTER
- ADDITIONAL LAVA ROCKS PLACED IN FILTER

- If you leave your fish in year-round, keep a spot open in the pond by running an aerator or fountain all winter. If your pond still freezes, buy a floating heater (less than $50). Keeping your pond open provides oxygen for fish and allows gases to escape.

- For convenience, leave hardy water plants in all winter. Bring tropicals or water plants from warmer plant zones inside for the winter.

- Fish, like teenagers, need their space. One inch of fish for

every square foot of pond surface is a good rule of thumb. For example, a 4-in. fish needs 4 sq. ft. of pond surface.

- Hardy fish—goldfish for example—don't require much attention. You don't even need to feed them once they're established, as long as your pond isn't overstocked. Hardy ones can survive by eating insects and the plant life in your pond. They actually help keep your pond clean. If you plan to stock your pond with more exotic species, you'll have to do more to ensure their survival.

EPDM LINER

LARGE ROCK

PUMP CONTAINER

LINE SIDES WITH BOULDERS

5 Lay in the liner so it loosely conforms to the contours of the hole. Don't worry about folds and ripples; they'll flatten out when you add water. Put rocks on one side to hold the liner in place while you adjust the other. Any excess material can be trimmed off with scissors or a utility knife after the pond is full of water and encircled with rocks.

6 Line the pond sides with boulders and set in the pump container. Wash down the rocks after they're in place and then empty the pond with your pump. For large rocks, lay a scrap piece of liner slightly smaller than the rock on top of the pond liner before positioning the rock. This helps prevent punctures.

Keep your pond healthy—make water fall

It's important for water to circulate and aerate throughout the pond. Buying a $10 fountain head and connecting it to the end of the water circulation pipe is the easiest way to accomplish this.

The most dramatic way to circulate and aerate water in your pond is to construct a waterfall and stream. Install a stream bed liner the same way as for your pond. Begin by digging a holding pool. The pool keeps water from spraying out of the circulation pipe and allows it to spill lazily into the pond. Next, dig the course for the water to flow in. Two feet wide is a good dimension. Lay the liner in place, overlapping the pond liner by at least 6 inches.

Creating an attractive water flow will take some trial-and-error adjustments of the rocks. But this is the fun part. Don't mortar your rocks in place. The mortar looks unnatural and makes it difficult to move rocks around to get the desired effect.

How to choose a 24-hour-per-day pump

Buy a pump that'll turn over the pond's entire volume once per hour. To size your pump, calculate the approximate volume in your pond: Multiply the length (ft.) x the width (ft.) x the average depth (ft.) and multiply by the conversion factor of 7.48. Also note the height and distance the pump needs to move the water between the pump and the water inlet.

With these figures in hand, consult your pump supplier for the pump size and circulation pipe diameter for your pond (see Resources, p. 252).

Once you've determined the pump size, decide whether to buy a high- or low-efficiency pump. High-efficiency pumps cost more but last longer and are less expensive to run. Since your pond pump will run 24 hours a day, seven days a week, the lower utility bills will soon make up for the higher price tag.

Place your pump in a pump container to keep it from clogging with leaves or debris. Either buy one from your pond dealer, install the pump in a skimmer container, or make one from a sturdy garbage can peppered with 1/4-in. holes (Photo 6). Don't be shy about drilling holes. The more water you allow through the can, the better.

Handy Hints®

Use a tablet-style fertilizer pressed into the soil around your nearby landscape plantings so the nutrients don't leach into the water.

Simple in-ground fountain

Inexpensive, simple to build and a great place for the neighborhood birds to freshen up.

—*Spike Carlsen*

This quaint fountain is proof that good things come in small packages. I was able to build it in an afternoon for under $100. It's a "disappearing fountain," so there's no exposed standing water. This means there's less maintenance, since there's less chance debris and critters will wind up in the water. Yet it provides the soothing sight and sound of running water people love. Another bonus—since birds love moving water, there's a chance you'll attract some of these outdoor friends.

You can personalize your fountain in a number of ways:

- Surround it with any type of rock. We used a natural wall stone, but you can use modular concrete retaining-wall blocks, boulders or flagstone.
- Top it off with any type of small stone. You can use pebbles, lava stone or special rocks you've collected in your travels.
- Use any bowl, dish or plate you want for the water to splash into. We used three pieces, so the water cascades from one piece into the next.

Let's get started

We used a whiskey barrel liner from our local home center for the catch basin, but any large plastic container will do (see Photo 1 on p. 38). Some garden centers sell special pond liners just for this purpose.

Regardless of your soil conditions, nestle your catch basin or liner into a bed of sand. This helps protect the bottom of the tub from sharp rocks and makes it easier to level the tub and the first course of rock.

We constructed our fountain so we could gain access to the pump by removing a handful of rocks along with the hardware cloth trap door (Photo 5). This allows us to easily remove the pump for maintenance and for storing it indoors over the winter.

Project at a glance

Skill level
Beginner

Special tools
Drill
Ceramic tile drill bit
Wire cutter

Approximate cost
$100

MULTIPLE SPRAY PATTERNS. All four of these interchangeable fountainheads, which provide different looks, came in one package. Use just one or switch them around from time to time for a new look and feel.

EASY FOR EVERYONE

1 Select a location where you'll enjoy your fountain, hollow out a 2-in.-deep area, then level in a bed of sand large enough to accommodate the plastic tub and the rock or block that will surround it.

2 Locate a sturdy plastic flower pot the same height as your plastic tub, cut a hole in the side near the bottom and feed the cord for the electric pump through it. Position this pot right side up in the center of your tub.

3 Cut a hole in the wire hardware cloth (available at home centers) large enough for the pump to fit through, then position the cloth over the tub and bend the edges over the tub lip.

Use a bag of sand as a workbench when drilling the holes in your bowls and dishes (Photo 6). It'll provide a cushion and help prevent breakage.

Many large garden centers and home centers sell water garden pumps and accessories (see Resources, p. 252).

Operating tips

Keep your fountain liner full of water and check the level every day or so, especially in hot weather. You can use any thin stick as a dipstick to check the water level.

Plug your pump into a GFCI-protected outlet—ideally one located next to the fountain. If you use an extension cord, leave it exposed so you know where it is and be careful with sharp garden tools and mowers.

As a precaution, unplug the fountain when you're not

around to watch it (or put it on a timer). If the pump runs dry, it'll burn out.

Most pumps will accept a variety of fountainheads. Bear in mind that with some spray patterns, all the water may not drain back into the tub. You'll have to refill your tub much more often with this type of fountain.

FIGURE A
How it all goes together

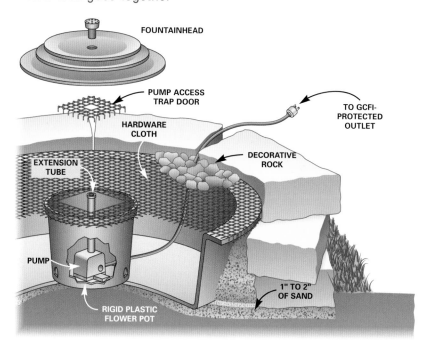

FOUNTAINHEAD

PUMP ACCESS TRAP DOOR

TO GCFI-PROTECTED OUTLET

HARDWARE CLOTH

DECORATIVE ROCK

EXTENSION TUBE

PUMP

1" TO 2" OF SAND

RIGID PLASTIC FLOWER POT

4 Surround the tub with flagstone or concrete retaining-wall blocks to match the rest of your landscape. The upper course should be about 2 in. higher than the top of the tub.

5 Cut a small piece of hardware cloth a few inches larger than the access hole to create a removable trap door, then cut a small opening for the pump stem. Cover the top of the hardware cloth with decorative stone.

SMALL OPENING FOR PUMP STEM

REMOVABLE TRAP DOOR

CERAMIC TILE BIT

BAG OF SAND

OTHER FOUNTAINHEADS

6 Drill a hole in your fountain dish by first scoring the glaze in the center of the bowl with a light tap of a nail (I said light!), then boring a hole using a ceramic tile bit. If you need to enlarge the hole, use a larger bit or small file.

7 Install the fountainhead of your choice. Most pumps can accommodate a range of heads including mushroom-shaped, cup-shaped and fan-shaped patterns. Then fill the tub, plug in the pump and relax.

Plan Smart

Have a little fun selecting your fountain dishes. It's the perfect opportunity to use those I-never-use-'em-but-I-can't-bear-to-throw-'em-out bowls, plates and even teapots.

Container water gardens

Great ponds in small packages.

—Bruce Wiebe

ontainer gardens with aquatic plants create more mystery than plants potted in soil. They make you want to go outside and have a look. Plus, they're extremely low maintenance. Top them off with water before you go on vacation, and they're still bright and beautiful when you come home. And if you add a spouting ornament or water movement of any kind, the kids will love it even more than you do.

Container water gardens are inexpensive and easy to build, too. So here's how to get into the swim of things with a container water garden.

What you need

For a basic garden, you need at least an 18- to 20-in. plastic container that's 7 to 8 in. deep, a small submersible pump, a spouting ornament, plants, clear vinyl tubing, clean kitty litter, pea gravel or small pebbles and a nylon stocking. Most items are readily available at larger garden centers or on-line.

EASY FOR EVERYONE

Project at a glance

Skill level
Beginner

Special tools
Drill

Approximate cost
$50–$100

WATER TUBE CONNECTOR

MOUNTING SPIKE

PEA GRAVEL

KITTY LITTER

1 Drill a small hole in the rim of the container to mount the spouting ornament. If you need to bend the support spike to level or position the spouter, grip it with two pairs of pliers so you don't crack the ornament.

2 Spread the soil of the lily or other deep-water plants in one half of the container, then add kitty litter to create a level floor.

How to do it

The photos show you how. Here are a few additional tips:

■ The floor is two tiered to allow for different types of plants; the lilies planted on the deep side have stems that float upward and extend horizontally, while the "marginal" plants—those that grow upright and favor shallower water—stand on the higher side. The partition that separates the two sides can be made from stone, bricks or other heavy material.

■ Pea gravel both beautifies your water garden and acts as a lid over the unpotted soil so it can't circulate and darken the water. Rinse the pea gravel before adding it to the container.

■ For extra protection, place the pump in a nylon stocking before putting it in the cup, then stuff the extra nylon over the pump. This filtering is crucial; otherwise pebbles

and kitty litter will be drawn into the pump and clog it. A well-filtered pump will run for months; a clogged pump must be dug up, which fouls the water.

■ Small submersible pumps have adjustable pressure, so before burying the pump, place it in a bucket of water, plug it in and adjust the pressure of the jet of water coming out of the spouter.

■ Fill a couple of buckets with tap water, then let them sit for a day or two to allow chlorine to evaporate and water temperature to moderate. Pour the water in gradually—it should be as clear as a mountain stream.

■ Aquatic plants thrive on direct sunlight, so a bright sunny spot is ideal. If possible, position the container near an electrical outlet for the pump.

Plan Smart

Wind can wreak havoc with tall plants by pushing the containers off their pedestals. Finding a wind-free space helps solve this problem and ensures the fountain arc from the spouting ornament looks and sounds the way you want it to.

MARGINAL
PLANTS

FLAGSTONE
PARTITION

PLASTIC
COVER

LOWER
SIDE

PEA
GRAVEL

3 Add a partition to divide the container into halves. Plant the shallow-growing marginal plants and spread more kitty litter over the soil. On the low side, nestle a plastic cup for the pump in the kitty litter, keeping it covered with plastic to prevent gravel from falling in.

4 Spread pea gravel over the kitty litter. Keep the floor on the lily side lower to allow the lily stems room to extend upward when you add water.

Care, maintenance and something fishy

Taking care of water gardens is a breeze. Top them off as water evaporates and scoop off the occasional dead leaf or bit of algae.

Plants maintain water clarity by absorbing decaying matter through their roots as food. But if the water starts looking gunky, remove the plants, rinse the container and refill.

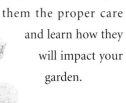

For any plants needing a boost, press a fertilizer pellet into the potting soil. You can also add a Mosquito Dunk (about $1 each at garden centers) a couple times in the summer to kill mosquito larvae without posing harm to people or pets.

MOSQUITO
DUNK

FERTILIZER
PELLETS

Smaller containers will only need a small piece.

For a small container, plant a dwarf lily so the pads don't completely cover the surface as they grow. For larger water gardens, you can add a floating plant like water hyacinth, duckweed or water lettuce.

A dish-style garden is too small for koi or goldfish, but larger containers, like whiskey barrels or larger terracotta pots, are ideal. (Note: Water in metal containers usually gets too warm for fish.) Fish help keep the garden clean by eating algae, decaying plant material and mosquito larvae. Make certain to read up on fish so you give them the proper care and learn how they will impact your garden.

Handy Hints®

You can overwinter hardy water lilies by wrapping them in a damp towel and storing them in a cool basement or garage corner. Other plants are relatively inexpensive and grow rapidly, so in cold climates, buy them anew each year and treat as annuals.

SECTION
OF 1/2"
TUBING

3/8"
TUBING

SUCTION
CUPS

NYLON
FILTER

5 Connect the pump to the spouter with vinyl tubing. Use a transition piece of 1/2-in. tubing if necessary to connect the 3/8-in. tube to the pump. Press the pump into the cup so that the suction cups anchor it to the bottom.

6 Cover the pump with a nylon stocking filter to keep gravel from clogging the pump, and then cover the pump with pea gravel.

The Super-Simple Approach

If you want an instant water garden, simply slip a plastic barrel liner into a decorative wooden barrel, set some pavers of various heights in place to act as pedestals and then perch a few potted aquatic plants on top. Just make sure to position the plants at the depth indicated on the plant tag or information sheet. The only drawback to this approach is that the container won't look as natural close up—you can see the plastic pots below the surface. You can even add a spouter to the barrel; the pump can simply sit on a pedestal without a cup.

If you can't find a plastic barrel liner, you can make a watertight terra-cotta container by plugging the drain hole with plumber's epoxy (left) and applying two coats of polyurethane.

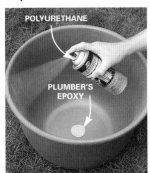

POLYURETHANE

PLUMBER'S
EPOXY

LINER

PAVER
PEDESTALS

Gallery of ideas

Whether it's a rugged stone fountain or a gently cascading bamboo sluice, water features hold one thing in common: the natural, comforting sound of flowing water.

For information on obtaining plans for building the water features shown here, see Resources, p. 252.

Fountain of stone

This fountain is simple to build and easy to maintain. The size can be customized to suit your yard and you can use nearly any type of stone without changing the basic construction procedures. You'll spend about $200 for the liner, pump and basin; all the materials are available at well-stocked garden or home centers.

Bamboo water garden

This bamboo water garden can add life to an existing garden or serve as the heart and soul of a new one. The water runs through a series of bamboo sluices, into a small pond containing a pump that recirculates the water back to its "source." Materials are available through mail order and Internet sources such as www.bamboo hardwoods.com or www.bamboo andrattan.com.

Millstone fountain

This quaint fountain, modeled after an old millstone, is built using sheet metal forms, concrete and copper pipe. Expect to spend about two days and $150 building this unique garden accent.

CHAPTER

Dream
decks

Maintenance-free deck

Composite decking, treated wood and special building techniques all add up to a durable, low-maintenance deck.

—*Travis Larson*

Who says natural is the only way to go? Occasionally humans invent something that not only lasts longer than Mother Nature's products but is easier to maintain. In this article, we'll tell you how to use some of these materials to build yourself a deck that will last a long time, look good and be easy to maintain. We'll also show you tricks and tips to make the building process simpler and "mistake-tolerant."

Decks are great do-it-yourself projects, and this one, big as it looks, is no exception. Although this multilevel deck looks complex, you can build it using standard tools. A circular saw, tape measure, chalk line, hammer and posthole digger can be adequate for building anything from a simple 12 x 12-ft. deck to an elaborate multilevel structure. But don't think you'll knock this one off in a couple of weekends. This deck took 12 skilled-carpenter days to build, so if you're new to carpentry, add a few days for the learning curve, weather delays, weekend-only work and family obligations. Realistically, a deck this size could turn into a summer-long project.

The plastic/wood composite decking (the planks you walk on) used for this deck is called Trex and costs about

Project at a glance

Skill level
Advanced

Special tools
Circular saw
Drill
Posthole digger
Level

Approximate cost
$11,000

1 Determine the size of your deck by laying out garden hose to mark its footprint (size and shape) on the yard exactly where it will be built. We used two garden hoses of different colors, one to lay out the deck and the other to lay out the planter boxes. Then pretend it's your finished deck by arranging chairs, tables, barbecue grills or whatever else you expect to keep on it.

$1.50 per linear foot. Using Trex in lieu of cedar added $420 to the project cost. That sounds like a lot of money, but when you figure that 15 years from now you'll be vacationing in Mexico instead of replacing the old deck, it doesn't seem so bad. For decking material pros and cons, see "The Case for Composite Decking" on p. 57.

The key ingredients that'll make your deck last (almost) forever

Decking: The floor bears the brunt of rot on decks. Because deck boards lie flat, water collects in cracks and knots and soaks into the end grain—especially at splices. Because these areas stay wet for long periods of time, they are the most vulnerable to decay. Although we used Trex for the decking, we chose rough-sawn cedar lumber for the privacy wall, planter trim and other exposed wood to give the project a more natural, tactile character. Because these items are largely vertical, they can be made of wood and will last a very long time.

   Lumber: The wood for all the above-ground framing is .40-grade pressure-treated lumber, which will last for

SHOPPING LIST
(Color-indexed with illustrations on pp. 51 and 53)

MATERIAL	USE
Lumber:	
.60 foundation-grade 2x4	Middle of posts, top and bottom plates, studs and braces for planters
.60 foundation-grade 2x6	Outsides of posts, footing plates for planters
.60 foundation-grade 1/2-in. plywood	Planter liner
.40 treated 2x12s	Stair stringers and deck beams
.40 treated 2x10s	Wall ledgers, deck joists, rim joists and stair plate
.40 treated 1x6s	Ground board for planters
5/4 x 6 Trex	Decking, stair treads
1x10 cedar	Trim that hides joists
1x8 cedar	Stair risers
2x4 cedar	Corner boards on planter, upper and lower rails on privacy wall
2x6 cedar	Center board and top cap on privacy wall panels
2x10 cedar	Planter top caps
2x12 cedar	Dress skirt
2x2 cedar	Privacy wall pickets, top trim for planters
4x4 cedar	Privacy wall posts
Siding	Planter box siding
Pine 1x4s	Batter boards

Hardware:	
3-in. stainless nails	Framing nailing
2-1/2 in. stainless ring or spiral-shanked nails	Decking and plywood liner fasteners
2-in. and 3-in. siding nails	Siding and cedar trim
3-in. stainless screws	Planter top cap and privacy fence
3/8 x 4-in. bolts, nuts and washers	Privacy fence posts
Joist hangers with exterior-rated 1-1/2 in. joist hanger nails	Joist attachment to ledger
Rafter tie hangers	Stair stringer to rim connections
3/8 x 4-in. lag screws	Ledger to house
3/8 x 3-in. lag screws	Planter braces and outside corners
1-1/2 in. drip cap	Over ledger, behind house siding
7/8-in. drip cap	Over planter ground board, behind siding

Miscellaneous:	
Premixed concrete	1 bag for each posthole
3/4-in. gravel	Planter box fill, planter and stair footings

FIGURE A
Main deck assembly

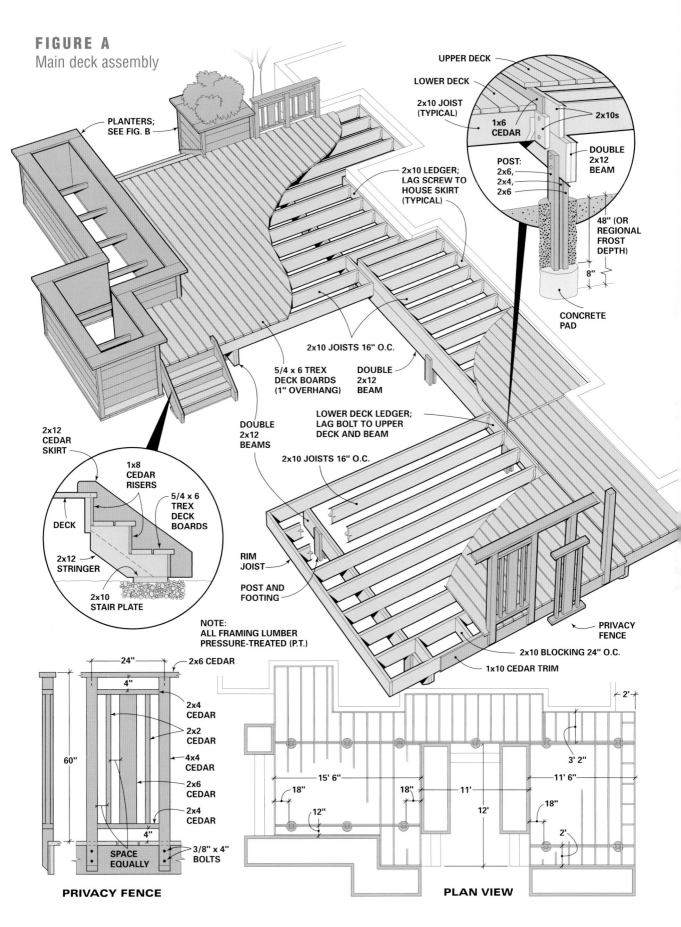

PLANTERS; SEE FIG. B

UPPER DECK

LOWER DECK

2x10 JOIST (TYPICAL)

1x6 CEDAR

2x10s

POST: 2x6, 2x4, 2x6

DOUBLE 2x12 BEAM

2x10 LEDGER; LAG SCREW TO HOUSE SKIRT (TYPICAL)

48" (OR REGIONAL FROST DEPTH)

8"

CONCRETE PAD

2x10 JOISTS 16" O.C.

5/4 x 6 TREX DECK BOARDS (1" OVERHANG)

DOUBLE 2x12 BEAM

LOWER DECK LEDGER; LAG BOLT TO UPPER DECK AND BEAM

2x10 JOISTS 16" O.C.

2x12 CEDAR SKIRT

1x8 CEDAR RISERS

5/4 x 6 TREX DECK BOARDS

DECK

2x12 STRINGER

2x10 STAIR PLATE

DOUBLE 2x12 BEAMS

RIM JOIST

POST AND FOOTING

PRIVACY FENCE

2x10 BLOCKING 24" O.C.

1x10 CEDAR TRIM

NOTE: ALL FRAMING LUMBER PRESSURE-TREATED (P.T.)

PRIVACY FENCE

24"

4"

2x6 CEDAR

2x4 CEDAR

2x2 CEDAR

4x4 CEDAR

2x6 CEDAR

2x4 CEDAR

60"

4"

SPACE EQUALLY

3/8" x 4" BOLTS

PLAN VIEW

2'

3' 2"

11' 6"

15' 6"

18"

18"

11'

12"

12'

18"

2'

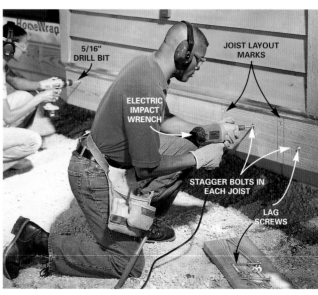

2 Cut out the siding with a circular saw to create a space for the deck ledger to attach to the house. Leave space for the decking to slide under the siding. Tuck drip cap under the siding. Level and tack the ledger to the rim of the house with 16d galvanized nails.

3 Draw joist layout marks every 16 in. on the ledger board. Drill a pilot hole, then install a 3/8-in. x 4-in. lag screw between each floor joist. (Screw length may vary, but the screws should extend through the house sheathing and the rim joist of the house.) Stagger the lag screws in every other joist space to prevent the ledger from splitting.

4 Install batter boards outside the perimeter of each corner of the deck so that the center of the batter boards is "eyeball" square to the left and right ends of the ledger board. Stretch a string line at right angles to the ledger board at each end using the 3-4-5 triangle squaring method (6-8-10 in this instance for more accuracy). Pound a small nail into the batter board where the string crosses it and tie the string to the nail. The string is a square reference guide parallel to the edge of the deck for laying out the rest of the framing.

decades without any maintenance. Posts and planter framing that are underground call for foundation-grade .60-treated lumber (stamped FNDN), the same material used for wood foundations. FNDN material may be a special-order item in your part of the country, but most lumberyards can get it for you.

Hardware: Plan on spending a few extra dollars to get quality hardware designed for outside use. That means using double-hot-dipped galvanized nails or, better yet, stainless steel nails for all nailing and exterior-rated joist hanger nails. Install drip cap above the ledger and behind the siding (Photo 2). Don't scrimp on hardware; remember that for the first time ever, the deck's structure could outlast the hardware.

Design: Take pains to plan your deck for

Work Smart

Flashing the ledger board is critical. Otherwise, the house framing will rot and the deck will eventually fall off the side of the house.

BEAM CANTILEVER

STRING IS OUTSIDE EDGE OF BEAM

DECK CANTILEVER

ADJUST TO MARK CENTER OF HOLE

POSTS ARE APPROX. 24" FROM INSIDE EDGE OF DECK

.60 FNDN GRADE 2x6, 2x4, 2x6 SANDWICH POSTS

24"

FUTURE DECK JOISTS

END POSTS ARE APPROX. 18" FROM INSIDE OF DECK

5 Measure from the deck ledger to position batter boards and strings for the beams that run parallel to the house. Mark the outside edge of the beam locations with the strings. Drive stakes into the ground to mark the center of each posthole (remember that the string marks the outside edge of the beam, not the middle).

6 Assemble the posts from FNDN 2x4s and 2x6s, nailing them below their future cut-off level—see Photos 8 and 9. Drop them into their holes and align them with the string line. Lay temporary 2x10s (joist material) alongside the posts to help position them. Plumb the posts both ways and tack them into the floor joists. Fill the holes, packing the dirt as you fill.

FIGURE B
Planter

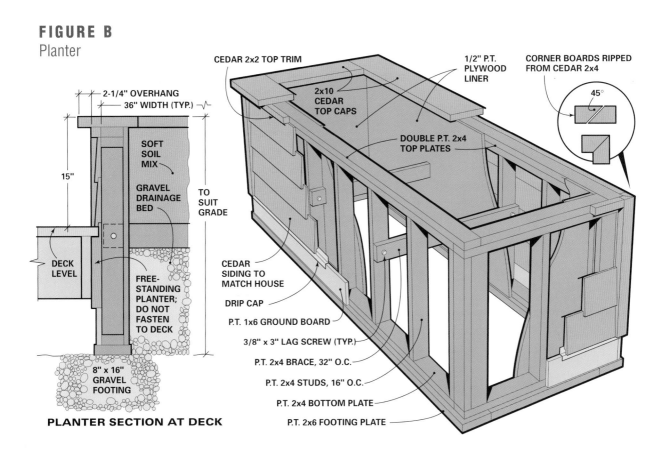

2-1/4" OVERHANG
36" WIDTH (TYP.)

SOFT SOIL MIX

GRAVEL DRAINAGE BED

15"

TO SUIT GRADE

DECK LEVEL

FREE-STANDING PLANTER; DO NOT FASTEN TO DECK

8" x 16" GRAVEL FOOTING

PLANTER SECTION AT DECK

CEDAR 2x2 TOP TRIM

2x10 CEDAR TOP CAPS

1/2" P.T. PLYWOOD LINER

CORNER BOARDS RIPPED FROM CEDAR 2x4

45°

DOUBLE P.T. 2x4 TOP PLATES

CEDAR SIDING TO MATCH HOUSE

DRIP CAP

P.T. 1x6 GROUND BOARD

3/8" x 3" LAG SCREW (TYP.)

P.T. 2x4 BRACE, 32" O.C.

P.T. 2x4 STUDS, 16" O.C.

P.T. 2x4 BOTTOM PLATE

P.T. 2x6 FOOTING PLATE

POWER POSTHOLE DIGGER

12" AUGER

STEEL BAR

CLAMSHELL POSTHOLE DIGGER

DRAIN-TILE SHOVEL

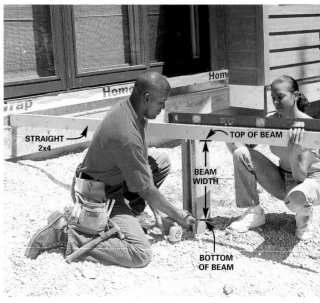

STRAIGHT 2x4

TOP OF BEAM

BEAM WIDTH

BOTTOM OF BEAM

7 Set aside the beam strings and dig 12-in. dia. postholes the correct depth for your area. Solidly pack the loose soil at the bottom of the holes with the end of a 2x4 and pour a 60-lb. bag of premixed concrete into the holes to form an 8-in. thick footing pad.

8 Level from the deck ledger to each post with a straight board. Measure down from the ledger level the depth of your beams to establish cut-off lines.

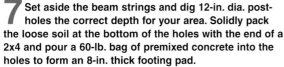

Digging postholes with fewer blisters

The soil at our site was a combination of loose sand, rocks and hard clay, so we ended up using a power auger, a steel bar to loosen rocks and a clamshell-style posthole digger to extract the rock and clean out loose soil at the bottom of the hole. A drain tile shovel is great for loosening the clay at the bottom of the hole and for dislodging rocks.

Power augers cost about $90 per day to rent, and they don't always make posthole digging a quick, easy chore. They take two strong people to run, and they bog down in heavy soil and skip over the top of any rocks bigger than a tangerine. They are, however, worth their weight in gold if you have lots of holes to dig—especially if you're digging in sandy soil. The corkscrew end on the auger will extract the dirt more efficiently than the clamshell digger because sand falls through the end of the clamshell blades when you're lifting the tool out of the hole. The pros usually end up hand-digging about 40 percent of the holes even if they do have a power auger at their disposal. If you choose to rent an auger, remember to hand-dig a pilot hole a few inches deep before firing up the machine. Otherwise the auger has a tendency to wander at startup and your hole might shift several inches off your layout.

Work Smart

Call building permit and contact utility companies to locate underground utilities before digging.

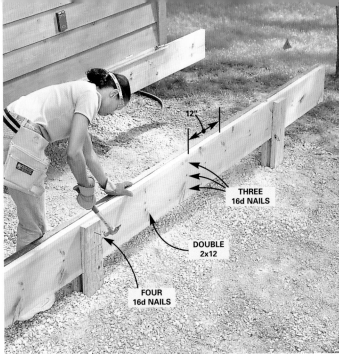

9 Cut off one 2x6 and the middle 2x4 with a circular saw. If your posts will show, you may want to cut off the 2x6 away from the house. Complete the cut with a handsaw. Cut off the longer 2x6 even with the top of the ledger.

10 Set the double 2x12 beam on the posts and fasten it to the long 2x6 with 16d galvanized box nails. Nail the 2x12s to each other with three nails every 12 in., one close to each edge and one in the middle. Be sure the beam projects several inches past the edge of the deck for later trimming.

the long term. Think far into the future to get the size and shape right. Think in terms of a room addition more than a deck. We hired an architect and spent $500, a sum that bought us a site visit, a couple of preliminary drawings and final plans. He had numerous suggestions and ideas we wouldn't have thought of. With the design fee only 6 percent of the total project, it was a bargain.

Footings: Make sure your footings are deep and wide enough for your climate. When you take your plans in to get a building permit, your inspector will let you know about the local requirements. In the upper Midwest, that means 42-in. deep footings, but we went 48 in. to ensure that the deck would be able to handle the next ice age.

Structure: Build with shorter spans, narrower spacing and heavier materials than you would for a normal, wood deck. Our deck spans called for 2x10 beams and 2x8 joists, but we supersized the structural members to 2x12 beams and 2x10 joists to give a more beefy, permanent feel to what we expect will be an often-used outside living room.

11 Nail the first end joist (A) into the end of the ledger and square it to the ledger with the 6-8-10 triangle technique (Photo 4). Mark the beam even with the outside edge of the end joist, slide the joist away from the cut mark, draw a square cut-off line and cut off the end of the beam. Toenail the joist into the beam and measure from the joist to make 16-in. layout marks on the top of the beam for joist placement. Use the joist layout marks on the ledger as a guide to transfer marks to the beam for setting the joists. Install the remaining joists, toenailing them into the rim and beam. After you're satisfied with the joist placement, secure them to the ledger with joist hangers.

12 Set end joist (B) parallel with end joist (A), mark for beam cut-off, slide the joist away and cut off the beam end.

13 Measure from the rim joist the depth of the deck, mark the end joists and snap a line for cutting off the ends of the joists. (When measuring, don't forget to subtract for the 1-1/2 in. thickness for the rim joist.) Draw cut-off lines with a carpenter's square and cut off the ends with a circular saw. If you're installing a rail, use a 2-ft. level to mark end cuts to get a perfectly plumb, true rim joist and a straight rail.

14 Nail the end rim joist onto end joist (A) and have your partner raise and lower the rim joist to make the top edge of the rim flush with the top edge of the joists. Nail each joist, working your way from end joist (A) to end joist (B). Cut the end of the rim off flush with the end of the last deck joist.

Plan your deck with a garden hose

Spend some time walking around on your "hose deck" (Photo 1) to get a feel for the adequacy of its size and shape. We decided to split our deck into three distinct areas. There's a small boardwalk next to the house for accessing the two lower decks, one of which is for lounging and the other, for a dining table and chairs.

Although a deck with different levels is more interesting visually, it also entails more complicated construction and shrinks usable space. If you're just planning on a 12 x 12 postage stamp–sized deck, you probably don't need any professional design work, but if you envision a large, elaborate, multilevel deck, consider hiring a professional designer to help with the plans. The pro's final design will have the correct structural details to make your deck strong and safe. Whether you do the drawing yourself or hire it done, you'll need drawings to get the building permit and order materials. If you draw your own plans, a helpful lumberyard or building inspector will assist in sizing and spacing all the important structural members of your deck.

No splinters. You can walk on this composite deck in your bare feet.

The case for composite decking

Decks used to be built solely of redwood, cedar or cypress because of their inherent wood preservatives. But as some of us have learned the hard way, all wood eventually rots—especially in shady, moist locations.

For the last 20 years or so, preservative-treated (green) lumber has been the accepted material for a long-lasting, rot-resistant deck. But treated wood has its downsides too. Besides not being particularly attractive, it has a tendency to split, warp and twist (and those treated splinters embedded in the bottom of your feet are no picnic either).

There are now alternatives to conventional treated and natural wood. Various manufacturers are now distributing their versions of plastic or composite plastic/wood decking. You'll find everything from simple Trex clones to elaborate space-frame vinyl and fiberglass extrusions with, of course, elaborate prices. These products are not available in all areas. You'll need to visit the lumberyards in your area to see what your choices are.

We chose Trex for this deck because of its wide availability and reasonable price. It's a 50/50 mix of surplus wood fibers and polymers

(plastics) that is molded into various shapes and sizes. The decking material we used is the classic 1-1/4 x 5-1/2 in. shape of conventional wood decking. In addition to decking, Trex comes in a variety of non-structural dimensions such as 2x6s and 2x4s, which you can use for benches, rails or privacy screens. But Trex can't be used for posts, beams, joists or any other load-bearing purpose. Trex decking is limited to 16-in. spans, so the joists need to be spaced every 16 in. instead of the more common 24 in. used for full 2x6s.

Although Trex comes in several attractive colors (tan, dark brown and gray), it does have a bit of that plastic Barbie dollhouse look. Gone are wood's subtle grain, color variegation and knots. In short, you sacrifice the natural character of real wood.

Trex is also denser and heavier than wood. Consequently, it's harder to haul around and a bit harder to drive fasteners into. The good news is that its monolithic nature means Trex won't split, warp, twist, cup or crack—ever. Its surface is skid-resistant even when wet, and you'll get that warm, fuzzy feeling knowing that fewer trees gave their lives for your deck.

Use conventional woodworking tools and techniques with Trex

All of the woodworking techniques you've learned over the years apply to Trex as well. Conventional saw blades, router bits, drills and fasteners work with Trex the same as they do with wood. Trex will also receive wood stains and paints like the real thing. Just remember before applying a finish that it will add that maintenance factor you're attempting to avoid. Except for cosmetic reasons, paint and stain are unnecessary. Trex achieves its final weather-adjusted color in 6 to 12 weeks and will be somewhat lighter than the installed shade. If you're planning to apply a finish, you'll need to wait until the fading is complete.

DISTANCE A

CEDAR FASCIA
BOARD

DISTANCE B

2"

15 Nail off the decking with ring-shanked 10d stainless steel nails, working from the outside of the deck toward the house using 16d nails for spacers. Let the decking hang over the end joists at least 2-1/2 in. Measure from the house side of the deck every five or six boards to confirm that the decking is running parallel to the house (distances A and B) and make small spacing adjustments as necessary. Leave off the last piece of decking because the house will block the last cut made by the circular saw.

16 Measure 2 in. from the end joists and mark the decking for cut-off by snapping a line. The 2-in. overhang allows for the 7/8-in. thick cedar face board and a 1-1/8 in. overhang.

Use construction-friendly building methods

Follow the photo series for step-by-step building techniques and keep these labor-saving tips in mind.

■ We employed cantilevers (beams hanging over posts, and joists hanging over beams) in our design because they make layout and construction much easier. They also give the deck a floating appearance by moving the main structural supports in from the deck's perimeter. Cantilevering also helps by providing "fudge factors" throughout construction. They allow you to fine-tune the dimensions of the deck as you build. Non-cantilevered decks require exact placement of posts at each corner from the moment you dig your first posthole. Unfortunately, all too often you discover only after setting the posts that footing and post placement are off by several inches. You're then faced with living with an out-of-square deck or making some very time-consuming fixes.

■ Begin construction by installing the ledger board. (Don't forget the drip cap!) Use the ledger for laying out the rest of the deck, including posthole placement.

■ Don't cut anything until you have to. If possible, install members before cutting them to length to give you the opportunity to make minor adjustments in the structure as you build. That means installing posts longer than they have to be, running beams longer than the deck is wide and attaching joists to the ledger before cutting them to their finished length.

■ Make your deck at least 6 in. smaller than the standard 2-ft. increments of lumber. We made our 12-ft. section of deck 11 ft. 6 in. and our 16-ft. section 15 ft. 6 in. This lets you trim bad ends on deck boards, maintain a 1-in. overhang along the edges and install cedar trim boards to hide the treated lumber framing.

Splice decking with a single seam

The typical way to handle a deck that is wider than the deck boards is to randomly butt the ends together and split them over a deck joist. Cutting and fitting all these joints takes a lot of time and forces you to butt two boards tightly together to share the 1-1/2 in. thickness of a floor joist. Nailing close to the ends makes wood split and rot prematurely because moisture gets into the splice and doesn't dry out for long periods of time.

A more elegant, longer-lasting way is to create a

17 Cut off the excess decking. Measure the final cut lengths of the deck boards and cut the last deck board to length, rip it to width if necessary, and install it.

18 Cut notches in a piece of decking so that it protrudes above the joists 1-1/4 in. (flush with the top of the decking), away from the deck edge and even with the decking overhang.

19 Nail the notched piece to the side of the joist. Nail a second joist against it and toe-nail the joist into the rims. Nail the decking, leaving a gap between the splice board and the end of the decking.

20 Dig trenches 6 in. deep and 12 in. wide and fill with gravel. Measure down from the deck to keep gravel levels within 1/2 in. of desired height. Lay down .60 foundation-grade lumber for footing plates a few inches longer than the intended planter length and width. To set the footing plates, measure down from the deck and pound on them with a heavy board. Use a 4-ft. level, working off the first plate when setting the plates that don't adjoin the deck.

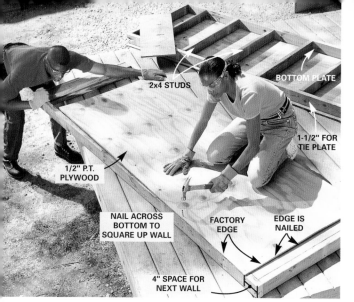

2x4 STUDS

BOTTOM PLATE

1-1/2" FOR TIE PLATE

1/2" P.T. PLYWOOD

NAIL ACROSS BOTTOM TO SQUARE UP WALL

FACTORY EDGE

EDGE IS NAILED

4" SPACE FOR NEXT WALL

PLANTER WALLS AGAINST DECK HAVE 2x4s INSTALLED BEFORE STANDING

1/2 HEIGHT OF WALL

2x4 BRACES

1/2" .60 PRESSURE TREATED WOOD

21 Lay out all pairs of plates on walls that face each other so that the braces are square when you attach them to the studs. Nail the studs to the top and bottom plates and nail on the plywood after first fastening it to an end stud. Then square the wall by working the plywood up and down to align the bottom of the plywood with the bottom of the plate, nailing across the bottom from the fastened end toward the other end. Finish nailing the plywood to the studs and the top plate every 8 in.

22 Cut 1-5/8 in. x 3-5/8 in. holes for the 2x4 braces halfway up the wall every 32 in. Cut 2x4 braces the same length as the width of the wall, slip them through the walls and lag-screw them to the sides of the studs before standing them against the deck (they may be inaccessible later, depending on the height of your deck and planters).

single seam with a dogeared length of decking perpendicular to the deck itself. Then toe-nail in another floor joist for nailing the ends of the next section. Having a full 1-1/2 in. of joist for nailing each deck board allows for a space between the end of the decking board and the splice board for drying, and helps keep nails away from the splitting zone.

Think through rail, planter and stair details or they'll trip you up later

Most building codes call for 36-in. high guardrails on any deck that's more than 30 in. above ground and any set of stairs that has more than three risers. Our deck had only one side higher than 30 in., so we decided to handle that area with a 5-ft. privacy wall (Photo 25) to provide a safety rail and to screen the deck from a nearby road.

For the rest of the deck perimeter, we built planter boxes in lieu of railings (Photos 20 – 24) because we

Work Smart

Using deck joists as straightedges will help keep the posts in line, assist in layout and hold the posts steady while backfilling.

didn't want our lake view obstructed. We also liked the idea of being surrounded by a deck-level flower garden. Frame the planters like a conventional stud wall made of foundation-grade lumber and rest them on a gravel footing. It's important to make the planters freestanding. The lack of a frost footing means they'll rise and fall with frost movement and will lift the deck if they're attached to it. Don't consider them as legal guardrails but as a passive barrier to keep people from accidentally stepping off the edge. They were designed so the tops were 15 in. above the deck to double as casual seating.

We added some cosmetic side stringers (Photo 26) to dress the stair sides and decked the treads with Trex. Rest the steps on a gravel footing topped with a treated 2x10 (Photo 26) using the same setting methods demonstrated for the planters (Photo 20).

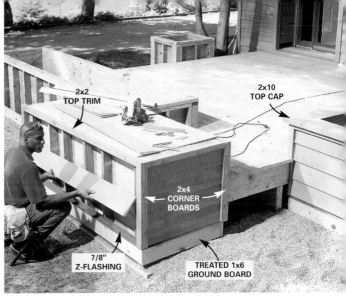

23 Tack the corners together with 16d nails. Fasten the ends of the walls with three equally spaced 3-in. lag screws to tie the corners together, and one 3-in. lag screw through each wall brace. Cut and nail tie plates so that the tie plates overlap adjoining walls. Nail with two 16d nails over each stud.

24 Install treated 1x6 boards at grade to protect cedar from ground contact, then top with 7/8-in. Z-flashing to keep water from getting behind the siding. Nail 2x4 corner boards, positioning the tops flush with the top of the framing and install 2x2 horizontal trim boards between the corners. Side the walls and cap with 2x10s.

25 Notch 4x4s and decking and cut 4x4s to length (4-ft. 10-1/2 in. above deck). Plumb posts with a 4-ft. level and bolt to rim of deck after predrilling 1-in. countersink hole and boring a 3/8-in. hole through the post, cedar trim and end joist. Nail on a 2x6 top cap and install premade panel assemblies by toe-screwing into the side of the posts.

26 Cut stair stringers and use them for positioning 2x10 footing plate for stairs to rest on. Tack stringers onto rim joist and install rafter tie joist hangers to permanently attach stringers. Nail stair risers to face of stringers and install treads.

Deck in the round

The fine art of building with curves.

—Art Rooze

If you're dreaming of a deck that's beyond the ordinary, take a close look at this one. It may be just the design you've always wanted, but couldn't plan on paper.

More than just elegant, our deck-in-the-round makes effective use of space, and its framing and structure are simple enough that it needn't scare you away even if you're a first-time deck builder.

Nor is this a super-expensive deck to build, considering its size and configuration. We built all the framing members with pressure-treated lumber and used D-grade cedar for the decking, steps and railing.

In this article, we don't tell you how to build the retaining wall and lay the pavers, but see "Circular Patio & Retaining Wall" on p. 112 for the basics on building both.

If you're a do-it-yourselfer with good building skills and experience, working alone, you could probably build this deck (not counting the retaining wall and pavers) in about 200 hours. That's a big chunk of your spare time!

The tools you'll need are quite ordinary. In addition to an assortment of basic hand tools, you'll need a circular saw, a heavy-duty power drill that you can also use to drive screws, a band saw or hand-held power jigsaw, a belt sander and a router. We chose to screw our decking boards to the joists. However, if you choose to nail them, consider renting a power nailer and compressor for a few days.

Project at a glance

Skill level
Advanced

Special tools
Circular saw
Jigsaw
Level

Approximate cost
$4,500 for deck materials, $2,100 for retaining wall materials, $1,000 for plantings

FIGURE A
Footing and beam layout

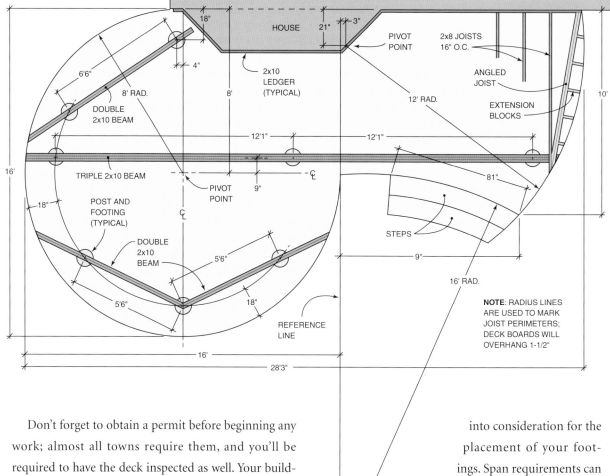

NOTE: RADIUS LINES ARE USED TO MARK JOIST PERIMETERS; DECK BOARDS WILL OVERHANG 1-1/2"

Don't forget to obtain a permit before beginning any work; almost all towns require them, and you'll be required to have the deck inspected as well. Your building inspector will help you avoid serious mistakes in design or construction and may even suggest shortcuts or better building methods for your region.

Footings

Our deck required eight frost-proof concrete footings. They are positioned to support the four main beams, as shown and explained in Photos 1, 2 and 3 and Figure A. In our deck's configuration, our central beam, consisting of pressure-treated, triple 2x10s, can span up to about 14 ft. A longer span would require additional footing support. The other three supporting beams, which are double 2x10s, can span up to 10 ft. The single 2x8 joists shown being installed in Photo 4 can span 9 or 10 ft., and possibly more, when placed on 16-in. centers.

If your deck differs in size or configuration from ours, you'll need to take span requirements like these into consideration for the placement of your footings. Span requirements can vary by locality, and also according to the type of wood used, so check this with your building inspector.

Concrete footings should flare out to about 16 in. at their base, as shown in Figure D. They must also extend below the frost line in your area. So if you live in a cold climate (where you may have to dig down 42 in. or more), consider renting a two-person power auger. Call your utility company to come out and check for power lines before you do any digging.

Deck framing

The deck is mounted to the house by means of a 2x10 ledger board (see Photos 1 and 3, and Figure E). Cut away the siding, and mount the ledger exactly level along its entire length using 4-in. galvanized lag bolts screwed securely into the rim joist of the house. Calculate the

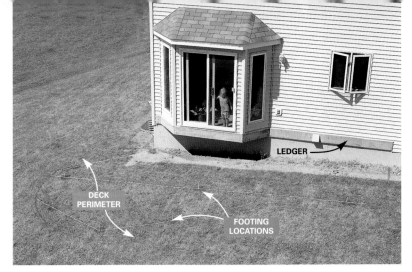

1 Lay out the perimeter of the deck, after finding the pivot points for all three curved sections as given in Figure A. Mark the perimeter with a can of spray paint, secured to one end of an unstretchable chain or wire; secure the other end of the chain or wire to the three pivot points, in turn, using a long nail driven into the ground. Next, determine the location for each footing according to the dimensions given in Figure A. The number of footings required is determined by the span limits for beams and joists, as explained in the text under "Footings."

2 Pour concrete footings using sections of 10-in. wide cardboard forms at the tops of the holes. Keep the footing tops level. Place 1/2-in. x 24-in. long steel rebar drift pins in the center of the wet concrete, extending about 4 in. above the footing. These hold the posts in place. Trowel the concrete smooth after positioning the rebar.

3 Nail the 2x10 beams together with three 10d nails every 16 in. Place the beams on notched 6x6 posts, as shown in Figure D. Drill 1/2-in. holes in the post bottoms for the rebar drift pins. Extend the beam ends about 6 in. beyond the spray-painted perimeter line; trim the beams to length later, after all the joists are in place (Photo 7). Make sure the beams are at the proper height in relation to the ledger, and that they are all level with each other, as described under "Deck Framing," p. 64. Then secure the beams to the post notches with 5-in. galvanized lag bolts and washers. Predrill lag bolt holes in the posts to avoid splitting.

4 Lay joists in place after marking the beams and ledger at 16-in. intervals. Mount joist hangers on the ledger. (Note 45-degree joist hangers on the angled bay.) Allow joists to overhang the deck's perimeter line by 3 or 4 in. all the way around. Secure the joists with two angle-driven decking screws at each beam.

FIGURE B
Deck configuration

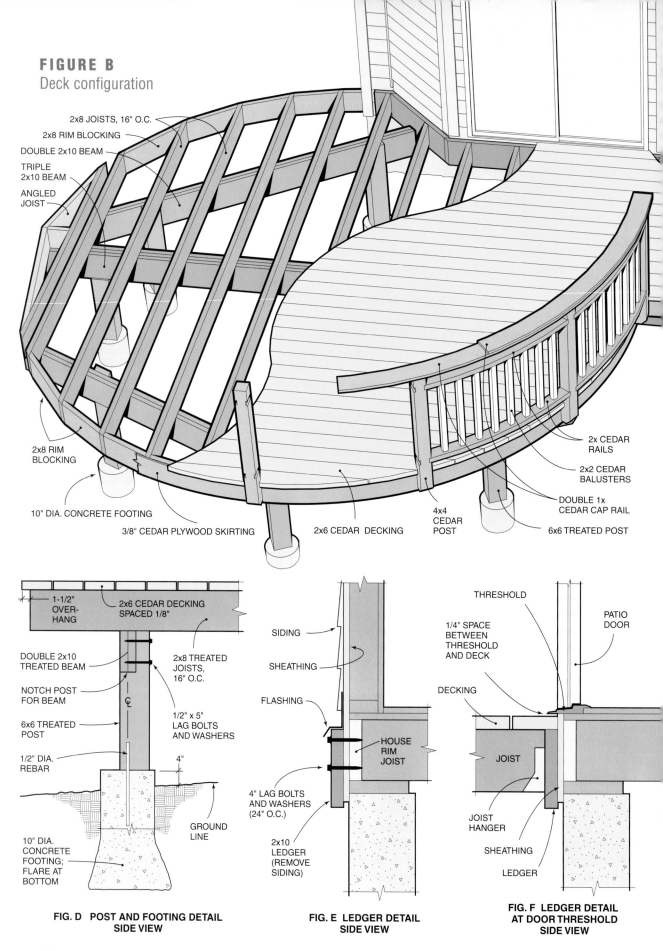

2x8 JOISTS, 16" O.C.

2x8 RIM BLOCKING

DOUBLE 2x10 BEAM

TRIPLE 2x10 BEAM

ANGLED JOIST

2x8 RIM BLOCKING

10" DIA. CONCRETE FOOTING

3/8" CEDAR PLYWOOD SKIRTING

2x6 CEDAR DECKING

4x4 CEDAR POST

2x CEDAR RAILS

2x2 CEDAR BALUSTERS

DOUBLE 1x CEDAR CAP RAIL

6x6 TREATED POST

1-1/2" OVER-HANG

2x6 CEDAR DECKING SPACED 1/8"

DOUBLE 2x10 TREATED BEAM

NOTCH POST FOR BEAM

6x6 TREATED POST

1/2" DIA. REBAR

2x8 TREATED JOISTS, 16" O.C.

1/2" x 5" LAG BOLTS AND WASHERS

4"

GROUND LINE

10" DIA. CONCRETE FOOTING; FLARE AT BOTTOM

FIG. D POST AND FOOTING DETAIL SIDE VIEW

SIDING

SHEATHING

FLASHING

HOUSE RIM JOIST

4" LAG BOLTS AND WASHERS (24" O.C.)

2x10 LEDGER (REMOVE SIDING)

FIG. E LEDGER DETAIL SIDE VIEW

THRESHOLD

1/4" SPACE BETWEEN THRESHOLD AND DECK

PATIO DOOR

DECKING

JOIST

JOIST HANGER

SHEATHING

LEDGER

FIG. F LEDGER DETAIL AT DOOR THRESHOLD SIDE VIEW

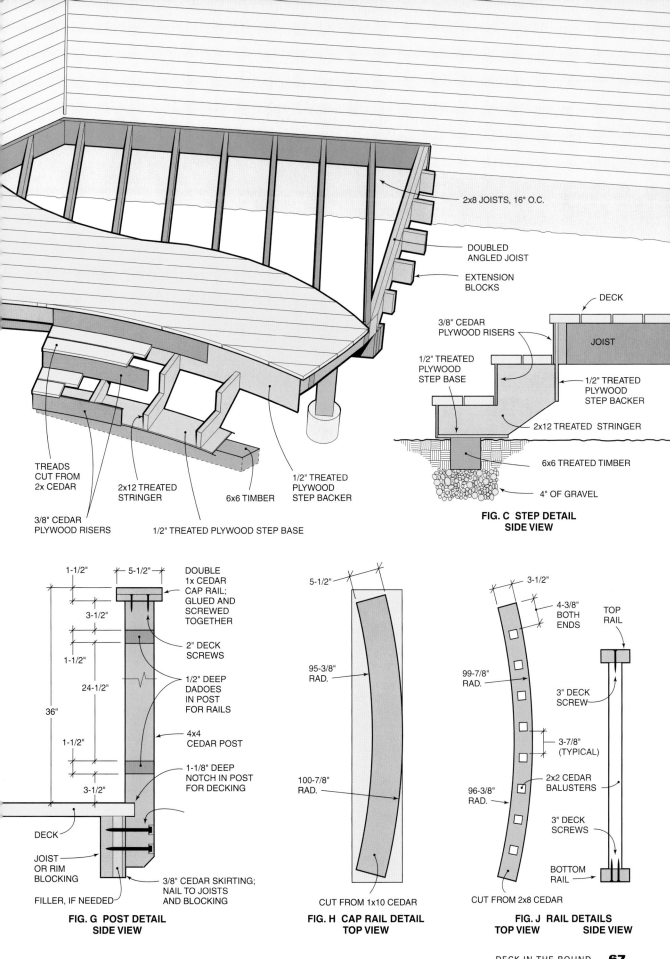

2x8 JOISTS, 16" O.C.

DOUBLED
ANGLED JOIST

EXTENSION
BLOCKS

DECK

3/8" CEDAR
PLYWOOD RISERS

JOIST

1/2" TREATED
PLYWOOD
STEP BASE

1/2" TREATED
PLYWOOD
STEP BACKER

2x12 TREATED STRINGER

6x6 TREATED TIMBER

4" OF GRAVEL

FIG. C STEP DETAIL
SIDE VIEW

TREADS
CUT FROM
2x CEDAR

2x12 TREATED
STRINGER

6x6 TIMBER

1/2" TREATED
PLYWOOD
STEP BACKER

3/8" CEDAR
PLYWOOD RISERS

1/2" TREATED PLYWOOD STEP BASE

1-1/2"   5-1/2"

DOUBLE
1x CEDAR
CAP RAIL;
GLUED AND
SCREWED
TOGETHER

3-1/2"

2" DECK
SCREWS

1-1/2"

1/2" DEEP
DADOES
IN POST
FOR RAILS

24-1/2"

36"

4x4
CEDAR POST

1-1/2"

1-1/8" DEEP
NOTCH IN POST
FOR DECKING

3-1/2"

DECK

JOIST
OR RIM
BLOCKING

FILLER, IF NEEDED

3/8" CEDAR SKIRTING;
NAIL TO JOISTS
AND BLOCKING

FIG. G POST DETAIL
SIDE VIEW

5-1/2"

95-3/8"
RAD.

100-7/8"
RAD.

CUT FROM 1x10 CEDAR

FIG. H CAP RAIL DETAIL
TOP VIEW

3-1/2"

4-3/8"
BOTH
ENDS

TOP
RAIL

99-7/8"
RAD.

3" DECK
SCREW

3-7/8"
(TYPICAL)

2x2 CEDAR
BALUSTERS

96-3/8"
RAD.

3" DECK
SCREWS

BOTTOM
RAIL

CUT FROM 2x8 CEDAR

FIG. J RAIL DETAILS
TOP VIEW   SIDE VIEW

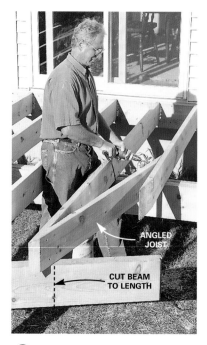

5 Mark joist ends with a pencil at the end of an unstretchable chain or wire. Secure the other end of the chain or wire with a screw at the deck's three pivot points, shown in Figure A. For accuracy, be sure to reuse your original pivot points, rather than using the imprecise spray-painted perimeter lines for a reference. Keep the chain or wire taut and your pencil exactly vertical as you swing your arcs. Double-check your curves for accuracy. Then trim the joist ends to length with a circular saw set to match the angle of the marks.

6 Add angled joists at both ends and the center of the deck, as shown here and Photo 7, to provide support for decking as close to the edges as possible.

ledger's height so the *finished* surface of the deck will fall 1/4 in. *below* the threshold of the door—just enough for a bead of caulk.

Before mounting the ledger, install metal flashing up and under the last course of siding, as shown in Figure E, to prevent water from penetrating behind the ledger.

Place the 6x6 support posts and the beams as shown in Photo 3. This is a critical and tricky step. The beams must be at exactly the right height in comparison to the ledger (in this case, lower than the ledger by the width of the 2x8 joists). They must also be exactly level, and all at exactly the same height. Here's how to accomplish this:

Run a line level (or use a long, perfectly straight board with a level) from the top of the ledger to each footing. Measure from this level line to the top of the footing. Subtract the width of your joists and beams. This gives you the length for each post—to the bottom of its supporting notch, as shown in Figure D.

Next lay joists in place across the beams as shown in

Photo 4. The exact placement of the angled joists, shown in Photos 6 and 7, is determined after the shape of the deck is clearly defined by all the other joist and beam ends.

Decking

We used 2x6 cedar for our decking, proceeding as shown in Photo 8. We spaced our decking boards 1/8 in. apart, since our lumber was quite dry and not likely to shrink excessively. Wetter lumber can be spaced a bit closer.

Buy decking boards of the longest practical length you can find (we used 16-footers). Long boards are often a bit more expensive per foot, but they look better because they have fewer joints to open up over time. Stagger these end joints (always centered over joists) as much as possible for both appearance and strength.

Mark the deck's shape on the decking boards from the three pivot points, the same way you marked the joist ends (Photo 5). Trim the joist ends with a circular saw (Photo 9).

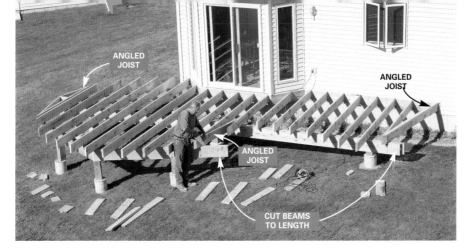

ANGLED JOIST

ANGLED JOIST

ANGLED JOIST

CUT BEAMS TO LENGTH

7 Cut the beam ends to length with a handsaw after all the joist ends are cut.

RIM BLOCKING

SQUARE USED AS SPACER

DECK PERIMETER LINE

8 Lay decking from the house outward, keeping the best side of the board face-up. We used a small square as a spacer to keep the boards 1/8 in. apart. Buy long decking boards to keep end joints to a minimum. Stagger these end joints as widely as possible between joists for both appearance and strength. Use two 3-in. decking screws at each joist. Let your decking boards run long on all the edges—extending at least 3 in. beyond the spray-painted perimeter line. Note the rim blocking placed between the joist ends. Angle-cut each of these rim blocks to length, and secure them with decking screws.

9 Mark the deck perimeter, once again using an unstretchable chain or wire from your pivot points, then cut the deck boards to length. The decking should overhang the joist ends by 1-1/2 inches. A circular saw with a 7-in. blade works best for cutting the curves, but watch out for saw kickback on the concave curve. A hefty jigsaw with a good blade guide will also work, but it takes longer. In either case, take your time and make a neat cut on this very visible part of the job.

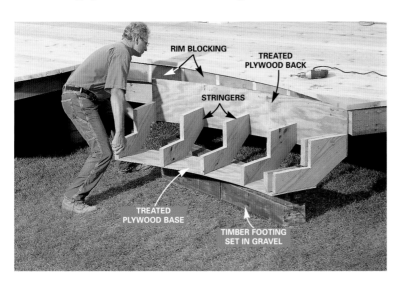

RIM BLOCKING

TREATED PLYWOOD BACK

STRINGERS

TREATED PLYWOOD BASE

TIMBER FOOTING SET IN GRAVEL

10 Build the step platform from five stringers cut from pressure-treated 2x12s and two pieces of 1/2-in. pressure-treated plywood, as shown above and in Figure C. Screw the stringers onto the treated plywood back, then mount this assembly temporarily onto the rim blocking to conform to the curved edge of the deck. Mark the treated plywood base to align with the bottoms of the stringers, and cut it to shape. Place the treated timber footing as described in the text under "Steps" on p. 70, and mount the assembled platform with screws through the plywood into the rim blocking and the timber footing. Place the treads and risers later, as shown in Figure B.

11 Cut strips for skirting from 3/8-in. cedar plywood, and nail it in place around the joist ends with 2-in. galvanized nails. Where there are no joist ends to support the curved skirting shape, cut extension blocks and screw them in place. This helps maintain a consistent 1-1/8 in. deck board overhang beyond the skirting all around the deck.

12 Assemble baluster sections to fit between the posts. First mark and cut the curved 3-1/2 in. wide middle and lower rails from 2x8s by this method: Tack-nail one 2x8 to the deck edge, and use your center pivot point one more time to scribe the inner and outer arcs. (Note from Figures G and H that our inner arc is 1-1/8 in. less than the deck radius; the outer arc is 2-3/8 in. larger.) While you're at it, scribe arcs on a length of 1x10 for the top railing (Photo 14). Cut all these arcs with a band saw or jigsaw. Use these cut sections as templates to form all the other curved railing pieces.

We assembled the baluster sections with the jig shown here in order to maintain a consistent 3-7/8 in. spacing between the 2x2 balusters. One screw at the top and two at the bottom of each baluster prevents them from twisting.

Steps

Our steps are 81 in. wide along the contour of the concave portion of the deck, as shown in Photo 10 and Figure C. The height and number of your steps will be determined by how high your deck is off the ground, but here are some general rules to follow:

Keep each step the same height. The standard height for a step is from 7 to 7-1/2 in.; the standard tread depth is from 11 to 12 in. However, you can reduce the height of each step to as little as 5 in. If you do this, increase the tread depth by the same amount you reduce the height.

Screw together the step unit as shown in Photo 10, matching the curve of the deck. Mount it in place temporarily, so you can determine the height and placement of the treated 6x6 timber on which the steps rest. Then roll back the sod, dig a trench and lay 4 in. of gravel for drainage, and embed the 6x6 timber in the gravel.

Cut the stair treads to their curved shape from cedar 2x8s. Step risers are cut from 3/8-in. cedar plywood, the same material used for the skirting (Photo 11). The skirting encircles the joist ends around the entire deck to form an attractive edge.

Railings and balusters

Our railing-in-the-round, while it's not a piece of cake, is not as daunting as it looks. The first step is to trace and cut out the curved middle and lower rails from 2x8s, as described with Photo 12.

Our balusters are 2x2 cedar, with 3-7/8 in. spacing between them, as shown in Figure J. Most codes require a maximum of 4 in. of space between balusters to prevent entrapment of a child's head. (See "Railing Design & Codes," p. 77.)

The assembly jig we used to make the baluster sections in Photo 12, cut from 1/2-in. plywood, saves time and assures accurate baluster spacing. We preassembled

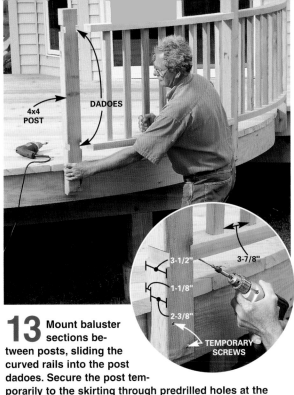

13 Mount baluster sections between posts, sliding the curved rails into the post dadoes. Secure the post temporarily to the skirting through predrilled holes at the post bottoms. Then screw the rails to the posts with angle-driven screws, as shown. Later, when all the posts are in place, remove the screws from the post bottoms, one at a time, drill the holes larger and mount the posts permanently with 6-in. lag bolts and washers. Wherever there is space between the skirting and rim blocking, cut shims to fill.

4x4 POST

DADOES

3-1/2" **3-7/8"**

1-1/8"

2-3/8"

TEMPORARY SCREWS

TOP RAILING

WATERPROOF GLUE BETWEEN LAYERS

14 Install the top railing after marking and cutting the pieces to shape from cedar 1x10s, as described with Photo 12. Screw the sections of the bottom layer to the post tops; splices between sections needn't meet over the posts. Then glue the top layer over the bottom layer using water-resistant wood glue, clamping it as you go and driving 1-1/4 in. screws up through the bottom layer into the top. Make sure the splices in the top layer are offset from those in the bottom by at least 4 inches. Round the corners and sand the edges as shown. We then used a round-over bit in a router to soften all the railing's top edges.

nine separate baluster sections like the one shown lying on the deck in Photo 12. We then installed them section by section, mounting the posts at the same time (Photo 13). The spacing between our posts worked out to be 46-1/8 in. along the circumference, taking into consideration both the baluster spacing and the overall circumference of the deck. Fit all the railing sections in place between posts before permanently securing the posts.

The top railing shown in Photo 14 is 5-1/2 in. wide, and is marked and cut the same way as the middle and lower rails. It's cut from 1x10s rather than 2x10s. The two layers, glued with water-resistant wood glue (Titebond II is a brand sold at most home centers), are screwed together from the bottom. That way the splices can be overlapped for both appearance and strength, and without visible screwheads.

Simple deck

Just follow these step-by-step photos.

—David Radtke

We can't promise you a beachfront view, but we know you'll enjoy relaxing on this simple deck wherever you choose to build it. Since it's at ground level and is freestanding, you don't have to fuss with challenging railings or footings. All you need are basic carpentry tools and a relatively flat area in your yard or garden. The foundation is nothing more than 4x6 treated timbers buried in the soil, with decorative treated joists and construction-grade cedar decking and a bench. Follow the instructions along with the photos for detailed measurements and building techniques.

Project at a glance

Skill level
Beginner

Special tools
Circular saw
Jigsaw

Approximate cost
$900

MATERIALS LIST

QTY.	SIZE	DESCRIPTION
2	4x6 x 12'	treated timbers
9	2x6 x 10'	cedar joists
2	2x6 x 10'	cedar for blocking
1	2x12 x 10'	cedar bench supports
2	2x6 x 10'	cedar bench tops
22	2x6 x 12	cedar decking
32		metal corner brackets
3 lbs.		galv. joist hanger nails
2 lbs.		No. 8 galv. box nails
10 lbs.		16d galv. casing nails
1 lb.		3-in. galv. deck screws

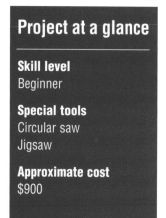

HERE'S ALL THE LUMBER YOU'LL NEED, COLOR-CODED TO OUR PLANS AND PHOTOS.

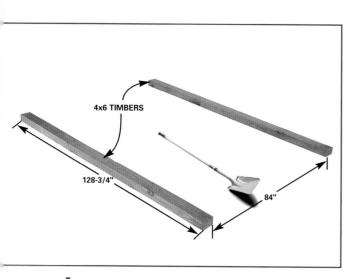

4x6 TIMBERS

128-3/4"

84"

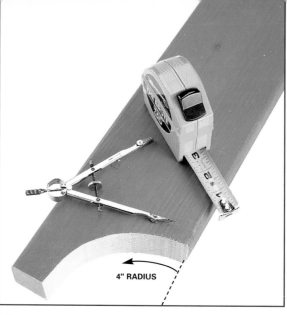

4" RADIUS

1 Dig the 4x6 timbers into the soil, leaving about 1-1/2 in. of the top exposed. The timbers must be parallel and the diagonal measurements must be equal.

2 Cut each treated 2x6 joist to 10 ft. Cut the decorative curve on each end, as shown, before installing them onto the 4x6 treated timbers.

FIRST BLOCK IS 13-1/4"

ALIGN FACE OF FIRST JOIST WITH END OF TIMBER

REMAINDER OF BLOCKS ARE 14-1/2"

Tool List

- Shovel
- Square
- Tape measure
- Level
- Compass
- Chalk line
- Jigsaw
- Hammer
- Circular saw
- Hearing and eye protection, gloves

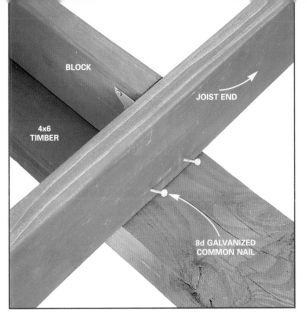

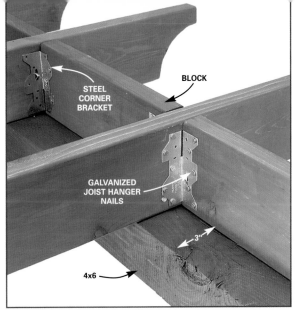

3 Lay out the joist spacing so the joists are on 16-in. centers. Cut the blocks to fit between the joists. The first set of blocks (one on each side) will be 13-1/4 in., while the remainder will be 14-1/2 in. long. Toenail each joist to the timber as shown. Be sure the ends of all the joists align with each other as you toenail them in place.

4 Nail your steel corner brackets to the joists and each block between with 1-1/4 in. galvanized joist hanger nails. The blocks add stability and give the deck a finished look.

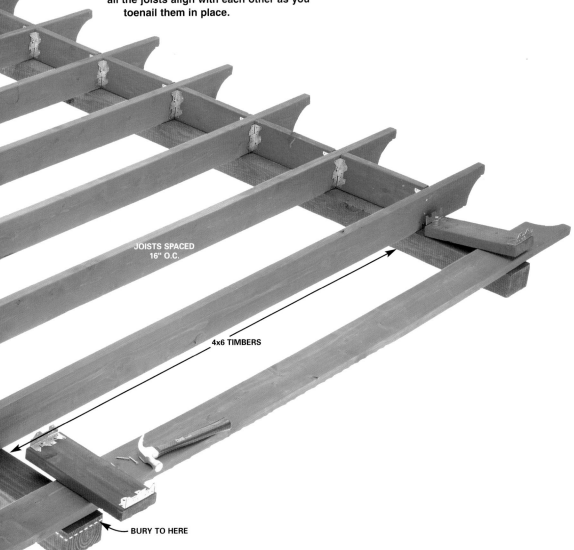

JOISTS SPACED 16" O.C.

4x6 TIMBERS

BURY TO HERE

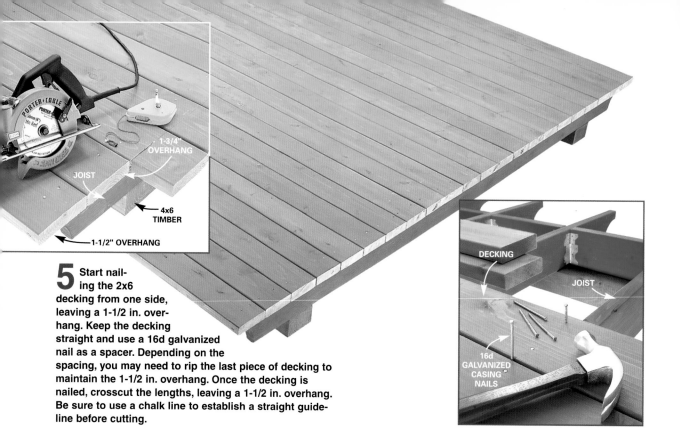

5 Start nailing the 2x6 decking from one side, leaving a 1-1/2 in. overhang. Keep the decking straight and use a 16d galvanized nail as a spacer. Depending on the spacing, you may need to rip the last piece of decking to maintain the 1-1/2 in. overhang. Once the decking is nailed, crosscut the lengths, leaving a 1-1/2 in. overhang. Be sure to use a chalk line to establish a straight guideline before cutting.

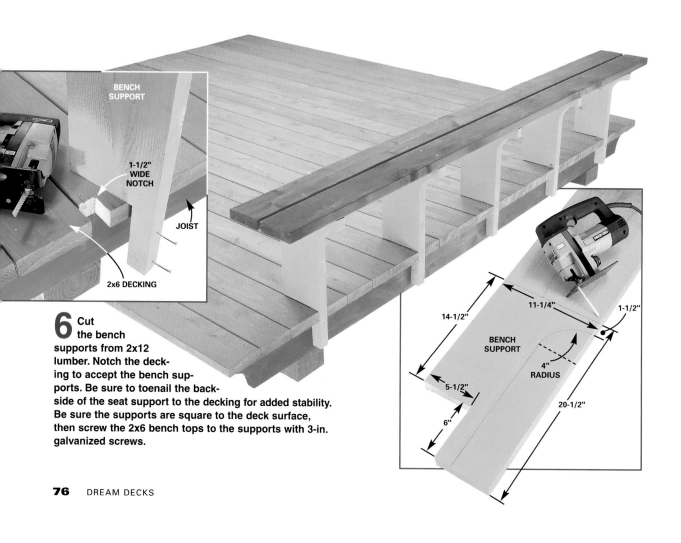

6 Cut the bench supports from 2x12 lumber. Notch the decking to accept the bench supports. Be sure to toenail the backside of the seat support to the decking for added stability. Be sure the supports are square to the deck surface, then screw the 2x6 bench tops to the supports with 3-in. galvanized screws.

Railing design & codes

Where function meets beauty.

—*Spike Carlsen*

Building the just-right deck railing is a real brainteaser; you want a railing enclosed enough to stop people from falling through or over it, yet open enough for them to enjoy the view beyond.

Figuring out the building codes and regulations to follow can be a brainteaser too. This article contains some general guidelines. But be aware that every community has its own guidelines; find out what they are before hammering the first nail.

The illustrations show some deck rail possibilities. Each railing is discussed in terms of its strength, code compliance and style. You'll find information about handrails too.

FIGURE A
Safe railing and stairway

ACCEPTABLE HANDRAIL

200 LBS. OF FORCE

UNACCEPTABLE HANDRAIL

36"

4" SPHERE

TREAD NOSE

4" SPHERE

6" SPHERE

30" OR MORE

RISER

A safe railing and stairway must meet many guidelines. Decks 30 in. or more off the ground must have a 36-in. high railing, a design in which a 4-in. sphere is unable to pass through, and strength to resist 200 lbs. of force. Stairways with a rise of 30 or more in. must include graspable handrails positioned 34 to 38 in. above the tread nose. In some jurisdictions, the triangular opening formed by the riser, tread and bottom rail must be designed so a 6-in. sphere is unable to pass through.

FIGURE B
Vertical spindle guardrail

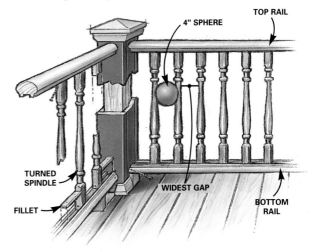

4" SPHERE

TOP RAIL

TURNED SPINDLE

WIDEST GAP

FILLET

BOTTOM RAIL

A vertical spindle guardrail comes in two common forms. A turned spindle version uses manufactured spindles, top and bottom rails, fillets and support posts as a system. Spindles fit into grooves on the horizontal rails. The 4-in. sphere must not be able to pass through the widest gap created by the contoured spindles.

The square spindle version (Figure A) uses 2x2 spindles of cedar, redwood or treated wood, with the top attached to a rail and the bottom secured to a rail or deck rim. The bottom rail must not be more than 4 in. above the deck. Remember to account for shrinkage; a 4-in. spacing with new wood can turn into a code-violating, 4-1/2 in. gap when spindles dry and shrink.

FIGURE C
Clear panel guardrail

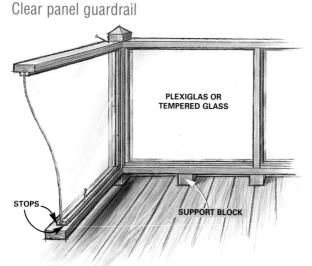

PLEXIGLAS OR
TEMPERED GLASS

STOPS

SUPPORT BLOCK

FIGURE D
Combination bench/guardrail

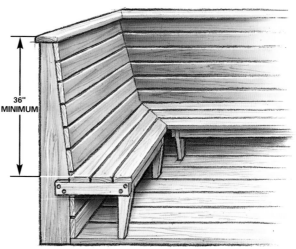

36"
MINIMUM

A clear panel guardrail using Plexiglas, tempered or laminated glass provides a clear view, wind protection and a sturdy barrier. Panels should be 1/4 in. thick for small areas; 3/8 in. for larger panels. Some inspectors require the panel to meet Consumer Product Safety Commission guidelines. A block supporting the bottom rail every 24 in. will minimize bowing. Clear panels should be held in place with 1 x 1-in. stops, secured every 8 in. with 2-in. galvanized screws. Some plastics yellow and become brittle with age; they also expand and contract more dramatically than glass.

The combination bench/guardrail provides both seating and fall prevention, but at a cost: Most inspectors measure the 36-in. guardrail height from the top of the seat. This can create an overall rail height of 52 in. or more. The space beneath the benches must be enclosed so a 4-in. sphere can't pass through.

Make it strong, make it last

In addition to written building codes, local inspectors may judge the suitability of a railing by local conditions: winds, earthquakes, snow loads and other factors.

Nonetheless, there are guidelines every deck builder should follow:

■ Always use galvanized, stainless steel or exterior grade fasteners.

■ Use screws, bolts, ring or spiral shank nails and other fasteners with threaded or contoured shanks. They'll grip better than smooth ones. This is important because exterior wood swells, shrinks and moves dramatically.

■ Secure your railings solidly where they meet the house. In many cases, a metal L-bracket or a metal framing anchor does the best job.

■ If you're adding on to an existing deck, bring the old part up to current codes. Your completed deck will be safer and look more uniform—and some building inspectors will require it anyway.

■ Use the right materials, fasteners and techniques. A deck and its railings will only be as strong as their weakest link. Often the right lumber and fasteners are used, but they're assembled in a shoddy manner, leading to structural failure.

■ If, by code, your deck isn't high enough to require a railing, but you include one anyway, most building officials will still require it to meet building code. Even though the railing isn't necessary to prevent falls, it still must be designed to prevent head entrapment.

FIGURE E
Steel cable guardrail

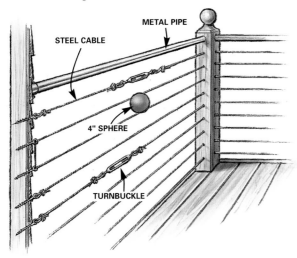

A steel cable guardrail using cable spaced every 3-1/2 in. provides fall protection and a minimally obstructed view. To meet code, inspectors will check to make sure cables can't be stretched to create a gap wider than 4 in.; that's a dangerous situation, particularly for head entrapment. To keep the cable taut, corner posts must be held rigid and the cable should have a turnbuckle system for tightening it. This has the drawback of any horizontal railing: It's climbable, putting anyone who climbs it at risk of falling an even greater distance. Many inspectors wouldn't allow this design.

FIGURE F
Lattice guardrail

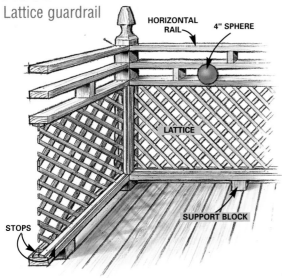

A lattice guardrail is quick, easy and inexpensive to install. But closely crisscrossing slats block the view, and some manufactured lattice is flimsy and easily broken. For rigidity, construct lattice panels in 4-ft., rather than 8-ft., long sections. Build a combination lattice-horizontal rail design, as shown, to provide a less obstructed view when you're seated.

FIGURE G
Stairs and handrails

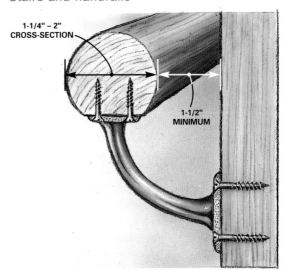

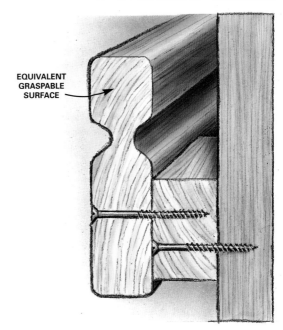

Stairs and handrails must also conform to regulations:
- Stairways must have handrails as specified in Figure A.
- Handrails on both sides, while addressed differently by different communities, do provide an extra measure of safety, especially on stairways exceeding 36 in. in width.
- The handrail must be 1-1/4 to 2 in. in cross-section (or an equivalent graspable surface), be spaced 1-1/2 in. away from the wall or railing, and have a smooth surface with no sharp corners.
- The 2x4 or 2x6 board used to cap many stairway railings doesn't create a graspable surface or comply with codes. An independent grooved or round handrail, as shown, is much safer.

Gallery of ideas

A deck creates that outdoor living, cooking and relaxing space many of us yearn for. Several of the projects include another feature most of us love—low maintenance. For information on obtaining plans for building the decks shown here, see Resources, p. 252.

Garden pond & deck

The heart of this outdoor structure is an in-ground pond constructed from treated wood and a flexible rubber liner. The surrounding deck has top boards of a tropical hardwood called Ipe. A sluice presents the soothing sound of water and connects the pond to a separate container housing a filter.

Wood/stone deck

This deck combines wood with a natural-looking stone wall crafted from manufactured stone veneer. The wall is a perfect height for sitting, and the two-level deck helps creates two defined spaces. It's a project best tackled by ambitious intermediate or advanced do-it-yourselfers. Expect to spend at least $4,000 for materials.

Dream deck

This small deck is big on special features. The upper deck is just the right size for entertaining small groups, the pergola offers shade and a place for climbing plants and the lower deck is a great place to lounge in the sun. The decking is a low-maintenance composite material with a tongue-and-groove design that allows you to hide the fasteners. The price of this gem? At least $7,000 for the materials alone.

Easy-care deck

This "new deck" is actually a resurrected old deck. The worn decking was replaced with a low-maintenance composite material, and a new railing with aluminum spindles was built. A lower landing, stairway and privacy screen make this deck better than new.

CHAPTER

Dream arbors, trellises & garden accents

Bent-sapling arbor

Create your own eye-catching garden sculpture.

—Travis Larson

People have been bending, weaving and lashing saplings ever since they figured out what opposable thumbs were for. Shelters, baskets, fish traps—you name it—were made with a bit of leather and a few green saplings or limbs.

The good news is that today you don't have to use dried beaver gut to lash sticks together. Using just about any fastener in your junk drawer and green (live) branches or saplings, you can create an arbor for your garden. Best of all, you don't even need much of a plan.

Rough out your ideas as you go and wing the actual construction. Let your imagination roam. Work in some hearts or decorate with some spider webs or butterflies made of twigs.

We suggest that you proceed in two steps. First, build a simple trellis to get the hang of sapling construction. We made just a wall section and leaned it against the house to complement the arbor. Then tackle the full-scale arbor.

You only need one power tool

The only power tool we used was a cordless drill to screw the side walls and top section together at the site. Besides that, you'll need a saw to cut large pieces (we used a bow saw; Photo 13), pruning shears for small pieces (Photo 7) and lopping shears for the in-between sizes (Photo 6).

A utility knife comes in handy both for easing the sharp edges on end cuts (Photo 3) and for cutting the plastic drain tile used for the footing (Photo 18). The willow bender who helped us preferred a ball peen hammer (Photo 10) to a conventional hammer for nailing because the former is less likely to damage the bark on errant back swings. He'd also place a hand maul behind the saplings he was hammering together to support the object being nailed. The maul was either hand-held for "up in the air" nailing or set on the floor under the pieces (Photo 1).

Cut saplings in the fall, winter or early spring

Before harvesting a lot of stock, test various diameters by bending them. The tighter the bend, the smaller the sapling you'll need to cut. That's why you should have some idea about the design before going into the woods. Plan on assembling your project within a few days of harvesting, when the wood is still fresh and flexible. If your project will stretch over several weeks, cut just enough saplings for that weekend's work.

Although sandbar willow

Plan Smart

It's best to do your harvesting during the months when the saplings are without leaves. The wood is more pliable and the bark is tougher and harder to damage during assembly. If you're eager to get started, go ahead and harvest your saplings anytime. But plan on using a bit more patience and care while bending, cutting and assembling.

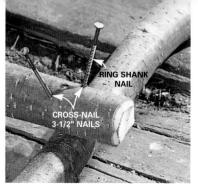

COMPLETE END FRAME

RING SHANK NAIL

CROSS-NAIL 3-1/2" NAILS

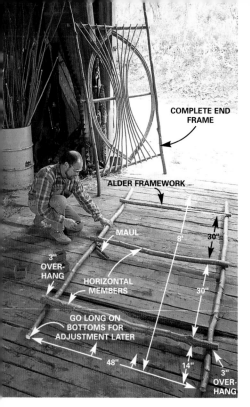

ALDER FRAMEWORK

MAUL

8'

30"

3" OVER-HANG

HORIZONTAL MEMBERS

30"

GO LONG ON BOTTOMS FOR ADJUSTMENT LATER

48"

14"

3" OVER-HANG

2 Cross-nail from two directions on all larger framing members. Cross-nailing will not only provide a strong anchor but also help prevent splitting at the ends.

3 Soften outer edges by beveling them with a utility knife. Shave off protruding nubs on ends that will be exposed.

BOTTOM

EVENLY SPACED SAPLINGS

1 Select four 8-ft. long, 2-1/2 in. dia. straight saplings for corners, and fasten evenly spaced horizontal members with 3-1/2 in. ring-shank nails. Leave plenty of extra length (at least 14 in.) on the legs for anchoring to the ground and for adjusting to uneven terrain. Overlap the 54-in. horizontal members 3 in. on each end to give a 48-in. wide end panel.

4 Gently flex pieces to be used for curved elements. A little initial coaxing will help keep them from splitting during assembly. Bend thicker ends more gradually to lessen the chance of kinking.

5 Flip the end frame over. Tack the center cluster and evenly space the sapling ends for decorative side spray. Position thicker ends at the bottom.

is a great material for bent structures, nearly any green sapling will do. Rustic artisans use dogwood, spirea, cherry, apple, cypress, cedar and bamboo. Weeping willow, with its fragile branches, is a poor choice for larger framing parts, but the delicate branches work well for intricate detailing. Birch is a great, straight sapling for bending but tends to have a shorter lifespan than other choices. Experiment to determine the bending qualities of the type of sapling you're considering. If it splinters easily, try another type of wood. A field guidebook is handy to have around to help identify species while you're scavenging.

If your lot doesn't include woods, try these sources for materials, *but make sure you ask permission first:*

■ Farms are good bets. We found our sandbar willow in a small drainage ditch next to a cornfield.

■ Utility lines are always monitored for invasive tree growth. You can contact utility companies to find out where they'll be cutting to gather downed limbs and saplings.

■ New housing developments are generally cleared prior to construction. It's even better if you can get there before they're cleared because it's easier to select and harvest while the wood is still standing than after it has been damaged by bulldozers or buried in dirt.

■ Nurseries or professional tree trimmers will often let you collect their prunings.

■ Orchards do a lot of pruning and are a great source of fruitwood cuttings.

6 Set the nails and trim ends evenly with lopping shears after you're satisfied with the placement.

7 Cut 45-degree angles on outwardly curving bent saplings, starting with the outside pieces first. Add the other two layers of saplings and fasten them to the horizontal members and to each other by nailing the sides together. Alternate butt ends on each row (thick-thin-thick).

8 Clamp rows together to hold them tightly for nailing.

9 Overlap the second half of each row to sight and match miter angle, then cut with lopping shears and nail into place.

Use thicker, straight saplings for posts, and mix wood species for the best results

On our arbor, we used sandbar willow for all of the curved elements. Small, highly curved decorative details are made of thinner, more flexible members. We chose alder for the framework on the sides and top section (Photos 1 – 3) because it's stiffer than willow and lends the arbor more rigidity. Our alder framework pieces had diameters between 1-3/4 and 2-1/4 in. Selecting straight posts isn't always easy, but we picked the best ones we could find. Try not to get too caught up in the frustration of perfection when building with saplings. When all is said and done, crooked parts will add personality to your sculpture.

Design your arbor, build it in the garage and finish assembling it in the garden

Initially we planned to build our arbor on-site, then realized it would be easier to prebuild the two sides and the arched top in the shop, then assemble the components later in the garden. We decided on the dimensions for our arbor by positioning some scrap wood on the ground. We eyeballed the size, scratched our heads and settled on a footprint (base dimension and shape) that is 5 ft. wide and 4 ft. deep with a height of about 6-1/2 ft. to the bottom of the arch.

Don't pay too much attention to our dimensions. (Our willow bender used his eye and hammer head for most measuring. After all, we are building with sticks.) But several of the measurements really count. The side wall posts must fit inside the outside width of the top

10 Cut the arch base out of the same material as the sides. Add 6 in. to the length so you can hang each side over 3 in. Nail the first arch piece 3 in. from the end, starting with the butt end of the sapling. The height of the arch is arbitrary; ours is about 2 ft. tall.

11 Add the last two saplings to the side of the main arch, nailing these pieces to the ends and to each other. Use the first arch framework as a template to ensure curve and height symmetry for both arches.

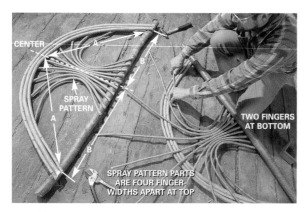

12 Measure to find the center of the arch's top and bottom. Distances A should be equal. Find B by dividing the length of the bottom by two. Tack the bottom of the two middle pieces and equally space and tack the tops of these saplings onto the outsides of the arched ends. Continue installing each right and left pair. Check spacing and set nails when satisfied. Trim ends flush.

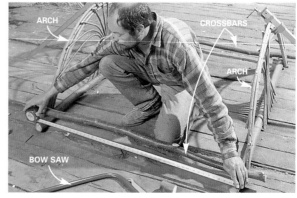

13 Prop up the arches side by side exactly the same distance apart as the width of the end panels. This is the only really important measurement for the whole project—remember, you'll be attaching the top to the sides. Nail the crossbar to the arch base. Cut and attach a doubled ridge and two intermediate purlins to the outsides of the arches.

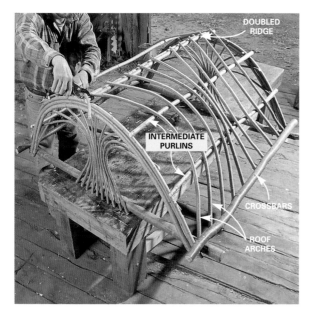

14 Nail roof arches to the inside of the crossbar, to the outside of the intermediate purlins and to one side of the ridge and cut to length.

panel for fastening. We made both end walls exactly the same width, then made the top arch to fit inside the corners (Photo 13). When you're cutting the corner posts to length, remember that at least 1 ft. will be in the ground (Photo 18), so make sure to cut the posts to accommodate the footing while still leaving plenty of headroom under the arch.

Put it together with nails and screws

We used a combination of 2, 2-1/2, 3 and 3-1/2 in. ring-shank, ungalvanized underlayment nails. Use the longest possible nails that won't split the wood or come out the other side. The ring shanks help hold the fasteners in the wood, especially when it's still green and under the stress of bending. There's no need to use outdoor-grade fasten-

15 Screw the side frames to the arch top with 3-1/2 in. drywall screws.

Labels: TOP ARCH, SIDE WALLS, 3-1/2" DRYWALL SCREWS

16 Cut 8-in. long corner braces and screw them to the bottom of the arch and the side framework on all four corners with 3-1/2 in. drywall screws.

Labels: 3-1/2" DRYWALL SCREWS, 8" CORNER BRACE WITH 45° ANGLES, SIDE FRAME, HORIZONTAL MEMBER OF TOP ARCH

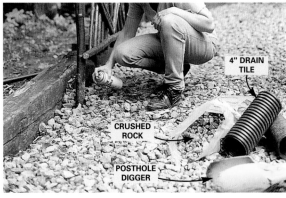

17 Position the arbor exactly in the desired location and draw circles around the legs with spray paint. Set aside the arbor and dig 8-in. wide by 18-in. deep postholes.

Labels: 4" DRAIN TILE, CRUSHED ROCK, POSTHOLE DIGGER

18 Cut 18-in. lengths of 4-in. perforated drain tile and lay them in the postholes. Pour in about 6 in. of crushed gravel, set the arbor in the drain tile and level it by adjusting the gravel at the bottom of the hole. When you're satisfied with the placement, fill around the corner posts with more crushed gravel.

Labels: CRUSHED ROCK, 4" DRAIN TILE

ers, because any fastener will outlive the woodwork, and rusted nailheads will add to the natural, rustic character of the work. If you decide to add decorative twig accents, use twisted light-gauge wire for fastening. For final assembly, use 3-1/2 in. drywall screws (Photos 15 and 16).

Crushed rock footings will make it last longer

Although you can simply stick the four legs in the ground, installing some cheap, easy footings made of 4-in. drain tile pipe with some 3/4-in. crushed gravel for drainage will help prevent rot and make the whole structure last longer (Photos 17 and 18). Nearly any gravel will work, but the rough, sharp edges on crushed gravel will lock together to keep the trellis more stable. Using this footing system will provide better drainage around the legs and prolong the life of your arbor. Soaking the legs in wood preservative will further lengthen the life of below-grade wood.

Enhance the beauty with an exterior sealer

A finish that repels water is optional, but it will add to the outdoor life expectancy of your arbor. A clear exterior-grade deck sealer will also enhance the beauty of the natural material. If you apply a finish, do it before final assembly to get better coverage and to keep the chemicals away from any plants.

Arbor
with seats

Create your own private garden getaway.

—David Radtke

I f you're looking for a weekend project to beautify your yard or garden and you want it to be solid, straightforward and built to last, this project is for you. This graceful arbor triples as a shade trellis to grow flowering vines overhead and a garden retreat to melt away the hubbub of our too busy lives.

This project may appear complex at first glance, but it's designed with foolproof methods for building the graceful arches, measuring and cutting the decorative lintel ends and getting the posts precisely positioned. The whole project is made from ordinary cedar dimensional lumber and four 2x4 posts of pressure-treated pine. The trellis and roof lattice parts are cut from cedar decking and provide sturdy yet graceful support for climbing vines. You can either build the arbor over an existing path or walkway, or complete the project by laying a footpath using your favorite stone.

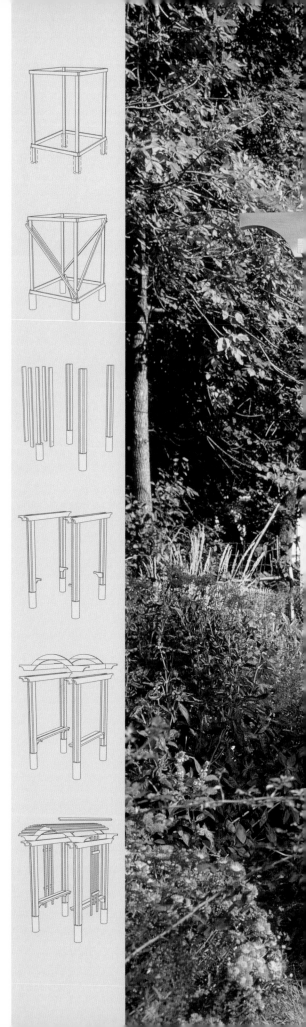

Project at a glance

Skill level
Intermediate

Special tools
Circular saw
Jigsaw
Doweling jig
Belt sander

Approximate cost
$400

1 Build the post framework first, then before you pour concrete into the 18-in. deep postholes, shim and level the assembly. Note: The red lumber pieces are temporary supports to hold the posts in position while you plumb and level and pour the concrete (see text below).

Image labels:
PRESSURE-TREATED 2x4 (A)
UPPER HORIZONTAL BRACES (aa and bb)
DIAGONAL BRACES (cc)
LOWER HORIZONTAL BRACES (aa and bb)
BENCH SIDE
OPEN SIDE
BOTTOM BRACE (cc)

The framework

When you're building any outdoor structure, setting and plumbing the posts can be a real pain. To make this task hassle free, I've designed a basic framework that resembles a cube (Photo 1) to hold the posts precisely in position while you mark the posthole locations. Then, once the holes are dug, this same framework allows you to easily plumb the posts as you pour the concrete. Here's how it actually works:

First, cut your posts to length. Next, check the width of your 2x4 posts. Pressure-treated wood is sometimes a bit wider than, say, 2x4 cedar. To prevent ugly gaps later, be sure the width of your posts is 3-1/2 in. (or just under to be safe).

Next, cut your braces (aa and bb) to length and screw the upper open-side horizontal braces (aa) flush with the top of the posts. Then measure up 18 in. from the bottom of each post and screw the lower horizontal braces to each pair of posts.

ITEM	QTY.
2x4 x 10' treated pine (parts A)	4
2x4 x 8' cedar (parts B)	8
2x6 x 8' cedar (parts C, H)	8
2x6 x 8' cedar (parts D, E, F, G)	8
2x6 x 12' cedar (parts Q, J, K)	3
5/4 x 6 x 10' cedar decking (L, M, N, P, R)	9
2x4 x 12' pine (horizontal braces)	4
2x2 x 8' pine (diagonal braces)	5
60-lb. bags of concrete mix	5
5-lb. box of 3" deck screws	1
5-lb. box of 2" deck screws	1
3/8" x 4" galvanized lag screws and washers	12
1/2" x 2" wooden dowel pins	16
Waterproof carpenter's glue (Titebond or Elmer's)	1 pint
Construction adhesive	1 tube

CUTTING LIST

KEY	QTY.	SIZE & DESCRIPTION
A	4	1-1/2" x 3-1/2" x 102" pressure-treated pine posts
B	8	1-1/2" x 3-1/2" x 84" cedar post wraps
C	8	1-1/2" x 5-1/2" x 84" cedar post wraps
D	2	1-1/2" x 5-1/2" x 41" cedar top arch members
E	2	1-1/2" x 5-1/2" x 54" cedar middle arch members
F	2	1-1/2" x 5-1/2" x 87" cedar bottom arch members
G	4	1-1/2" x 5-1/2" x 96" cedar lintels
H	4	1-1/2" x 5-1/2" x 11-1/2" cedar seat supports
J	2	1-1/2" x 5-1/2" x 61" cedar back seat planks**
K	2	1-1/2" x 5-1/2" x 66" cedar front seat planks
L	2	1-1/16" x 2-5/8" x 10" cedar middle seat supports
M	4	1-1/16" x 2-5/8" x 85" cedar outer trellis slats
N	2	1-1/16" x 2-5/8" x 74-1/2" cedar middle trellis slats
P	4	1-1/16" x 2-5/8" x 18" cedar horizontal trellis supports
Q	2	1-1/2" x 5-1/2" x 69" cedar stringers
R	11	1-1/16" x 2-5/8" x 120" cedar roof slats
aa	4	2x4 x 61" open-side horizontal braces*
bb	4	2x4 x 68" bench-side horizontal braces*
cc	5	2x2 x 96" diagonal braces

*Cut these braces to exact length
**Cut to fit

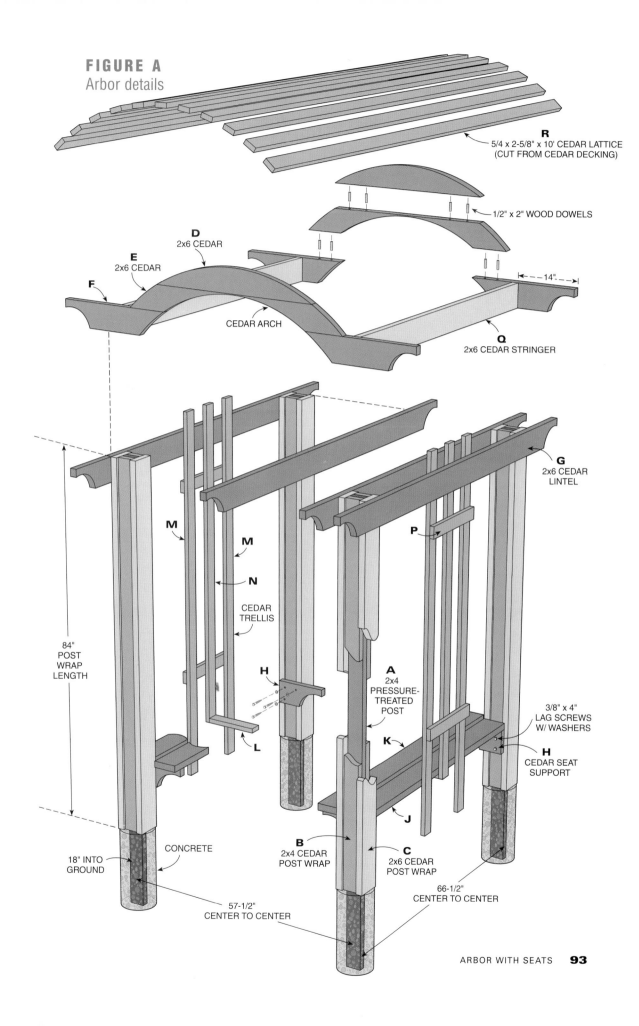

FIGURE A
Arbor details

R
5/4 x 2-5/8" x 10' CEDAR LATTICE
(CUT FROM CEDAR DECKING)

1/2" x 2" WOOD DOWELS

D
2x6 CEDAR

E
2x6 CEDAR

F

←— 14" —→

CEDAR ARCH

Q
2x6 CEDAR STRINGER

G
2x6 CEDAR
LINTEL

M

M

N

P

CEDAR
TRELLIS

84"
POST
WRAP
LENGTH

H

A
2x4
PRESSURE-
TREATED
POST

3/8" x 4"
LAG SCREWS
W/ WASHERS

K

H
CEDAR SEAT
SUPPORT

L

J

18" INTO
GROUND

CONCRETE

B
2x4 CEDAR
POST WRAP

C
2x6 CEDAR
POST WRAP

57-1/2"
CENTER TO CENTER

66-1/2"
CENTER TO CENTER

ARBOR WITH SEATS **93**

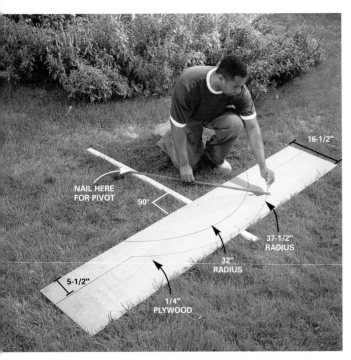

2 Scribe an arc onto a piece of 1/4-in. plywood 96 in. long to form the template for the arched ends of the arbor. Center, then fasten a board to the back side of the plywood. Then make a beam compass with a straight piece of wood. Nail one end of the compass strip (21 in. from plywood) on the board and drill two 1/4-in. holes for your arcs: one at 32 in. from the nail and the other at 37-1/2 in. Draw the arcs onto the plywood and cut the shape with a jigsaw.

3 Lay parts D, E and F onto the sawhorses and push them together tightly. Lay the template over the pieces and trace the arch shape onto the pieces. Next, mark the dowel hole locations so they fall within the arch. Drill 1/2-in. dowel holes using a self-centering doweling jig. Coat the dowels and surfaces with outdoor carpenter's glue and clamp them overnight.

Next, stand the end panels upright as shown in Photo 1 and screw the other pairs of horizontal braces to the posts. Next, add the diagonal brace. The diagonal braces will "square up" the cube. Make sure the diagonal measurements of each opposite cube side are equal before you screw them to the framework.

Once your framework is complete, move it around the garden to define your exact location. Once you've chosen the position, mark the posthole locations and dig

Work Smart

It's important to apply an oil-based deck finish within a day after assembly or at least finish the cut ends to keep them from checking in the hot sun.

postholes 18 in. deep and 8 in. wide. With the holes completed, set the framework legs into the holes (Photo 1). Level each lower horizontal brace by shimming it where necessary. (Don't drive yourself crazy trying to get it exact; close is good enough.) Then, mix up concrete (about a bag per hole) in a tub or wheelbarrow and fill each hole. Make the top of the concrete fairly flat to the ground level because you'll be adding 2x4s and 2x6s to the posts later.

The arches are the defining element of the arbor (like tail feathers on a peacock)

The secret to making the arches is to first make a template like the one shown in Photo 2. Draw the template with the beam compass and cut the shape with a jigsaw. Lay the 2x6 cedar pieces D, E and F onto a set of saw-

4 Cut the remaining pieces using the Cutting List on p. 92. Trace a curve on the ends of the arch assemblies, the lintels and the seat supports. We used a 9-1/2 in. section of the base of a 5-gallon pail with a radius of 5 in. Cut them out with a jigsaw and smooth the edges with a belt sander.

5 Wrap all sides of the pressure-treated 2x4s with cedar. Screw 2x4 cedar on the open sides of the posts and 2x6 on the bench sides of the posts using 3-in. deck screws. Be sure the tops of all the pieces are flush.

horses (Photo 3). Draw a line down the center of each piece and lay them edge to edge. Set the template onto the 2x6 pieces and trace the shape with a template. When you remove the template, you'll easily see where to position the dowels so they fall within the arch. Drill the 1/2-in. holes with a drill and doweling jig to 1 in. deep. (Use 2-in. long precut dowel pins available at a home center or hardware store.)

Once you've drilled the dowel holes, spread glue onto the 2x6s only in the areas that are within the arch. Roll the dowel pins in glue and insert them into the holes, and clamp each assembly (Photo 3). Set them aside to dry overnight and then cut each arch along the marks with a jigsaw. Smooth the curves with a belt sander. To complete the arch assemblies, mark and cut (Photo 4) the curved ends and smooth them with sandpaper.

Building the lower section of the arbor

Cut the 2x4 and 2x6 cedar wrap pieces (B and C) to length and then screw them to the posts as shown in Photo 5. The 2x6s will overlap the 2x4s a half inch on each side. Next, cut the lintels to length and the decorative shapes at the ends using the same technique as you did for the arch ends. Screw the lintels flush with the tops of the posts.

Don't mount the seat supports flush with the posts. Instead, measure back 1 in. from the outer edge of the wrapped posts to allow room for mounting the trellis later. Clamp the top of the seat braces 16 in. up from the bottom of the posts and then predrill and attach them to the posts with lag screws.

Note that the seats have a center support (L) connecting the 2x6 planks beneath for stability. Make this piece

6 Center the lintels along the posts and screw them flush (four screws per post) with the top of the posts with 3-in. deck screws.

7 Fasten the seat supports securely to the posts. Predrill the holes with a 5/16-in. drill bit. Then cut and screw the seat planks to the tops of the supports with 3-in. deck screws. Assemble the trellis and screw it in place.

as well as the trellis and roof lattice by ripping 5/4 x 6 decking in half and then cutting the pieces to length. Screw piece L flush to the back of the seat planks.

Next, preassemble the trellis (parts M, N and P). Glue and screw (use construction adhesive here and 2-in. deck screws) the top horizontal tie 16 in. from the top of parts M and N. Screw the lower tie 22 in. from the bottom of parts M. Make sure the lattice assemblies are square. Set them aside for a couple of hours while the glue sets and then screw them to the seat and stringer above. Screw the center slat of the trellis over the center seat support (L) and then attach the outer slats to the back of the seat and at the top into the outer lintels.

Fasten the roof assembly to the posts and lintels

Fasten the arches together with parts Q. Lift this assembly over the lintels (Photo 8), center it side to side and end to end, then toe-screw it in place. Note: Be sure to clamp braces to the posts before screwing the roof assembly in place. The clamps will help hold the posts parallel during the process.

Now you're ready to fasten the roof slats (Photo 9) cut from 5/4 x 6 decking that you've ripped in half. Note: Buy extra pieces of 5/4 decking for the roof lattice. You'll find that even though you picked straight lumber from the pile at the lumberyard or home center, some pieces will spring out of shape when you rip them with your saw.

Apply a quality exterior finish

We chose an oil stain/sealer that mimicked weathered wood, so even as the finish degrades over time, the appearance will be the same. Before you stain, spread a dropcloth below, especially if you have a patio or stone path under the arbor!

8 Fasten the stringers (Q) to the front and rear arches to form the arbor roof assembly. Clamp the top of the posts to temporary spacers to keep them parallel while you lift the roof assembly onto the lintels. Toe-screw the roof assembly to the posts and the lintels with 3-in. deck screws (three screws at each location).

9 Rip 5/4 x 6 cedar decking in half to make the roof lattice. Round the cut edges of each piece with a hand plane. Start in the middle and work each way, spacing the slats 2-5/8 in. apart. Screw them to the arches with 2-1/2 in. screws.

Buy pressure-treated lumber with the right amount of treatment for the job

Pressure-treated lumber is the logical choice for the structural part of your arbor. Pressure-treated lumber can support more weight and span longer distances than cedar, redwood or other woods commonly used for their appearance. It's also much less expensive.

Pressure-treated lumber is rated according to the pounds of preservative retained per cubic foot of wood;

"ABOVE GRADE"
.15 TO .25 LBS./CU. FT.

"GROUND CONTACT"
.40 LBS./CU. FT.

"BELOW GRADE"
.60 LBS./CU. FT.

the higher the number, the better the protection against fungi and insect attack. Select boards with the preservative suitable for their use.

The three common ratings:

1. **Above-ground use** (.25, sometimes 1.5). Typically used for decking, fence and railing material.
2. **Ground-contact use** (.40). Typically used for posts, beams, joists and, again, decking.
3. **Below-grade** (.60). Typically used for support posts that are partially buried below grade and for permanent wood foundations and planters.

Your boards will be tagged with the concentration and treating solution used. Use .40 material if you can't find .25. CCA (chromated copper arsenate) is being phased out because of health concerns. ACQ (Alkaline Copper Quat) and other preservatives are replacing it.

Copper trellis

A garden project with a twist.

—Ken Collier

The first reaction of my neighbor when she saw this trellis was, "Wow! I love it!" The second reaction was, "How in the world did you make it?"

Well, there's a trick to bending the wire, that's for sure, but once you understand it, this trellis goes together pretty easily. When you're done, you've got an elegant garden ornament that looks great even when the plants that climb on it have died back.

Give it a year or two outdoors and the wood will turn gray and the copper will turn a beautiful dark brown, and then eventually green. It wouldn't be hard to customize this trellis, forming the copper wire into initials or even more fanciful shapes.

Materials and tools

The copper scrollwork is made from No. 6 solid-copper wire, which is used for grounding electrical panels and is available at most home centers. This wire is stiff enough to hold its shape on the trellis, but soft enough to bend easily. The rest of the trellis is made from 2x2s and 1/2-in. copper pipe.

In the tool department, you'll need a drill and a 5/8-in. spade bit, a pair of medium to large wire-cutting pliers (test 'em out on the copper wire to see if they can cut it), a miter box or electric miter saw and an electric sander.

When you're shopping for the 2x2s, the best choice is clear D-grade cedar, typically stocked for deck railings. You can use pressure-treated lumber, which will be more economical, but you may have to sort through a lot of 2x2s to find straight, rela-

1 Drill holes in the legs using a wood scrap cut at 80 degrees to guide you. With all four legs clamped together, it's easy to get the holes to line up.

ANGLE GUIDE

DEPTH MARK

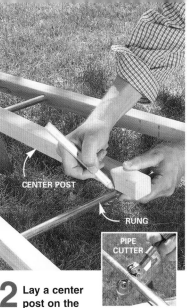

2 Lay a center post on the rungs, which are cut from copper pipe, and mark the rung holes directly on the post. Be sure the post is centered top-to-bottom and side-to-side.

CENTER POST

RUNG

PIPE CUTTER

3 Your bending jig for the wire scrolls is a piece of scrap wood with a copy of the scroll pattern (p. 100) tacked to it. Two finish nails in the middle hold the pieces of copper wire.

FINISH NAIL

tively knot-free ones. If you have a table saw, you can often cut fairly knot-free 2x2s from the edges of a wider board.

Made from treated lumber, this trellis will cost around $70. Using clear cedar will bump it to $90.

Begin with the legs and rungs

Begin with the four legs, the wooden center posts and the copper pipe rungs that connect them.

Place your four 2x2 legs on sawhorses, get the top ends even and clamp them all together. Mark one end as the top, and measure from that end at 28 in., 41-1/2 in. and 59 in. to mark where you will drill the holes. Use a square to transfer the marks to all four legs and to the adjacent side of one leg. Make an angle guide by cutting a piece of scrap wood at an 80-degree angle (Photo 1). An inexpensive protractor works fine to set the angle. Drill angled holes at each mark, using your guide, so you're drilling three holes in each leg (Photo 1). Mark your drill bit to indicate the 1-in. depth for the holes, and be sure the drill is always "leaning" toward the top of the legs. Flip each leg 90 degrees, clamp them together and repeat the whole process. The marks

Project at a glance

Skill level
Beginner

Special tools
Drill
Wire cutter
Miter saw
Electric sander

Approximate cost
$90

you made on the second side of one leg will allow you to transfer your hole locations. Be careful—the drill may be a bit jumpy as the second hole meets the first.

Cut six pieces of pipe (C, D and E), as shown in Photo 2. Note in the Cutting List (on p. 100) that there are two sets of pipe rungs; one set is slightly longer. Cut the longer set now. Temporarily assemble one side of the trellis—two legs and three pieces of pipe. Tap the legs to get the pipe seated. The tops of the legs should be within 1/4 in. of each other. Cut the center posts (B) to length, and use a miter box or miter saw to cut points on the ends. A line marked around all four sides will help guide you. Lay the center post on top of the assembled side. Be sure the post is centered and equidistant from the legs. Mark the post for the pipe holes, then transfer the marks to the other three center posts and drill the holes at 90 degrees. Drill from one side until the point of the spade bit pokes through, then drill the other side. This gives you cleaner holes.

Be careful inserting the pipe

Assemble two sides. The easiest approach is to put the

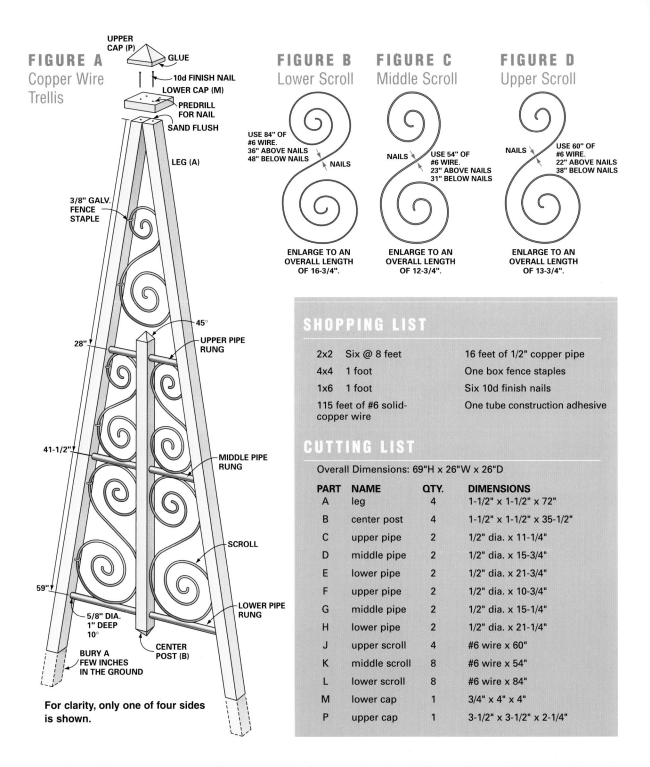

FIGURE A
Copper Wire Trellis

- UPPER CAP (P)
- GLUE
- 10d FINISH NAIL
- LOWER CAP (M)
- PREDRILL FOR NAIL
- SAND FLUSH
- LEG (A)
- 3/8" GALV. FENCE STAPLE
- 45°
- UPPER PIPE RUNG
- 28"
- 41-1/2"
- MIDDLE PIPE RUNG
- SCROLL
- 59"
- LOWER PIPE RUNG
- 5/8" DIA. 1" DEEP 10°
- BURY A FEW INCHES IN THE GROUND
- CENTER POST (B)

For clarity, only one of four sides is shown.

FIGURE B
Lower Scroll

USE 84" OF #6 WIRE.
36" ABOVE NAILS
48" BELOW NAILS
NAILS

ENLARGE TO AN OVERALL LENGTH OF 16-3/4".

FIGURE C
Middle Scroll

NAILS
USE 54" OF #6 WIRE.
23" ABOVE NAILS
31" BELOW NAILS

ENLARGE TO AN OVERALL LENGTH OF 12-3/4".

FIGURE D
Upper Scroll

NAILS
USE 60" OF #6 WIRE.
22" ABOVE NAILS
38" BELOW NAILS

ENLARGE TO AN OVERALL LENGTH OF 13-3/4".

SHOPPING LIST

2x2	Six @ 8 feet	16 feet of 1/2" copper pipe
4x4	1 foot	One box fence staples
1x6	1 foot	Six 10d finish nails
115 feet of #6 solid-copper wire		One tube construction adhesive

CUTTING LIST

Overall Dimensions: 69"H x 26"W x 26"D

PART	NAME	QTY.	DIMENSIONS
A	leg	4	1-1/2" x 1-1/2" x 72"
B	center post	4	1-1/2" x 1-1/2" x 35-1/2"
C	upper pipe	2	1/2" dia. x 11-1/4"
D	middle pipe	2	1/2" dia. x 15-3/4"
E	lower pipe	2	1/2" dia. x 21-3/4"
F	upper pipe	2	1/2" dia. x 10-3/4"
G	middle pipe	2	1/2" dia. x 15-1/4"
H	lower pipe	2	1/2" dia. x 21-1/4"
J	upper scroll	4	#6 wire x 60"
K	middle scroll	8	#6 wire x 54"
L	lower scroll	8	#6 wire x 84"
M	lower cap	1	3/4" x 4" x 4"
P	upper cap	1	3-1/2" x 3-1/2" x 2-1/4"

pipes through the center posts, get them centered and then place the ends of the pipes in the legs. Be careful as you insert the pipe in the center post. It's possible to split out a chunk of the wood as the pipe exits the post. When you're done, the tops of the legs should be within 1/4 in. of each other.

Lay an assembled side upside down on sawhorses so the remaining holes in the legs are pointing up and sup-ported. Using a bolt, an old screwdriver or similar tool, mash the end of the pipe where you can see it at the bottom of each hole. This will lock the pipe in place and make room at the bottom of the hole for the other pipes.

Cut the remaining pipe rungs (F, G and H) and then fit the rungs and remaining center posts between the two assembled sides to form the complete trellis structure. If any of the joints are loose, put a bit of epoxy in the hole.

FENCE
STAPLE

4 Bend the scrolls with your hands, following the pattern. The copper wire is soft enough to bend easily. When you've bent one side, weight it down and bend the other.

5 Attach the scrolls with small fence staples. You can bend the scroll out of the way temporarily to make room for the hammer.

6 Sand the top where all four legs come together, using coarse sandpaper, so they form a flat surface for nailing on the cap.

Bend the scrolls

Now the fun part: making the wire scrollwork. Make your bending jig out of a 2x12 or a scrap piece of plywood at least 11 in. x 18 inches. Enlarge the patterns in Figures B, C and D until the dimensions are correct, and tack a pattern to the jig (Photo 3). Nail two 10d finish nails on either side of the scroll shape to hold the wire (see Figures B, C and D).

Cut one piece of wire to the appropriate length for the scroll you're working on. Measure from one end to find the point that goes between the two finishing nails (see pattern drawing), mark that spot and lay the wire on the jig so your mark is between the two nails. Using your hand only, bend the wire to the shape on the pattern (Photo 4). There should be a few inches of extra wire on each end to give you something to hold. When you've got the first half bent to shape, snip the end. Put a weight or a clamp on the part you've done, then bend the other side. You don't have to be fussy about matching the pattern; close is good enough.

If your first scroll was a success, cut the remaining pieces of wire and bend the rest of the scrolls. For each of the three different shapes, I suggest doing one for practice before cutting all the remaining wire. If you have trouble, cut the wire a little long and you'll have more to work with.

Final assembly

Lay the trellis on its side and use fence staples to attach the scrolls to the 2x2s (Photo 5). Be sure to get the pairs of scrolls on each side of the trellis to be symmetrical (a right and a left), and to reverse the direction between the lower and middle scrolls (see Figure A).

When all the scrolls are attached, stand the trellis up, find yourself something to stand on, and sand the tops of the legs flat and even (Photo 6). If the pieces vibrate too much, tape them all together with duct tape or packing tape.

Cut the cap pieces (M and P). For the facets on the topmost cap piece (P), start with a 1-ft.-long piece of 4x4 so you have enough wood to hold on to while you cut the facets. Then trim off the finished cap piece. You can also buy deck caps at a home center to avoid the cutting completely. When both cap pieces are cut, drill pilot holes in M, nail it on, then glue on part P with construction adhesive or epoxy.

Install the trellis in your garden. Dig the bottoms of the legs into the earth and get the trellis plumb. You'll have to do it pretty much by eye. If your location is windy, anchor the bottoms of the legs into the ground. One way is to bend a couple of 3-ft. pieces of 1/8-in. rod into a U-shape, so they can be driven in around the legs. Then fasten them to the legs with fence staples and cover with dirt or mulch.

Plant markers

Unique, simple and really cheap.

—Jeff Timm

That favorite plant of yours deserves more recognition than a Popsicle stick with black ink spelling out its name. Try making these unique plant markers, which hold a label or a seed packet with bent copper wire set in a decorative base. They're easy to assemble, so let your creativity flow. Decorate them with rocks, glass beads or even seashells. They're also great gifts for friends and relatives, and at $2 apiece, you can make dozens of them.

You've probably got all the tools you'll need around the house to make these markers. A 2-gallon bucket and a wooden spoon are all you need for mixing the mortar. We used a 4- x 8- x 2-in. disposable plastic container as a form, but you could also try a cut-off milk carton or a bread pan. You should

Project at a glance

Skill level
Beginner

Special tools
Wire cutter

Approximate cost
$2–$5 each

EASY FOR EVERYONE

1 Bend the copper wire. Hold a dowel 8 in. up from the end of a 5-ft. piece of wire folded in half. Wrap the wire around it as shown, forming a loop. Move the dowel over 3-1/2 in. (or the width needed to fit your seed packet) and wrap it again, making a second loop in the opposite direction. Cut the wire off even with the first leg, and bend a 1/2-in. 90-degree turn at the bottom of each leg to anchor it in the mortar.

2 Add the mortar. Mix up the mortar to the consistency of cookie dough, slowly adding water to the dry mix as needed. Mix the mortar thoroughly, let it sit for about 3 minutes, then remix, adding a dash more water if needed. Coat the plastic form with cooking spray. After filling the container, give it a few quick shakes to settle the mortar. Then form a mound using a spoon or small trowel so it resembles a loaf of baked banana bread.

also round up a pair of pliers, wire cutters and a utility knife for working with the wire.

For supplies, you'll need a bag of premixed mortar (60 lbs. is plenty), a dust mask, a can of nonstick cooking spray, and 12-2 electrical cable with the plastic sheathing stripped off the wires.

For decoration, use rocks, glass beads or seashells—about 1/3 lb. of rocks per holder. Craft stores are loaded with materials. We added a latex bonding agent to the mortar. It's not absolutely necessary, but it'll make the mortar stick better to smooth rocks and glass. Buy it from a masonry supplier and follow the directions for mixing.

3 Push the copper marker into the mortar so the 90-degree bends are about 1/2 in. up from the bottom and centered. If the mortar is too wet to support the wire, have a cup of coffee and let it stiffen up a little.

Now arrange the rocks or beads to your liking. When arranging the rocks, it's best to start at the edges and work toward the center. Embed the decorations at least halfway into the mortar so they're held tight. If you don't like how a rock looks, remove it, rinse it off and reposition. Once you're done with the arrangement, let the marker set for at least 24 hours before removing it from the form.

Hose-reel hideaway

A charming accent that looks great alone or covered with vines.

—Eric Smith

I designed this latticework structure as a hideout for my clunky plastic hose reel—but, unexpectedly, it turned into a fun shady hideout for our kids and pets as well. In a few years, the lattice will be covered with a dense mound of vines, and I'll be the only person who knows there's a hose hiding underneath.

The construction is straightforward. To keep the wood from splitting, predrill all the holes with a countersink drill bit, then drive in rust-resistant deck screws. Or use a pneumatic brad nailer or narrow crown stapler. Follow the step-by-step photos on the following pages to build your own.

Project at a glance

Skill level
Beginner

Special tools
Drill
Saw

Approximate cost
$50

ITEM	QTY.
1x4 x 8 pine (for assembly jig)	1
2x4 x 8 treated	1
2x2 x 8 treated	5
1x2 x 8 treated	14
2-1/2" deck screws	1 lb.
1-5/8" deck screws	1 lb.
1-1/4" deck screws	1 lb.
polyurethane glue	4 oz.

CUTTING LIST

KEY	QTY.	SIZE & DESCRIPTION
A	2	2x4 x 31-1/2" (base)
B	1	2x2 x 31-1/2" (ridge)
C	6	2x2 x 31-3/4" (rafter)
D	6	2x2 x 17-1/4" (stud)
E	4	1x2 x 13" (base filler)*
F	26	1x2 x 30" (slats)
G	1	1x2 x 40" (cross tie)
H	3	1x2 x 11" (rafter tie)
J	4	1x2 x 7-3/4" (rafter brace)
K	2	1x2 x 33-3/4" (roof lattice-left)
L	2	1x2 x 34-1/2" (roof lattice-right)
M	4	1x2 x 16" (wall lattice)
N	1	2x2 x 35-1/4" (vertical brace)
P	2	1x2 x 41-3/4" (diagonal brace)
Q	3	1x4 x 31-3/4" (assembly jig)
R	3	1x2 x 2-7/16" (spacers for slats)

*Actual wood sizes vary. Our 2x2s averaged 1-5/16 in. sq., and the 1x2s were only 11/16 in. thick. Adjust the length of the base plate fillers (E) and the size of the spacers (R) if the wood you buy is a different size.

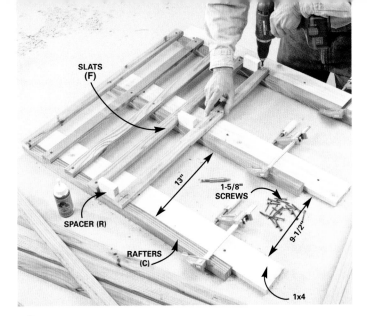

1 Build the roof lattice on a jig, which is simply three 1x4s screwed to a square corner of your work surface. Clamp the rafters (C) to the jig, then predrill and screw the slats (F) to the rafters, using spacers (R) to keep the slats parallel. A drop of polyurethane glue at each joint makes the structure rigid. Repeat for the other roof section.

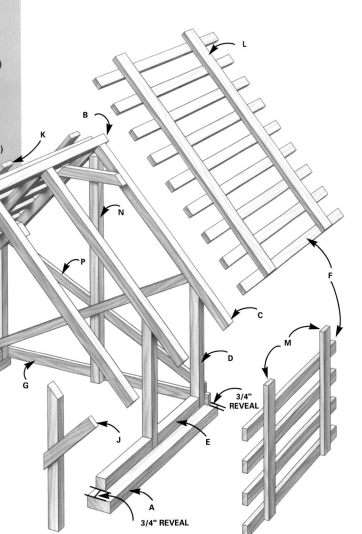

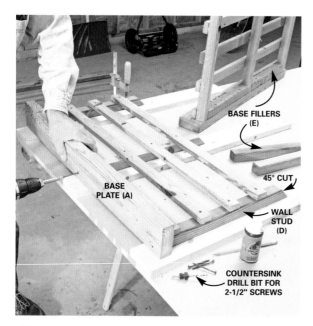

BASE FILLERS (E)

45° CUT

BASE PLATE (A)

WALL STUD (D)

COUNTERSINK DRILL BIT FOR 2-1/2" SCREWS

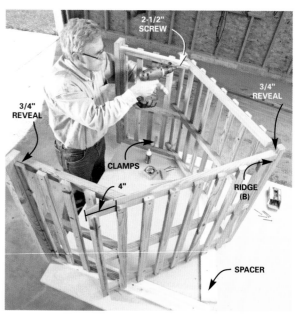

2-1/2" SCREW

3/4" REVEAL

3/4" REVEAL

CLAMPS

4"

RIDGE (B)

SPACER

2 Assemble the walls by screwing the 2x4 base plates (A) to the bottom of each wall stud (D), leaving a 3/4-in. reveal on each end (see illustration, p. 105). Reinforce the joint by cutting 2x2 base fillers (E) to fit between the studs, and then gluing and screwing them in place.

3 Attach the walls to the roof. Begin by attaching the 2x2 ridge (B) to one roof section. Clamp the sides upright on the worktable 36 in. apart, then set the roof sections in place. Predrill and screw the sides to the roof assembly, letting the roof hang over the walls by 4 in., as shown. Finally, join the roof pieces with screws through the ridge.

RAFTER BRACE (J)

CROSS TIE (G)

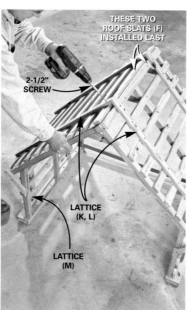

THESE TWO ROOF SLATS (F) INSTALLED LAST

2-1/2" SCREW

LATTICE (K, L)

LATTICE (M)

VERTICAL BRACE (N)

4 Reinforce the structure by first attaching the horizontal cross tie (G), then cut and install the short rafter ties (H) just below the ridge (see illustration, p. 105). Next, hold each rafter brace (J) in place, mark the 45-degree cut on the one end and secure them in place. Use a dab of glue and one screw to secure both ends of each brace.

5 Screw the last two roof slats (F) to the 2x2 ridge. Attach the lattice pieces (K, L and M) perpendicular to the roof and wall slats with 1-1/4-in. screws. Use 2-1/2-in.-long screws at the top to secure the lattice, roof slat and 2x2 ridge together.

6 Mark the center of the back cross tie and rafter tie, and then attach the vertical brace (N). Hold the diagonal braces (P) in place, then mark, cut and secure them to the walls, roof and one another as shown. Apply an exterior stain if desired.

Gallery of ideas

How does your garden grow? Well, it could grow beautifully on a trellis or pergola. The bridge, table and planter add that backyard accent that turns "nice" into "knockout!"

For information on obtaining plans for building the projects shown here, see Resources, p. 252.

Arched bridge
This graceful bridge combines pressure-treated lumber for strength with cedar for appearance. The arcs are so gradual they can be cut using a circular saw. It's a moderately difficult project, but if you've built a deck before it's a great "step up" project.

Mix 'n' match planters
Each of these planters starts as a simple plywood box, then a beveled cap, legs and siding are added. A standard-size plastic liner contains the moist soil. Expect to spend $50 to $80 and about a day building each planter.

Gallery of ideas

Classic columned pergola

Pressure-treated 2x8s and 2x10s create the upper framework, while columns made of composite material provide support. Lattice strips and add-on decorative rafter tails complete the project. Expect to spend about $3,000 for this homemade shade. Search the Internet or visit a site like www.hbgcolumns.com to find a column supplier in your area.

All-weather table

Building this outdoor table requires intermediate carpentry, metalworking and tile laying skills. You can personalize the tile design to your liking. Expect to spend about $150 and 12 hours on this project.

Arched trellis

This trellis can be used to block the wind, create privacy and provide footholds for vines to climb. It can be integrated into a porch or built as a freestanding structure supported by stout 4x4 posts.

Porch privacy trellis

The larger openings in this trellis let the breezes flow easily through to the open porch. Half-lap joints and a tall oval cutout create a long-lasting, attractive structure.

Dream paths
& patios

Circular patio & retaining wall

Hilly, small or ho-hum yard? Modular pavers and blocks let you carve out a unique retreat darn near anywhere!

—*Jeff Timm*

There may be circles, angles and curves everywhere, but if you think this patio and retaining wall are difficult to build, you're wrong. In fact, this is as simple as landscape construction gets. The free-floating circular patio is built from specially designed pavers that fit together like a simple puzzle. The surrounding wall is made from modular concrete blocks. You simply stack them—you won't have to measure or cut a single block.

While the step-by-step process is straightforward, this project entails a lot of hard work. You'll never have to lift more than 60 lbs. at a time, but you'll be handling literally tons of material. So you could probably skip your weight training while you're building it!

Project at a glance

Skill level
Intermediate

Special tools
Plate compactor
Level
Masonry saw

Approximate cost
$2,700 for retaining wall block, patio pavers and rental equipment

We'll show you everything you need to know to install this concrete block retaining wall system and circular patio. Once you complete the "ground-work," the blocks and pavers go in surprisingly quickly. Allow at least two long, sweaty weekends of labor, one for the patio and one for the wall. When you're finished, you'll have the satisfaction of having an attractive patio that'll last for generations. Do one or both parts of the project, as your site and needs dictate.

Getting Started

Design your space and estimate the material

Use garden hoses to represent the patio and wall, and move them around until you find a design and size you like. Use marking paint to establish the outlines (Photo 1). To estimate the wall block quantity, begin by pounding in stakes at the highest and lowest points of the wall, then stretch a string with a line level horizontally between the two. Measure down from the string to the sod at the stake on the lower side of the hill, then add 3 in. (to allow for burying the lowest course of block halfway). Round up to the nearest full block to get the approximate wall height. For the length, simply measure the painted wall layout line (Photo 1) with your tape. Multiply the length by the height to get the total square feet of wall face. The supplier will calculate the block quantity from the square-foot calculation. You'll have some extra because the wall steps down on the ends, but you might need it if any of the blocks are damaged. Plan on two corner blocks per row for the ends (Figure A). Tell the supplier that your top row will be cap blocks.

To order the patio pavers, just provide your supplier with the diameter; they'll put together a package containing the right quantity of each stone shape.

WALL BLOCKS

FIGURE A
Patio and retaining wall

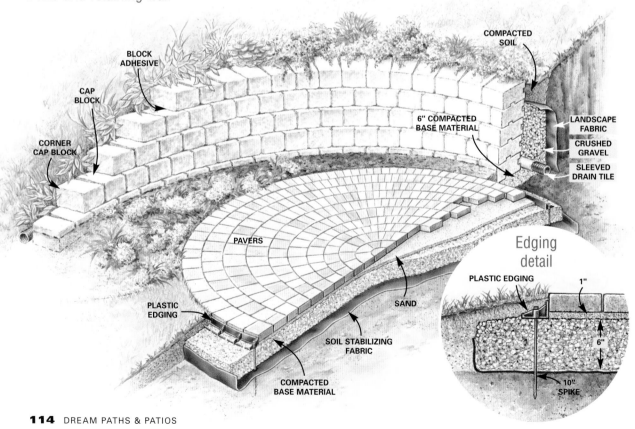

COMPACTED SOIL

BLOCK ADHESIVE

CAP BLOCK

6" COMPACTED BASE MATERIAL

LANDSCAPE FABRIC

CRUSHED GRAVEL

SLEEVED DRAIN TILE

CORNER CAP BLOCK

PAVERS

SAND

PLASTIC EDGING

SOIL STABILIZING FABRIC

COMPACTED BASE MATERIAL

Edging detail

PLASTIC EDGING

1"

6"

10" SPIKE

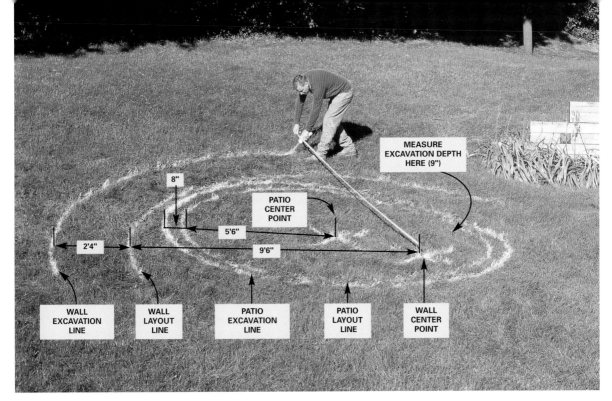

8"

PATIO CENTER POINT

5'6"

2'4"

9'6"

MEASURE EXCAVATION DEPTH HERE (9")

WALL EXCAVATION LINE

WALL LAYOUT LINE

PATIO EXCAVATION LINE

PATIO LAYOUT LINE

WALL CENTER POINT

1 Position 10-in. spikes to mark the center points of the patio and wall. Swing a tape measure hooked on the spikes and spray-paint arcs to mark the actual face of the wall and edge of the patio. Paint a second set of arcs to indicate outer excavation lines, adding 2 ft. 4 in. to the wall radius and 8 in. to the patio radius.

At first glance it might look complicated, but the manufacturer has directions telling how many of each shape to put in each ring. Ask for the paver layout plan when you order; it's not packaged with the pavers. We selected a style called "Cobble." (See Resources, p. 252.)

Tools (and the perfect excuse to rent a Bobcat)

You'll need several heavy-duty tools to do the job right. You'll have to rent a plate compactor (Photo 4). This 200-lb. beast is the secret of a long-lasting patio. Rent it and move it around with a dolly. You'll need it for two days: one day to pack the gravel footing for the retaining wall and a second day for the patio.

For excavating, you've got two choices: a good shovel and strong back or a skid-steer loader (commonly called a Bobcat; see Photo 2). If you're just doing the patio, dig it by hand. But for cutting into a hill like we did, a skid-steer is the only way to go. If you're a tool junkie, you can rent one. Bear in mind, though—by the time you're done

SHOPPING LIST

RETAINING WALL	QUANTITY
Crushed base material	3 tons
Retaining wall blocks	52 sq. ft.
Cap blocks	30 lin. ft.
Corner blocks	10 blocks
Crushed gravel backfill	3 tons
Construction adhesive	3 tubes
Landscape fabric	4 x 50-ft. roll
Drain tile	50-ft. roll

CIRCULAR PATIO	QUANTITY
Base material	6 tons
Coarse washed sand	1 ton
Pavers (main patio only)	96 sq. ft
Stabilization fabric	16 sq. yds.
Edge restraint	40 lin. ft.
3/8 x 10-in. spikes	One 50-lb. box
Bagged dry sand	Six 50-lb. bags

2 Dig into the hill to create a flat area for the patio and wall. Dig 9 in. below the sod, using a point 3 ft. in from the lowest edge of the patio as a reference point. Hire or rent a skid-steer loader (a Bobcat) to make quick work of removing the bulk of the material. Clean up the perimeter and flatten the bottom with a shovel.

3 Check your patio area using a straight 10-ft. 2x4 and 4-ft. level. It should have a slight slope (about 1/4 in. every 4 ft.) away from the wall and be level side to side. Use a plate compactor to compact any soil you've added or loosened.

Buy Smart

Our wall is made up of individual blocks that interlock. We chose a tumbled block because we liked the soft, aged look. But it came at a cost—33 percent more than standard untumbled block. Interlocking block, which has a tongue and groove, is easy to install on curved walls. You use a smooth-topped "cap" block to finish the top row, and corner blocks with a textured face on two sides to finish the ends.

Compare block at square-foot prices. Small blocks might seem cheap, but when you do the math they often end up costing the same as larger ones. Most blocks are 8 or 12 in. deep. Use 12-in. blocks for all but short garden walls; they're heavier, but the weight ensures a longer-lasting wall.

Ask the supplier what size radius you can make with the block, then make sure it accommodates your design. You'll have four or five colors to choose from. Lighter-colored blocks will maintain color better than darker ones.

If a wall will be more than 48 in. high, has a large hill behind it, or is supporting heavy clay soil, you need additional reinforcement. You may need to install a product commonly called "geogrid" and have an engineer help you with the design.

hauling it, learning how to operate it, using it and replacing the neighbor's hedge you destroyed, you can probably get the job done cheaper and faster by hiring a contractor. A skid-steer loader will rut your lawn, so plan on filling in the path with topsoil and grass seed when you're done.

To get rid of the excavated soil, you can rent a trash container, ask the contractor to haul it away, fill in a low spot or persuade a neighbor to take it. If you rent a trash container, keep it until you're finished so you can throw in any extra gravel or sand.

Rent or buy a hand tamper (Photo 6) for compacting the gravel behind the wall, and get a sturdy contractor's wheelbarrow for moving those 300-lb. loads of gravel.

Dig in

Spray-paint the "footprints" of your wall and patio (Photo 1), dig just inside the outer layout lines and then reestablish the center points of your arcs after excavation. Dig about 9 in. below the patio's center point to provide room for the gravel, sand and pavers. Photo 1

4 Relocate the spike that marks the wall center point; it may take a little trial and error. Spray-paint a new arc 6 in. shorter than the radius of the face of the wall. Then spread a 2-ft. wide swath of base material from this line to the back of the excavation. Start with two 2-in. thick layers, compacting each. Spread about 2 in. more and use your straight 10-ft. 2x4 and 4-ft. level to make it roughly level. Compact again.

5 Spray-paint another arc, representing the face of the wall. Align and level each block. Cut a notch out of a 14-in. 1x3 to bridge the "tongue" on top of the block for leveling the block front to back. Make slight adjustments by tapping a corner with the butt end of the hammer, and larger adjustments by adding or removing base material. If you add more than 1 in. of base material, compact it with the hand tamper before setting the block. Install landscape fabric to separate the soil from the gravel you'll use as backfill.

shows you where to measure your depth. Because of the sloping hill, the front edge of the patio will be a little high compared with the lawn. (You won't dig out as much soil here.) Add soil when you're done to blend the elevations. The bottom of the excavation has to be flat and slightly sloping (Photo 3). Be sure you compact any loose soil. If you don't, it will settle over time and the patio will end up with a dip.

Wall Construction

Install the gravel footing

A wall is only as sturdy as the base you build it on—in this case, crushed gravel that ranges in size from 3/4 in. down to a powder. Suppliers may refer to this material as crushed Class II or any of a number of other names. Build a 6-in. deep layer by spreading 2 in. of base, dampening it, compacting it, and repeating the process (Photo 4).

Compact the gravel at least four times. The compactor's tone will change from a dull thud to a sharp whack, and the machine will start to hop when the surface is hard enough. If you're unsure if it's packed well enough, pass over it a few extra times. The gravel layer should be 3 in. or more below the sod on the ends of the arc and be within an inch of level all the way around.

Set the first row of block flat as a pancake—and the rest is easy

Set the first block, level it in both directions, then add the next. Tweak each block when you set it to make it perfectly level (Photo 5). Setting just one slightly out-of-level block will haunt you on consecutive courses. Lay the entire first row. On the ends, place a cap block and a corner block to create a finished look where the wall steps down (Photo 6).

Work Smart

Lay and compact the gravel for the patio at the same time as the wall. It'll give you a nice, clean surface to work from when constructing the wall.

HAND TAMPER

STAGGERED BLOCK JOINTS

CRUSHED GRAVEL

CAP BLOCK

CORNER BLOCK

DRAIN TILE

SOIL

CAULK GUN

CONSTRUCTION ADHESIVE

CORNER BLOCK

CAP BLOCK

FABRIC

6 Place 4-in. drain tile behind the bottom row of block from end to end. Fill behind the block with 3/4-in. clean, crushed gravel and compact with a hand tamper. Add subsequent layers of block, starting at the middle of the arc. Center the first block over the joint below and work toward each end. Fill behind the wall with gravel after each course and compact with a hand tamper.

7 Secure the cap blocks and corner blocks with a bead of special construction adhesive. (Wrap the fabric over the gravel before placing the cap blocks.) Backfill behind the caps with soil and compact it with the hand tamper. Slope the soil to drain water around and away from the wall.

Place 4-in. perforated drain tile with fabric wrapped around it at the base of the wall. Bring it from end to end and leave the ends open. Don't worry about drowning your petunias; water will never gush out. The pipe just relieves water pressure against the wall.

Modular blocks stack fast

You'll amaze the neighbors with how fast the wall goes up. Fill behind each layer with 3/4-in. crushed gravel and hand-tamp it (Photo 6). Don't use extra base material for behind the wall; it doesn't drain well. To be sure the gravel continues to drain well, place landscape fabric between the soil and gravel to keep the dirt from mixing in (Photo 5).

Before placing each course, sweep off stray gravel on the block below. Since the blocks automatically step back with each layer, the wall's radius increases with each course. To keep the joints evenly staggered, start setting each row of block at the center of the arc and work toward the ends (Photo 6). Use construction adhesive formulated for concrete block to secure the cap and the

corner blocks in place (Photo 7).

Wrap the landscape fabric over the gravel and fill behind the top layer of block with soil. Grade the soil so water flows around, rather than over, the wall (Photo 7). To prevent water and soil from washing through the joints of the cap block, lay 6-in. squares of fabric over the joints to seal them.

Patio Construction
Laying the base

After excavating, we laid a special woven "ground stabilization fabric" over the patio area. (It's cut off a roll from the landscape supplier.) You don't need it in stable sandy or gravelly soils, but in other soils, it's cheap insurance for a flat patio for years to come.

Reestablish the patio's center point. Keep the spike in until you start laying the pavers; it'll mark the starting point for the paver circle. Mark out the patio perimeter plus an extra 8 in. with marking paint. Add and compact two layers of base material in 2-in. layers (Photo 8). Position and slope the screed pipes so the patio will drain

Planning, paperwork and materials

We carved our patio into a gradual hill, using the retaining wall to hold back the slope. The main wall is a 30-ft. long arc, 30 in. high. The patio is 11 ft. in diameter. This combination creates a cozy area for a couple to enjoy a cup of coffee and creates a nice space for flower beds and plantings. If you plan to entertain, or want room for the kids to cruise around with the Big Wheel, you can easily stretch the patio's diameter to 16 ft. without complicating the job. Increase the wall diameter accordingly.

Most communities don't require a building permit for patios or for retaining walls under 4 ft. high. They can usually be placed anywhere on your property, which makes them a great alternative to a deck in small yards. But keep them out of easements, which are bands of property left open for drainage or for access to buried utilities. Your local building or planning department can tell you, or your survey will show you, if there are any on your property. Review your plans with them to be safe. Also call the local utilities and have them mark their underground lines, even

if you don't think there are any in the area. The service is free, and it could save you from an injury or from having to dig up your patio later.

Don't locate a patio beneath a mature tree. Even though the tree makes for a nice shady spot and nothing will grow under it anyway, the patio can damage the roots (and vice versa). Locate it outside the tree's canopy; anything closer, consult a tree specialist.

Our expenses came to about half what a contractor would charge. The material costs may vary substantially depending on your location and delivery costs.

We suggest buying all your materials from a landscape supplier (see "Landscape Materials" in the Yellow Pages) and having them delivered. A landscape supplier will have a better selection than a home center, and you can see the different styles of pavers and retaining wall block firsthand at the displays in their yard. Plus they can provide expert advice for any questions you might have.

FIGURE B
Bird's-eye view of completed project

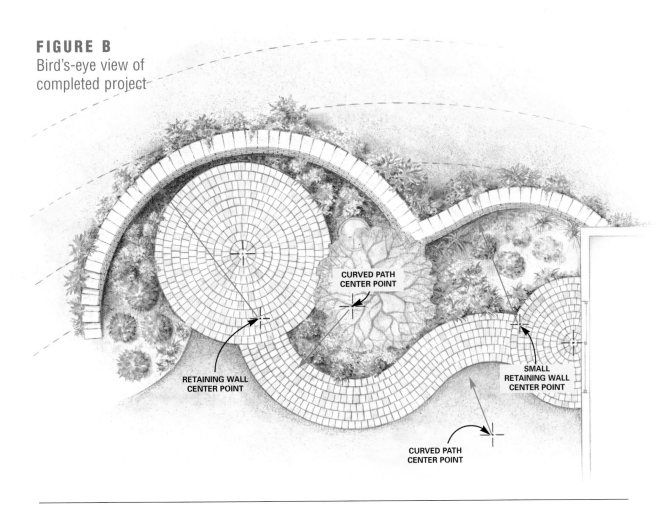

CURVED PATH CENTER POINT

RETAINING WALL CENTER POINT

SMALL RETAINING WALL CENTER POINT

CURVED PATH CENTER POINT

STABILIZATION FABRIC

SOIL

PLATE COMPACTOR

PATIO EDGE PLUS 8"

1" DIA. STEEL PIPE

PIPES SPACED 6' APART AND LEVEL TO ONE ANOTHER

4' LEVEL

3/4" BLOCK

SLOPE

8 Reset a spike at the center point of the patio and spray an arc 8 in. larger than the radius of the patio. Spread two 2-in. layers of base material over the stabilization fabric, compacting each layer with the plate compactor. Build up the perimeter with soil to keep the base material from spreading outward as you compact.

9 Set two 1-in. steel pipes about 6 ft. apart on top of the compacted base material. Orient them in the direction of drainage, away from the wall. Slip base material under the pipe until a 4-ft. level with a 3/4-in. block slipped under the low side reads level. Set the other pipe level and parallel to the first.

water away from the wall (Photos 9 and 10). The third layer should be no more than 3 in. below the sod at any point. A few inches higher than the sod is better. Add more base material to raise the entire patio if necessary. Slide the 2x4 side to side along the pipes to distribute the base material and create a flat surface. Compact this final layer four times, changing direction each time—north to south, then east to west (Photo 11).

Lay the sand bed

Leave enough time—at least one half day—to set the sand bed and lay the pavers. Leave your meticulously

screeded sand overnight and the neighbor's cat, a stray dog and a rain shower are guaranteed to disrupt your hard work.

Lay the pipes on the compacted base (the pipe diameter provides for 1 in. of sand). If you spot gaps larger than 1/2 in. anywhere under the pipe, add gravel in the depression and compact. Pour a few wheelbarrows of

1:30 p.m.

CENTER PAVERS

1:45 p.m.

TAPERED PAVERS

1:55 p.m.

FILL IN FOOTPRINT

10 Shuffle a 10-ft. 2x4 side to side along the pipes as you level the final layer of base material and pull it away from the wall. Fill in any depressions and remove any high spots as you work. Remove the pipes and fill the troughs with gravel.

11 Compact this last layer, making certain the soil is built up on the sides and the base material is perfectly flat.

coarse washed sand between the pipes, spread it out with a shovel, and screed it the same way you did the base (Photo 10). Work your way out from the wall so you have room to work. You won't compact the sand layer until after the pavers are laid.

Laying the pavers—the fun part

Laying the pavers is the easiest and most rewarding part of the project. You'll need five different shaped pavers to build this exact circular patio (Figure C, p. 122). The manufacturer's chart tells you how many of each shape to put into each ring. Alternate the shapes if a ring has more than one paver shape.

Since you start in the center and work out, you'll have to disrupt that flat sand layer with a few footprints. Minimize the damage by staying in the same footprints, then trowel them flat when the paver rings get close. After you've laid three or four rings, stand on the pavers and have a helper pass you the next pavers. Don't step on the very edge or you'll create a dip. Once you get the first five rings in, it's pretty methodical and will go quickly.

If you end up with a gap where a ring comes together, distribute it by spacing several bricks up to 1/8 in. apart. To get an even color mix throughout the patio, draw the

2:20 p.m.

2:45 p.m.

3:00 p.m.

PIPES REMOVED

TROWEL

ADDED SAND

12 Place the pipes in the same location as shown in Photo 9. No leveling should be needed, since the slope is established from the gravel layer. Repeat the procedure shown in Photo 10, using sand instead of base material. Remove the pipes, fill the troughs with sand and trowel the area smooth. Fill in your footprints as you back out. Remove the center spike.

13 Position the center pavers, then install outer rings using the shapes and patterns specified in the manufacturer's plan. Stagger the joints. Use only one footpath so you disturb the sand as little as possible. Stand on the pavers once you have a few rings placed and have a helper pass or throw you the next rings. Add a little sand and trowel out the footprints when you reach them with the installed pavers. Work out to the final size.

pavers from more than one pallet. If you're just using one pallet, you can blend the colors well by drawing from opposite sides; one half is usually darker than the other.

The final details

To contain the pavers and sand, install a paver edging around the perimeter (Photo 14). We used Snap-Edge (see Resources, p. 252). It costs a little more, but it installs easier and offers better support than less expensive alternatives. Before installing the edging, be sure to scrape the sand away to expose the base material. Conceal the edge

with soil or mulch when you're finished.

Run the compactor over the patio to set the pavers, compact the sand and vibrate sand up into the joints, locking the pavers together (Photo 15). The steel plate won't hurt the pavers, but it will make your ears ring. Wear hearing protection. (If a paver does break or chip during this step, gently wiggle it out with a pair of flat screwdrivers and replace it.) Spread coarse, dry sand over the patio to fill the joints and repeat the compacting. *The sand has to be thoroughly dry to jiggle into the joints.* Don't try to save money on a tamper rental by

FIGURE C
Circular patio components

SAFETY GLASSES

MALLET

SNIP EDGING HERE TO CREATE CURVES

10" x 3/8" SPIKE

EDGE RESTRAINT

TROWEL

14 Pull the sand away from the perimeter of the patio with a steel trowel until you reach the base material. Snip the back side of the edging with garden pruners to bend it to the arc of the patio. Hold the edge restraint tight to the pavers, then drive 10-in. long, 3/8-in. spikes every foot through holes in the edging. Connect the edging, leaving no gaps between the pieces.

15 Run the plate compactor on top of the pavers. Pass over the patio four times, switching direction after each pass. Compact around the outer edge after each pass.

skipping this step. The last tamping will vibrate the sand into the joints, locking all the bricks together.

No maintenance!

This type of patio and wall requires little to no mainte-
nance. Don't let dirt build up on them or you'll provide a home for weeds, and be sure to wash the patio down periodically. Sealers are available for enhancing the paver color, but once you apply them, you need to repeat the process every few years.

Garden path & steps

This easy-to-build natural stone path will last a lifetime.

—Jeff Gorton

Stonework doesn't have to be complex or require special masonry skills. In most regions, you can buy flat flagstones that you can easily lay for paths and stack for solid stairs. We'll show you how to plan, lay out and build a set of natural stone steps using flat flagstones for the treads and solid blocks of stone, called wallstone, for the risers.

Our steps are built on a gradual slope, but by changing the riser and tread sizes, you can build them on slopes as steep as about 40 degrees. Rustic steps like these are well suited for informal garden paths like ours, but we wouldn't recommend them for entry or other steps that get heavy daily use.

In addition to the basic gardening tools, leather gloves and carpenter's level, you'll need a few special tools for breaking and moving stone. Buy a 4-lb. maul (Photo 7) to chip and break stone. If you have to cut a few stones, buy a dry-cut diamond blade, available at home centers for $40. To move the stone, rent or buy a two-wheel dolly with large wheels.

Project at a glance

Skill level
Intermediate

Special tools
Two-wheel dolly
Garden tools
Level
Maul

Approximate cost
$1,800 for project shown

1 Outline the steps with spray paint and drive stakes at the top and bottom. Tie a level string line to the stakes. Measure the total run between the stakes and the total rise from the ground to the level line. Calculate the length of each tread (see Figure A and text below) and mark them with spray paint.

Stone steps don't have to be exact

Make a rough sketch of the plans for your steps, including the approximate number of risers and any retaining walls you might have to build.

Begin by measuring the total horizontal distance the stair will travel along a level line (Photo 1). This is called the "run" of the stair. Then measure down from this level line to determine the total vertical distance, or "rise." Your goal is to arrive at a set of comfortable steps with rises of 6 to 8 in. and treads at least 12 in. deep.

First figure out how many step risers you'll need. Gentle slopes like ours require short risers and long treads, while steep slopes require taller risers (up to a maximum of 8 in. and short treads). If your hill has both steep and gentle slopes, break it up into sections and calculate the step layout separately for each area (Figure A). Divide the total rise by about 6 in. for shallow slopes, up to a maximum of 8 in. for steep slopes, to arrive at the approximate number of risers. In our case, the total rise was 29 in. Dividing

by 6 yielded 4.83, which we rounded up to 5 risers.

Subtract 1 from the number of risers to determine the number of treads. Then divide the total run by this number to arrive at the depth of each tread. We divided the total run of 145 in. by 4 treads to arrive at a tread depth of a little more than 36 in. Using this information, mark the location of each stair riser on the ground with spray paint as shown in Photo 1.

FIGURE A
Steep slope

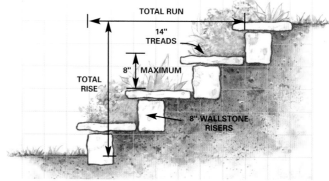

2 Dig a trench for the first stone riser. Plan to leave enough of the riser stone exposed so the step will be at the correct height when you set the stone tread on top.

3 Level the riser stones by removing soil or adding gravel as needed. Set the distance from the ground (or future path) to the top of the first riser stone equal to the riser dimension less the thickness of the tread.

There's no margin for error when you're building wood steps, but luckily you can cheat a little on these rustic stone steps. You'll still have to calculate the height of each riser and the depth of the treads, but if you're off by an inch when you reach the top, it's not difficult to adjust the level or slope of the landing to make up for it.

If your route includes a space where the grade levels out, make this spot a small seating area (photo, p. 124).

Buying stone

A visit to your local stone supplier is the quickest way to find out what types, sizes and shapes of stone are available in your area. Look for flat stones called flagstones that range in thickness from 2 to 3 in. to use for your treads. Ours are limestone, but you may find that another type of stone is more readily available. You'll need some 6- to 8-in. thick blocks of stone, called wall-

Gentle slope

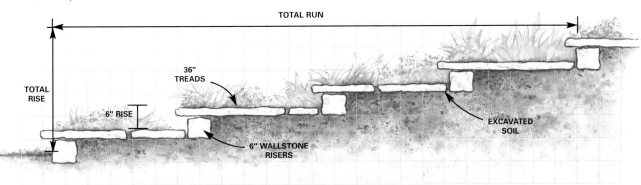

TOTAL RUN

TOTAL RISE

36" TREADS

6" RISE

6" WALLSTONE RISERS

EXCAVATED SOIL

4 Dig straight back, level with the top of the first riser stone to 10 in. beyond the mark for the second riser. Set the next riser stone so the distance from the dug-out ground to the top of the stone is equal to your riser height. Adjust the height of the riser by burying a bit of the stone or adding gravel under it. Level the top.

5 Move heavy flagstones by tipping them up on end and rocking them onto a two-wheeled dolly. Keep your back straight and lift with your legs.

stone, for the risers (Photo 2). Follow our instructions for figuring your riser height (Photo 1). Then pick out wallstones of this height to use for your risers. Try to find flagstones of consistent thickness. It will make it easier to keep the stone steps all the same height.

Our project required about 3 tons of stone for the treads and landing and another 2-1/2 tons for the risers and wall. In addition to the stone, order 1 ton of crushed

Buy Smart

Since stone is usually sold by the ton, and the number of square feet a ton will cover depends on the thickness of the stone, figuring quantities is best left to someone with experience selling natural stone. Note the dimensions on the sketch and take it with you to order the stone. Order about 15 percent extra to provide more shapes to choose from and avoid having to pay for a second delivery. You'll have no trouble finding uses for the extra stone.

gravel with aggregate 3/4 in. and smaller for leveling the treads and risers (Photos 3 and 4).

Start with level risers

With the tricky planning out of the way, you're ready to dig in and start building steps. Spread out some of the stone so you'll have many shapes to choose from. Then build one step at a time, starting at the bottom and working your way up. Photos 2 – 11 show how.

The first step is the trickiest to build. After that you just repeat the process until you reach the top. Set the first riser in place (Photos 2 and 3). Remember to bury it a few inches so the first riser won't be too tall. Now use the top surface of this riser stone to guide your shovel as you dig straight back into the hill to make a level spot for the first tread and the second riser. Be sure to dig out all of the sod. When the first two risers are in place, you're ready to set stones for the first tread. Pick larger stones to overhang the riser (Photo 9). The extra weight will keep them from tipping. Then fill in behind them with

6 Arrange large flagstones to overhang the lower riser about 2 in. Remove soil or tamp gravel into low areas to level the tops of the stones. You can leave gaps between stones up to 2 in. wide.

LARGE STONE OVERHANGS

SMALL STONE IN BACK

2x4 BLOCK FOR TAMPING

7 Trim stones for a better fit by chipping away at protruding pieces with a heavy maul. Wear safety glasses.

3- TO 4-LB. MAUL

CHIP OFF POINT

SECOND RISER

GRAVEL TO LEVEL RISER

8 Shim unstable flagstone treads with stone chips. Tip the tread stone out of the way and glue the stone shims to the risers with polyurethane construction adhesive.

POLYURETHANE CONSTRUCTION ADHESIVE

STONE CHIP SHIM

RISER STONE

9 Cut 16-in. squares of sod from alongside the steps with a flat-blade shovel and lift them out. Remove enough soil to slope and blend the surrounding yard into the new steps. Replace the sod and water it.

16" SQUARE OF SOD

CUT AND SLICE SOD

DIRT LEDGE TO REMOVE

SMALL STONES AT BACK

LARGER STONE AT FRONT

PRESS INTO CRACKS

50/50 SOIL AND COMPOST

10 Build a small retaining wall by stacking smaller stones and filling behind them with dirt. Stagger the joints and step each layer back a couple of inches from the one below.

11 Fill cracks with a 50/50 mix of soil and compost, and plant creeping groundcover such as thyme in the larger spaces.

Work Smart

To avoid moving stones more than necessary, we found it helpful to arrange the stones into the shape of the treads near the stone pile, and then move the pieces to their permanent location on the steps.

smaller stones.

For a safe set of steps, it's important to keep all the risers the same height. Compensate for variations in flagstone thickness by adjusting the height of the riser. If the stone you pick for the tread is extra thick—say, 3 in. rather than 2 in.—bury the riser an extra inch so the total rise will be consistent. The same goes for keeping the top surface of the treads even. Put a little gravel under thin stones to raise them, or excavate under stones that are too thick. If a stone tips or rocks when you step on it, shim it with stone chips (Photo 8). Take your time adding gravel and removing soil until your step is just right. Then move on to the next one.

Blend the steps into the landscape

Notching into the hill will leave bare ledges of soil along the edge of each tread. You can either remove soil to slope the surrounding landscape down to the steps or add stones along the edge to retain the soil. Photo 9 shows how to cut out the sod and regrade the soil. On the three steps leading from the landing to the top of the hill, we buried wallstone along the edge to hold back the dirt (Photo 10 and photo, p. 124).

Filling the cracks between stones is the final step in the project. Experts we talked to had varying opinions on the best material to use. Sand is easy, but it will wash out. Pea gravel looks good but tends to fall out and get under your feet, and it's like walking on ball bearings. We settled on a 50/50 mix of compost and soil. It packs easily into the cracks and looks natural. And if you want, you can plant a durable creeping groundcover, like creeping thyme, in the large spaces. Besides looking great, it will fill in the spaces to keep out weeds and hold the soil in place.

Work Smart

CUTTING STONE

You'll probably get through the project without having to cut any stone. But if you need an exact fit or just can't find the right shape, cutting is an option. Buy a diamond blade (about $40 at home centers) to fit your circular saw.

GFCI-PROTECTED PLUG

DIAMOND BLADE

LUMBER CRAYON

SAW KERF

Mark the stone with a crayon. Set the abrasive blade to cut about 1/2 in. deep and saw along the line. Increase the depth in 1/2-in. increments and make repeated cuts until you've sawed at least halfway through the stone. Direct a stream of water from a garden sprayer onto the blade as you saw to reduce dust and cool the blade.

CAUTION: Plug the saw into a GFCI-protected outlet or into a special portable GFCI plug.

Turn over the stone and gently tap along the cutting line with a heavy hammer until it breaks.

Crushed stone path

Build an informal pathway to meander through your yard or garden.

—*Art Rooze*

A path can do wonders for a backyard. It can invite you directly inside a garden or into a shaded area, or attract your attention to a rose-covered trellis, a busy bird feeder or your favorite maple. There's something relaxing about walking along a pleasantly contoured garden path, listening to the crunch of crushed stone underfoot. You may feel as if you've been away on a short trip.

Designing a pleasant path calls for a bit of imagination. And building one will give you some sore muscles by the time you finish, but it doesn't require any great skill or know-how. The path we show here is simply packed crushed limestone bordered by edging stone set into the soil. For a rundown on path materials and costs and how much you'll need, see "Buy Smart" on p. 135.

Project at a glance

Skill level
Beginner

Special tools
Mason chisel
Sledgehammer
Compactor

Approximate cost
$10–$15 per foot of
32-inch wide path

30" TO 38"

APPROX. 4' 6"

1 Lay out the path perimeter with non-kinking garden hose or rope. Make your curves gentle and natural looking. The overall width of our path varies from 30 to 38 in., including the edging. The end of the path flares out to about 4-1/2 ft.

Planning a path

The first step is to form a general idea of where you want to place your path. Look at the contours of your yard, and go with its flow as much as possible. For any dramatic rises in elevation, you might want to create a serpentine or winding path to make the rises gradual.

A garden path doesn't necessarily have to lead to a destination, but it should take you along or toward attractive spots. You can vary the width of the path to take advantage of these spots; widened areas encourage you to pause in your walk. Our path varies from 30 to 38 in. wide, including the edging stone—wide enough to walk on comfortably, yet narrow enough to feel cozy and intimate.

Even though a garden path doesn't need to go to a specific destination, it does need to start and stop some-

Plan Smart

Avoid routing your path too close to trees and large shrubs. The roots will make digging difficult, and if you cut too many of them, you could kill the plant.

where. Ideally, it should join in a crisp edge with a surface of a distinctly different material, such as a lawn or patio or deck. You'll probably want to avoid a loose-stone path that leads directly to a door of your house, however, or you'll be tracking stones inside. Consider curving the line of edging stones so that they flare out at each end of the path, forming a sort of open invitation to come and walk on it.

Once you have a general idea of the shape and direction, lay out both sides of the path with a long garden hose or rope, as shown in Photo 1. Use hose or rope that will lie flat, without kinks or awkward bends. Leave the outline in place for a few days. Walk the pathway several times, and make adjustments in the contours until you like the way it looks and feels. Then drive stakes into the ground (Photo 2) to mark the outer edges of the path.

2 Drive stakes into the ground along the perimeter—wood shims work well—keeping them close enough to each other to maintain smooth-flowing curves.

3 Dig out the soil 6 in. deep between the stakes. Use a square-nose spade to trim the edges neatly. Dig a deeper trench bed for the edging stones to a depth of 1 in. less than the width of your edging stones.

Buy Smart

The stone that you can use for a path—both the edging and the surface stone—will vary considerably from region to region in color, texture and the name it goes by. You'll find distributors listed under "Stone" in the Yellow Pages. Visit a distributor's yard to see exactly what you're getting before you order.

The crushed limestone we used in our path, yellowish in color, is common in most of the Midwest and in some areas of the East, South and West. Its colors may vary from gray to reddish brown. The nearest substitute is crushed gravel—sometimes called pea gravel or screened gravel—which is usually grayish in color.

Our path was 70 ft. long by 32 in. wide on average. With a path depth of 5-1/2 in., we required 4-1/2 cu. yds.—about 6 tons!—of limestone, crushed to 3/8-in. or smaller particles. (It's the smaller particles that help it pack.)

Edging stone can go by a multitude of names: fieldstone, cut

stone, wallstone, bluestone and many other names and types unique to specific regions. The edging stone we used is called lannon stone in the Midwest.

Our 70-ft. long path required 140 ft. of 8-in. wide by about 3-in. thick edging stone. (It was plunked down on our driveway on wood pallets, and we wheelbarrowed it to the path site.) Stone, depending on color, quality and the fineness of its cutting, can vary greatly in cost.

4 Place all the edging stones loosely in the dug trenches. Select stones with end shapes that more or less fit together. The stones come in random lengths; use the shorter lengths on the curves.

5 Dig out or fill in the trench bottom to fine-tune the leveling of each stone as you final-fit the stones end-to-end. A 4-ft. level helps you get an overall feel for the leveling, but because the stones are so irregular, you'll have to rely mostly on your own eye.

Digging the path and laying edges

We dug out the soil 6 in. deep, then a trench 1 in. deeper along the edges to accommodate the edging stone. Our edging stone was about 8 in. wide by about 3 in. thick. Our goal was to have the edging stone extend above the surrounding soil surface by about 1 in. (see illustration). If the stone you use is a different size, you'll need to vary your trench size.

The 5-1/2 in. of crushed limestone or gravel that forms the path (Photos 7, 8 and 9) will almost always provide enough drainage to prevent pooling of rainwater. However, if your soil under the path is heavy clay that doesn't absorb water, or if your path is in a very low-lying area, consider digging out an additional 3 in. for the pathway and adding 3 in. of coarser gravel (about 1/2-in. size) as a drainage base.

Unless you have a place on your property where you can use the dug-out soil, you'll have to haul it away or hire someone to do it. Or if it's good topsoil, you may find some takers in your neighborhood.

Path cross-section

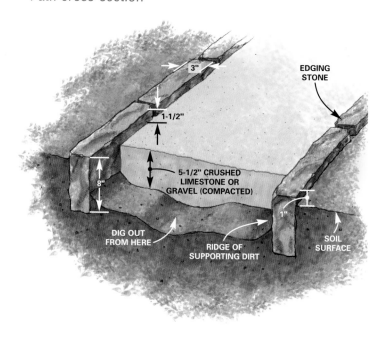

3"

1-1/2"

8"

5-1/2" CRUSHED LIMESTONE OR GRAVEL (COMPACTED)

EDGING STONE

1"

SOIL SURFACE

DIG OUT FROM HERE

RIDGE OF SUPPORTING DIRT

RIDGE OF
SUPPORTING DIRT

CRUSHED
LIMESTONE—3/8" OR
SMALLER PARTICLES

6 Anchor each stone in place by mounding a ridge of supporting dirt about 2 in. up against the inside bottom edges. Dig dirt out from the middle of the pathway for this as you need it. Stamp the dirt tight along the bottom of the stones with your feet. Then fill in with dirt behind the stones, as shown. Work the dirt tight behind the stones with the shovel edge, but don't overfill to the point of dislodging the stones.

7 Dump crushed limestone or gravel in the pathway. Level the material with a rake as you go so that you can wheel each succeeding wheelbarrow load over it.

Cutting stone

SCORE ON
ALL SIDES

WIDE
MASONRY
CHISEL

Cut the stones only where necessary to get an approximate fit. Score the stones with a wide masonry chisel and a sledgehammer on all four sides, then continue to strike along the width with the chisel until the stone cracks. Wear full-surround safety glasses and gloves.

Chip off small irregularities or protuberances as necessary for end-to-end fit. Don't get too fussy about this.

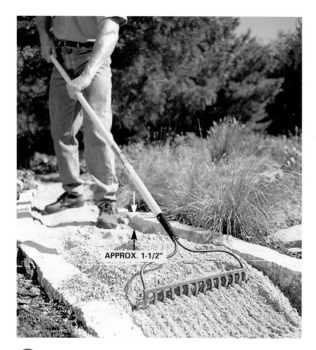

APPROX. 1-1/2"

8 Fill and level the entire path to within about 1-1/2 in. from the tops of the edging stones. Continue using a garden rake to spread and even out the material.

POWER PLATE COMPACTOR

9 Tamp the crushed limestone or gravel with a power plate compactor. Make three or four passes. Use your feet to stamp down spots the compactor can't reach. Next, spread another layer over the already compacted layer, leveling it to about 1 in. below the tops of the edging. Then make another series of passes with the compactor.

Lay the edging stones as shown in Photos 4 – 6. Keep in mind that you're not building the Taj Mahal here. The look of the path is meant to be informal, so don't struggle for a perfect end-to-end fit. Pick stones that naturally fit fairly well together; cut or chip stones only when absolutely necessary for an approximate fit (see "Cutting Stone," p. 137). Take a bit more care, however, in leveling the top edges of the stones (Photo 5), since you want the horizontal appearance of the path to have a smooth flow.

Putting down the path

You'll probably have the crushed limestone or gravel delivered to your driveway, and then you'll have to wheelbarrow it to the path site. If you need to cross areas of very soft lawn, lay down sheets of plywood to avoid forming ruts with the wheelbarrow.

Level the material as you dump it, to about 1-1/2 in. below the top of the edging stone, then tamp it down with a power plate compactor (Photo 9). You can rent a power compactor from most tool rental outlets. Or if you still have lots of energy left, even after laying all that edging stone, you can compact the path by hand with a heavy tamping tool that you can rent for a couple of bucks.

Make several passes with the compactor, then lay down another layer of crushed limestone or gravel and compact again (Photo 9). The compacted surface should end about 1-1/2 in. below the tops of the edging stones. Over time you can expect the path surface to compact by itself about another 1/2 in.

Path in a wheel-barrow

There's no heavy lifting, no fancy tools and it's really, really cheap!

—*Spike Carlsen*

EASY FOR EVERYONE

This garden path is as easy to build as it is to look at and walk on. A bundle or two of cedar shakes, a roll of landscape fabric, a few bags of mulch and a couple of hours are all it takes to build it. You'll spend less than $5 per foot of 30-in.-wide path.

To create the path edging, we cut 18-in.-long cedar shakes in half, then pounded the 9-inch sections about halfway into the ground. Shakes are naturally rot-resistant and should last 5 to 10 years or more. And since they're tapered, they're

Work Smart

Place a scrap 2x6 on top of each shake and pound on that if you find you're breaking shakes as you drive them in. The 2x6 will help distribute the blow more evenly across the top of the shake.

easy to install. Bear in mind, shakes will split and break if you try to pound them into soil with lots of rocks, roots or heavy clay; this path works best in loose garden soil.

The landscape fabric helps prevent weeds from growing up into the path and creates a barrier so the dirt below remains separate from the path materials above.

The path material itself can be wood chips, shredded bark, decorative stone—just about anything.

Here's how to do it in three steps:

WEAR YOUR SAFETY GLASSES

CEDAR SHAKES

1 Pound the cedar shakes into the soil using a small mallet. Stagger every other shake, overlapping the previous shake by about 1/2 in.

2 Trim or fold the fabric so it follows the contour of the cedar shake edging. On sloped ground, use U-shaped sod staples to hold the fabric.

MULCH

3 Install a 2- to 3-in. layer of wood chips, shredded bark or stone over the landscape fabric.

Gallery of ideas

Brick and stone structures are long lasting, eye-catching and virtually maintenance free. Isn't that what you want in your backyard?

For information on obtaining plans for building the projects shown here, see Resources, p. 252.

^

Brick & Stone Patio
This walkway consists of brick pavers meandering through a field of natural stone, all set on a solid base of gravel and sand. You can use just about any kind of flat stone and pavers for this project.

Stone Path
A 3-in. layer of sand creates the base for this flagstone path. Creeping thyme planted in a 50/50 mix of potting soil and compost fills the space between the stones.

Perfect Stone Patio & Wall
It takes a strong back, good stone laying skills and a hefty budget (around $8,000 for materials alone) to craft this bluestone patio and blue ledge stone wall duo. The curved, limestone-capped wall provides plenty of space for informal seating.

CHAPTER 5

Dream gazebos & sheds

Gingerbread gazebo

Solid construction, decorative trim and a complex roof made simple.

—David Radtke

Besides gracing the backyard with its splendor and calming presence, a gazebo is the perfect place to entertain. One look at this beauty and you'll be picturing it filled with family and friends, celebrating a graduation or even a backyard wedding.

We designed this 12-ft. dia. gazebo with plenty of eye-pleasing trim, from the pattern-cut rails that surround the seating area to the ball-shaped finial atop the cupola. Yet it's easy to build if you follow our special hints, tips, technical illustrations and Cutting List.

You're no doubt wondering what this gem costs to build. Well, you could pay $15,000 to $20,000 and let a contractor have all the fun, or you could build it yourself for about $5,000. You can pocket the savings—or throw one *really* great party.

This gazebo is builder-friendly

This project is not as difficult as it looks. Think of it as a series of several shorter projects with an end goal in sight for each. You can make all the decorative parts in your garage or shop (especially on rainy days). If you have several friends help you with the slab and framing (promise them anything), you can spread these two tasks over several weeks. A project like this would take two experienced carpenters nine working days from start to finish. An intermediate do-it-yourselfer who has built a deck should plan this as a whole summer project.

The slab

You don't have to get the slab dimensions perfect, but the closer they come to it, the easier things will be later. If you hate doing concrete work, skip this section, photocopy it and give it to your concrete mason. A crew can do the work while you're out shopping for lumber or cutting parts. Follow Figure B closely if you decide to do it yourself.

Begin by driving a 2-ft. piece of rigid electrical conduit at the intended center of the gazebo. Drive it in 18 in. Remove the sod with a rented sod cutter. You'll need to excavate a 9-in. deep area radiating out about 78 in. from the conduit. After that you'll set forms and put in a layer of 1/4-in. gravel to the dimensions shown in Figure B. The idea is to have the outside foot or more of the slab thicker to support the weight of the structure.

Build your forms after carefully examining Figure B. Set your circular saw at 22-1/2 degrees and cut eight 2x8 exterior forms with the short side measuring 57-1/2 in. Screw the forms together with 3-in. deck screws. Have a friend help you

Plan Smart

You must have a site that slopes less than 4 in. over 12 ft. (any more than this will require some excavating).

SHOPPING LIST

DESCRIPTION	QTY.
4x4 x 10' cedar (posts)	8
2x6 x 10' cedar (top plates)	4
1x4 x 14' cedar (wrap)	7
1x4 x 8' cedar (wrap)	1
1x6 x 14' cedar (wrap)	7
1x6 x 8' cedar (wrap)	1
2x4 x 10' cedar (rails and headers)	20
1x6 x 14' cedar (balusters)	10
1x4 x 8' cedar (pickets)	11
1x6 x 10' cedar ripped (3/4"strips)	6
5/4 x 10 x 8' cedar (corner braces)	4
2x6 x 10' cedar (rafters)	8
2x8 x 8' cedar (rafter buildups)	2
1x2 x 12' cedar (parts L)	2
2x6 x 8' cedar (cupola rafters)	3
4x4 x 5' cedar (octagonal hub)	1
2x4 x 8' cedar (outer ties P)	3
2x4 x 14' cedar (horizontal ties Q)	1
1x10 x 12' cedar (lower fascia)	4
1x6 x 8' cedar (upper fascia)	2
5/4 x 6 cedar decking 10-ft. lengths	50
Shangles (asphalt shingles)	3-1/2 squares
15-lb. roofing felt	1 roll
Roofing nails	10 lbs.
Simpson straps, No. LSTA12	16
Simpson angles, No. A23	16
Simpson standoffs, No. APS4	8
Joist hanger nails (galvanized)	5 lbs.
1-1/8" x 1/8" x 8' steel (anchors)	1
3/8" x 3" carriage bolts	8
3/8" x 3" hex bolts	8
3/8" nuts and washers	16
6d galvanized casing nails	5 lbs.
8d galvanized casing nails	5 lbs.
4d galvanized casing nails	5 lbs.
8d galvanized common nails	5 lbs.
Hook blades for shingle cutting	3
3" galvanized screws	5 lbs.

CUTTING LIST

KEY	QTY.	SIZE & DESCRIPTION
A	8	3-1/2" x 3-1/2" x 102" posts
B	8	1-1/2" x 5-1/2" x 56-1/2" top plates
C1	16	7/8" x 3-1/2" x 31" cedar wrap*
C2	16	7/8" x 3-1/2" x 36" cedar wrap*
D1	16	7/8" x 5-1/4" x 31" cedar wrap*
D2	16	7/8" x 5-1/4" x 36" cedar wrap*
E	8	1-1/2" x 3-1/2" x 50-3/4" cedar headers
F	30	1-1/2" x 3-1/2" x 50" cedar rails
G1	56	3/4" x 5-1/2" x 27" balusters
G2	96	3/4" x 3-1/2" x 8" spandrel pickets
G3	16	3/4" x 3-1/2" x 13" cupola pickets
H1	280 ft.	3/4" x 3/4" retainer strips (cut to fit)
H2	16 ft.	3/4" x 3/4" retainer strips (cut to fit)
J	16	1-1/8" x 9-1/4" x 22-1/2" corner braces
K1	8	1-1/2" x 5-1/2" x 102" lower rafters
K2	8	1-1/2" x 7-1/4" x 24" rafter tail buildups
L	8	3/4" x 1-1/2" x 34" inner vertical rafter ties
M	8	1-1/2" x 5-1/2" x 32" cupola rafters
N	1	3-1/2" x 3-1/2" x 50" octagonal rafter hub
P	8	1-1/2" x 3-1/2" x 32" outer vertical rafter ties
Q	16	1-1/2" x 3-1/2" x 10" horizontal rafter ties
R1	8	7/8" x 8-1/2" x 6' lower fascia (cut to length)
R2	8	7/8" x 5-1/2" x 2' upper fascia (cut to length)
S1	1	See Figure A
S2	2	See Figure A
T1	300 ft.	1" x 2-3/4" lower roof sheathing (5/4 decking cut in two)
T2	320 ft.	1" x 5-1/2" upper roof sheathing (5/4 decking)

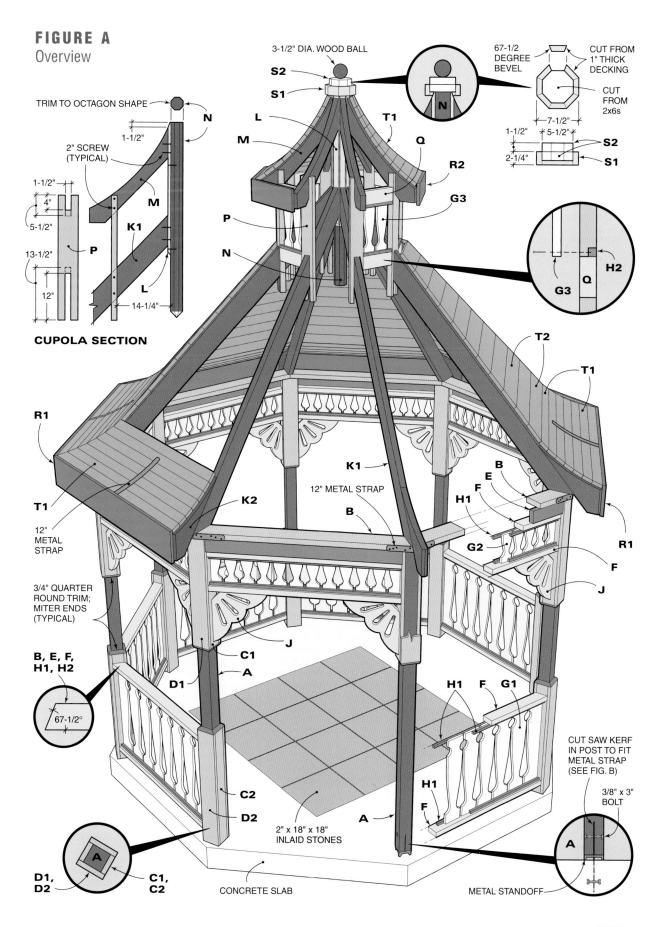

FIGURE A
Overview

FIGURE B
Concrete slab and paver detail

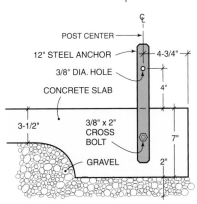

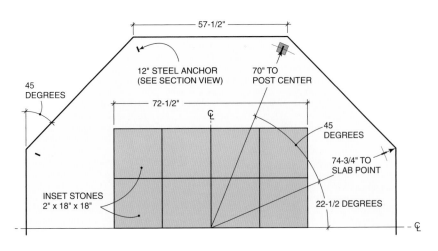

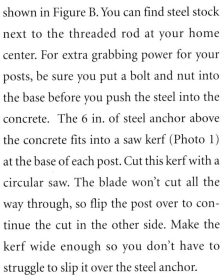

align the forms so the eight corners of the forms are all the same distance from the conduit center. If these measurements are all equal, your slab will be a perfect octagon—get it as close as you can. Drive 3/4 in. x 2-1/2 in. stakes along the outside of the forms at each intersection, level the forms and screw the forms to the stakes.

Now build a square inner form for the patio inlay, 72-1/2 in. on each side. Center it as shown and drive in the stakes on the inside of the forms and screw them together.

The slab will require about 1-1/2 yds. of concrete and four 10-ft. pieces of No. 4 rebar. Have plenty of help (at least three strong backs and two heavy-duty wheelbarrows). Wheelbarrow the concrete and dump it into the forms, lay rebar 4 in. in along the perimeter, screed the concrete with a straight 2x4, then run the hand float over it. Set your anchors in at the locations shown in Figure B. Wait until the concrete is firm (you should have to push hard to leave a thumbprint). Smooth it with a steel trowel, cover it with 4-mil clear plastic and let it set for two days. Keep kids and pets away.

Cut your posts to length and bolt them to the steel strap anchors

Make the anchors by cutting 12-in. lengths of 1/8-in. x 1-1/8 in. steel and boring 7/16-in. dia. holes into them as shown in Figure B. You can find steel stock next to the threaded rod at your home center. For extra grabbing power for your posts, be sure you put a bolt and nut into the base before you push the steel into the concrete. The 6 in. of steel anchor above the concrete fits into a saw kerf (Photo 1) at the base of each post. Cut this kerf with a circular saw. The blade won't cut all the way through, so flip the post over to continue the cut in the other side. Make the kerf wide enough so you don't have to struggle to slip it over the steel anchor.

Before you mark your anchor hole locations, screw the aluminum post standoff to the base of the post. These standoffs keep the post elevated for protection against rot. Mark the anchor hole locations as shown in Photo 1, then drill a 1-1/4 in. hole 1/2 in. deep on each side of the post, followed by a 3/8-in. hole all the way

CONCRETE SLAB

18" x 18" PAVERS INSET

1 Cut the posts to length and mount the aluminum standoff underneath. Transfer the hole locations in your steel anchors to the sides of the post. Drill a 1-1/4 in. recessed hole followed by a 3/8-in. hole for the 3-in. carriage bolt, washer and nut.

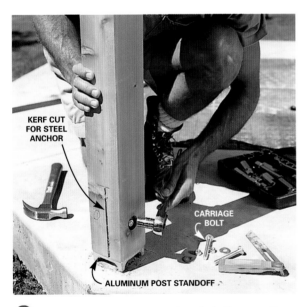

KERF CUT FOR STEEL ANCHOR

CARRIAGE BOLT

ALUMINUM POST STANDOFF

2 Tighten the nut onto the carriage bolt. Temporarily brace the 4x4s if necessary. Be sure you have the standoff screwed to the posts before you mark and drill the hole.

2x6 TOP PLATES

4x4 POSTS (A)

3 Screw the 2x6 top plates to the 4x4 posts with 3-in. galvanized screws. If your posts are set properly, the top plates should all be the same length. Make any adjustments to ensure the posts will all be plumb. Use a level to plumb the posts and install temporary bracing (shown in Photo 7). Cut and install the post wraps C1 and C2 at this time.

BALUSTERS (G1)

JIGSAW

4 Cut the balusters and the pickets from 1x6 and 2x6 material. See Figure C. Sand, prime and paint the pieces before installing them.

FIGURE C
Picket and baluster patterns

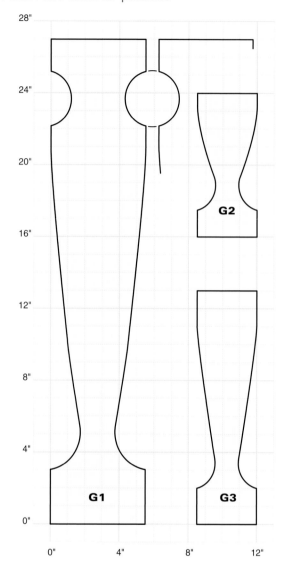

through. The 1-1/4 in. hole recesses the bolt head and nut to make room for the piece you'll nail over the post later. Grab a buddy to help set the post while you push the bolt through the hole and tighten it. Once all the posts are in place, cut the 2x6 top plates and screw them to the top of the posts with a pair of 3-in. deck screws. Plumb this framework with some temporary braces.

Nail the 1x4 (C1 and C2) cedar wrap onto the posts first, then measure this width and rip-cut the wider 1x6 to fit (D1 and D2). Nail the wider wrap to the post with 8d galvanized casing nails.

Set up and cut out the gingerbread pieces

These ornate parts do take time, but there's nothing difficult about cutting them. Use the scale drawing in Figures C and D to make a full-size template and trace the shapes onto boards. Don't think you have to cut all of them in one day. This is the kind of task you can chip away at by knocking off several pieces every day after work. Cut the lower balusters from 1x6 pine and the upper pickets (G2 and G3) from 1x4 pine. Use a circular

saw for end cuts and a jigsaw for curves. Once you've finished cutting these pieces, sand the edges and prime and paint them.

Cut the corner braces (J) from 5/4 (1-1/8 in. thick) pine (Photo 5). After you cut the shape, bevel-cut one side with your circular saw set at 22-1/2 degrees. Keep in mind that there's a left and a right corner brace for each post. Prime and paint these as well. Nail the corner braces to the post and rail with 8d galvanized casing nails after you install the rails, lower balusters, upper pickets and all the cleats. Use 4d galvanized casing nails to nail the cleats to the rails.

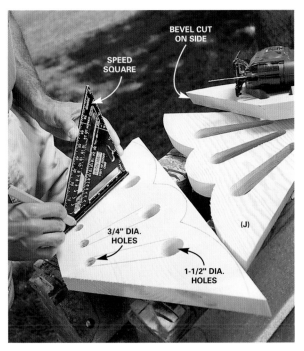

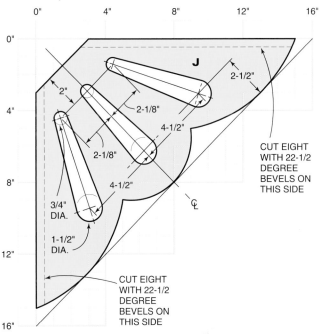

FIGURE D
Bracket patterns

FIGURE D
Bracket patterns

0" 4" 8" 12" 16"

J

2-1/2"

2"

2-1/8"

4-1/2"

2-1/8"

4-1/2"

3/4"
DIA.

1-1/2"
DIA.

CUT EIGHT
WITH 22-1/2
DEGREE
BEVELS ON
THIS SIDE

CUT EIGHT
WITH 22-1/2
DEGREE
BEVELS ON
THIS SIDE

BEVEL CUT
ON SIDE

SPEED
SQUARE

3/4" DIA.
HOLES

1-1/2" DIA.
HOLES

(J)

5 Cut the 16 corner brackets from 5/4 x 9-1/4 in. pine (which is 1-1/8 in. thick). Note that there are eight left- and eight right-hand pieces.

F

H1

F

BALUSTER (G1)

CEDAR WRAP (C2)

6 Miter and screw the rails and headers to the posts with 3-in. galvanized screws. Nail the balusters (G1) to the cleats, which are nailed to the cedar rails. Use 1-1/4 in. galvanized nails. A power finish nailer is handy here.

TOP PLATE

TEMPORARY
UPPER BRACES

TEMPORARY
LOWER
BRACES

7 Screw upper braces to the top plates (B). These will help stabilize the structure as you assemble the roof. Be sure the posts are anchored with braces as well.

8 Cut the cupola rafters from the template shown in Figure E. Cut the rafters and the curved rafter tail buildups using the information in Figure F.

FIGURE E
Cupola rafter

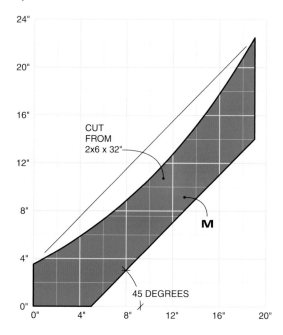

CUT FROM 2x6 x 32"

M

45 DEGREES

FIGURE F
Rafter assembly

Study Figures A, E and F and Photo 10. Cut your lower rafters (K1) and screw curved rafter tail buildups (K2) to the ends of the lower rafter. Cut the 1x2 inner and outer vertical rafter ties (L and P). Notice that these 2x4 outer vertical rafter ties have slots cut in them to slip over the upper and lower rafters. You can cut these slots with a table saw or circular saw, working from each end. First cut one side with multiple passes and then flip the rafter tie over and cut multiple passes from the other side. You'll get an angled slope at the end of the slot from the roundness of the blade.

Lay out the rafter parts (not including the center octagonal piece N) on a large flat area like a garage floor or a driveway (look at the upper left diagram of Figure

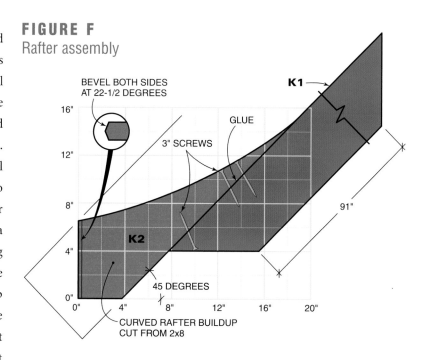

BEVEL BOTH SIDES AT 22-1/2 DEGREES

K1

GLUE

3" SCREWS

91"

K2

45 DEGREES

CURVED RAFTER BUILDUP CUT FROM 2x8

A). Fasten the upper and lower rafter to the 1x2 (L) with 2-in. screws. These rafters run parallel, with a 14-1/2 in. space between them. Next screw part P into the sides of the upper and lower rafter so that it's parallel to part L.

SAW BEVEL
SET AT 45°

4x4 BLANK FOR
CENTER HUB (N)

9 Shape the center hub (N) into an octagon. Measure in from each side about 1 in. and cut along this line with your saw bevel set at a 45-degree angle. The finished octagon should be about 1-1/2 in. on a side.

NOTE: DON'T DO THIS ON A WINDY DAY

CENTER HUB (N)

RAFTER ASSEMBLY SCREWED TO CENTER HUB

TEMPORARY BRACE

10 Attach two opposite rafters to the center hub. Then grab a partner and carefully walk the assembly up to position. See Photo 11 for nailing detail.

RAFTER TAIL BUILDUP (SEE FIGURE F)

ANGLED PLATE

STEEL STRAP

11 Nail the angled plates (see Resources, p. 252) to the rafter and to the top plates to secure the rafters to the structure.

UPPER RAFTER (M)

VERTICAL RAFTER TIES (P)

CENTER HUB (N)

12 Fasten each rafter system to the center octagonal hub. Install opposite sides one after the other to maintain the shape of the octagon.

13 Screw the horizontal rafter ties to the sides of each outer vertical rafter tie.

14 Nail the lower fascia (R1) to the rafter tail ends. Miter the ends with the saw set at 22-1/2 degrees.

15 Nail the roof decking to the rafters with 8d nails. Be sure to screw (use 3/4-in. screws) the steel strap to the lower roof boards for extra support. The strap ties the narrower boards together to prevent sagging.

Build the rest of the assemblies and then mount a pair to the center hub (N; see Photo 9). Follow Photos 10 – 12 to mount the rafter assemblies to the top plates.

Work Smart

Attach the rafter tails to the rafters before hauling them to the roof.

Deck the roof

Cut your lower fascia from 1x10 cedar. Hold it 7/8 in. above the ends of the rafters so your roof decking will be flush with the fascia.

Rip 5-1/2 in. decking in half for the first seven courses so they'll be able to bend around the lower curved section. Cut each end of the decking at 22-1/2 degrees for the first course and change the angle slightly until you finally reach about 16 degrees for the rest of the full-width courses.

There are a few things you need to know about using the Carriage House Shangle (see Resources, p. 252) roof-

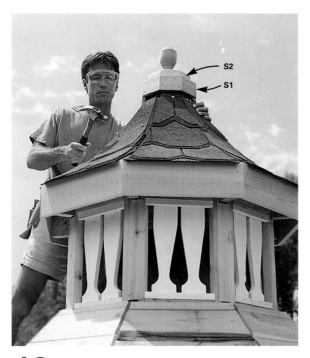

16 Shingle the cupola before shingling the lower roof. Otherwise, you'll damage the lower shingles when you go up and down.

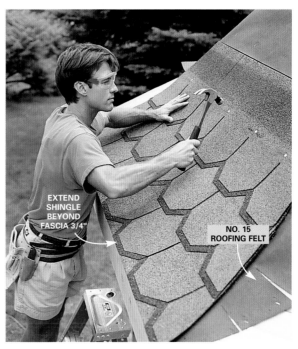

17 Shingle each lower roof section, then move to the opposite side. Keep the exposure consistent from side to side by measuring as you go.

ing material. First of all, these shingles are heavy and a bit tougher to work with than ordinary asphalt shingles. They also cost about twice as much, but we thought the finished look was well worth it. Don't buy the special cap shingles for the ridges; full cap shingles will look out of place. Instead, buy a matching color of ordinary asphalt shingles. You can cut these to fit the width and proportion of this small structure.

At the cupola where the surfaces are all curved, you'll need to remove the top one-third of each shingle to get it to lie flat. The cap over the seams should be cut narrower and shorter to follow the concave curve. Another thing to remember for the lower section: The cap shingles should be full width, but the length on the bottom four rows of cap needs to be cut down several inches to make the curve.

Painting your gazebo

Prime and paint if you please, but keep in mind that painting the gazebo means a lot of prep and repainting work in the future. It's best to paint just the gingerbread

features as accents, and then seal the unpainted parts with a brush-on oil sealer. I'd recommend applying the oil first, then painting the next day. Don't bother oiling the underside of the roof. Because it's out of the weather and direct sun, it'll look fresh for years to come.

Open-air gazebo

The perfect setting for picnics, parties—even outdoor concerts!

—David Radtke

I can still remember the first gazebo I saw as a kid. This lacy wood structure in my local park seemed to miraculously climb its way up from eight posts to a single point at the peak of the roof. And the best part was, I could see out in any direction.

Our gazebo has eight sides just like the first one I saw. Building any shape other than a rectangle can be a real head scratcher, but we've got the kinks worked out for you. This isn't a project for beginners, but you don't need a journeyman's card to qualify either. So if you've got basic carpentry tools and have tackled a project like a deck somewhere in your past, it's very doable.

The gazebo is built from dimensional treated wood and cedar.

Tools and time

You'll need a measuring tape, chalk line, hammer, shovel, two 8-ft. stepladders, electric or cordless drill, 1-1/2 in. and 3 in. hole saws, handsaw, jigsaw, circular saw, 4-ft. level and protractor-style cutting guide. Plan on using a full week's vacation (and for some of us, several weekends to finish up).

Project at a glance

Skill level
Intermediate

Special tools
Level
Drill
Circular saw
Jigsaw

Approximate cost
$3,000

Planning

It's easiest to consider the building process in five steps, each taking about a full day (eight hours, with a short lunch break) or more to finish:

1. Building the foundation using 12-in. round patio blocks stacked and mortared together to form a level surface.
2. Building the deck with the joists and decking.
3. Prestaining or painting the rafters, side slats and roof caps.
4. Assembling the walls and roof.
5. Cutting and installing the side slats, cleats and lattice.

1 Position the patio blocks with the location of the entry in mind. Align the first block on one side of the entry and then set the opposite block using the center of the layout circle as a guide. See Figure B for proper positioning of the patio blocks.

You'll also need a relatively flat spot to build the gazebo. Our site had a slope of 3 in. in 10 ft., so we had to build up our foundation on the low sides. If you have more than an 8-in. slope in 10 ft., consider a different site or a change in landscaping before you build.

Foundation

The success of any structure lies in a good foundation, so don't hurry through this part. You'll have to wait a day anyway for the mortar to set before you can build. The foundation is nothing more than round patio blocks (12 in. dia.) set level to each other at 10 key points. You'll probably have to stack and mortar some of the patio blocks to get the foundation level.

To lay out the foundation, scribe a 65-in. circle in the grass using a mason's string and a landscaping spike or stake as the center pivot. Mark out a circle as you go around with the string pulled tight from the stake. The center of each block along the perimeter will intersect with this line.

For a firm foundation, remove the sod under each block. Start with the highest elevation and level all the patio blocks to it using a long, straight 2x6 with a level on top of it (Photo 2). Keep in mind that you'll need 3/8-in. mortar joints between the patio blocks.

Framing the deck

This is a lot easier than it looks. The best way to start is to make the I-shaped beam assembly (Photo 3). Nail the rest of the joists, including the outer rim joists, to the beam assembly. Use the joist hangers (Figure A) and nail

FIGURE A
Gazebo details

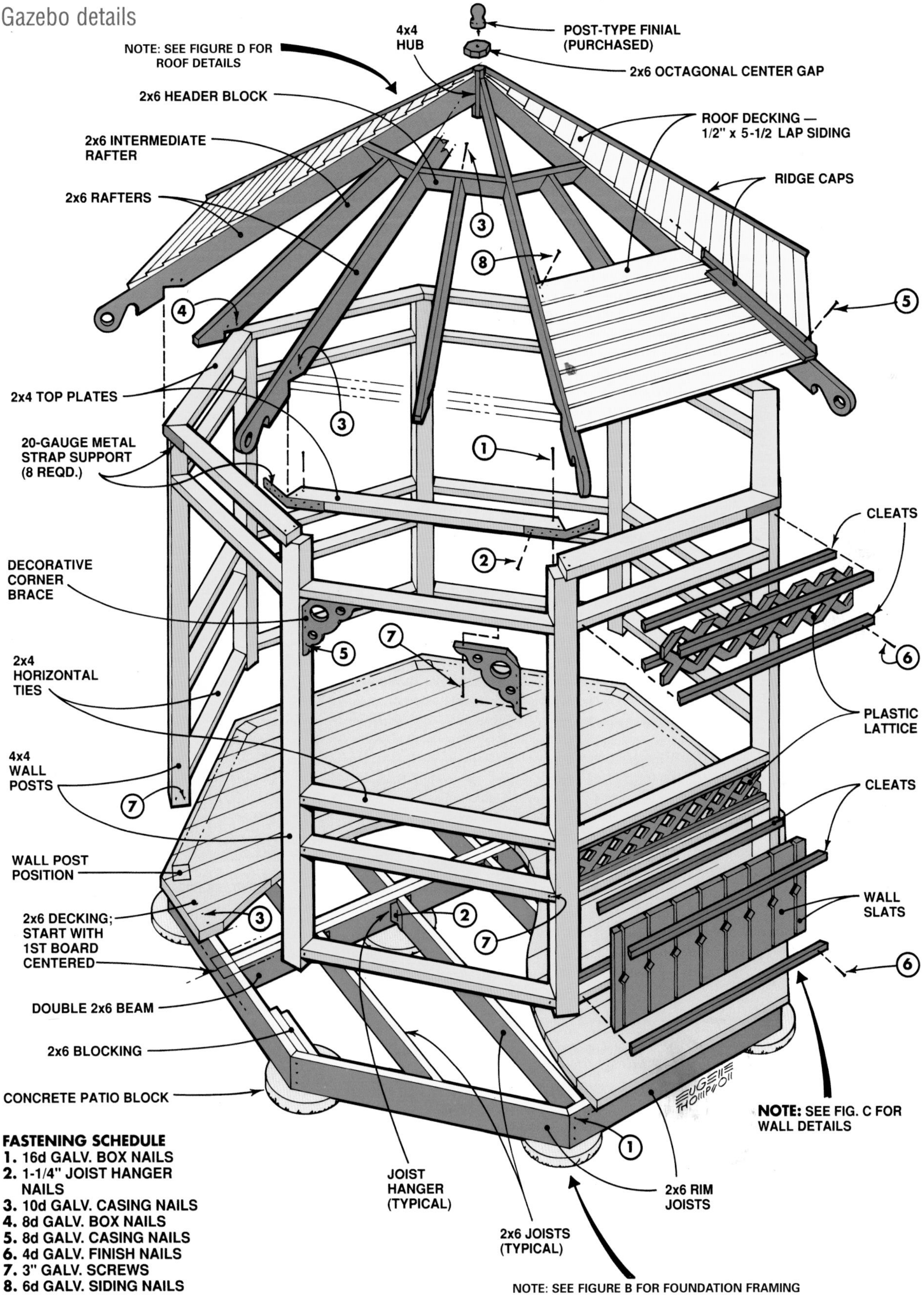

NOTE: SEE FIGURE D FOR ROOF DETAILS

POST-TYPE FINIAL (PURCHASED)

4x4 HUB

2x6 OCTAGONAL CENTER GAP

2x6 HEADER BLOCK

ROOF DECKING —
1/2" x 5-1/2 LAP SIDING

2x6 INTERMEDIATE RAFTER

RIDGE CAPS

2x6 RAFTERS

③

⑧

④

⑤

2x4 TOP PLATES

③

①

20-GAUGE METAL STRAP SUPPORT (8 REQD.)

②

CLEATS

CLEATS

DECORATIVE CORNER BRACE

⑤

⑦

⑥

2x4 HORIZONTAL TIES

⑦

PLASTIC LATTICE

4x4 WALL POSTS

⑦

CLEATS

WALL POST POSITION

③

②

WALL SLATS

2x6 DECKING; START WITH 1ST BOARD CENTERED

⑦

⑥

DOUBLE 2x6 BEAM

2x6 BLOCKING

CONCRETE PATIO BLOCK

NOTE: SEE FIG. C FOR WALL DETAILS

FASTENING SCHEDULE
1. 16d GALV. BOX NAILS
2. 1-1/4" JOIST HANGER NAILS
3. 10d GALV. CASING NAILS
4. 8d GALV. BOX NAILS
5. 8d GALV. CASING NAILS
6. 4d GALV. FINISH NAILS
7. 3" GALV. SCREWS
8. 6d GALV. SIDING NAILS

JOIST HANGER (TYPICAL)

①

2x6 RIM JOISTS

2x6 JOISTS (TYPICAL)

NOTE: SEE FIGURE B FOR FOUNDATION FRAMING

2 Level all of the patio blocks so they're at the same height. To raise the low spots, stack the patio blocks and mix and apply mortar (available in 60-lb. bags at home centers) between them. Remove any turf under the stones and dig down only deep enough to level them. Mix the mortar to a soft ice cream consistency and make the joint about 3/8 in. thick. Let the mortar set overnight before continuing.

3 Position the I-shaped beam assembly onto the center beam supports. The assembly is made from treated 2x6s nailed together and two outside rim joists. Cut and nail the remaining rim joists to each other with galvanized box nails as you set them across the patio blocks.

the rims together with three 16d galvanized box nails each.

Check the framing for level. Now's the time to do any shimming or adjusting. If you need shims, use treated scrap. Be sure to nail the blocking in the corners (Figure B) to later support the posts. At this point, make sure all of the diagonal measurements are equal. If not, tweak the framing with a few blows to the corners until you're satisfied.

Decking

Nail down the 2x6 decking (Photo 5). Start in the middle and work your way to each end. Let the deck boards "run wild" and after nailing, cut them 1 in. beyond the rim joists (Photo 6).

FIGURE B
Foundation framing

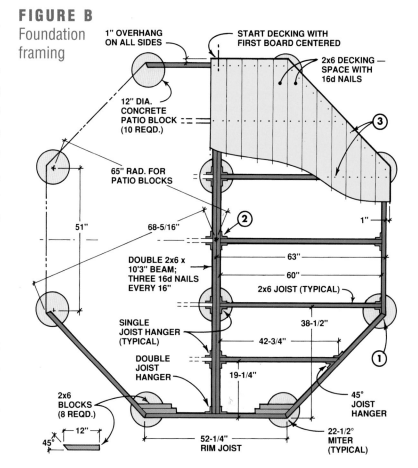

4 Install the joists inside the outer rims. Use joist hangers as shown in Figure B for support and strength. Make sure the measurements of all the diagonals (opposite points) of the octagon are equal before nailing the joists to the rims. Nail the blocks in the corners as shown in Figure B to help support the posts.

5 Nail the decking to the joists with 16d galvanized finish nails. Start in the middle and work your way out, and be sure the decking is perpendicular to the joists. Use 12-ft. lengths in the middle, then 10-ft. and finally 8-ft. lengths to minimize waste.

6 Trim the decking with a circular saw. Be sure to snap the chalk line 1 in. to the outside of the rim joists.

7 Prebuild the four wall sections by screwing the horizontal ties to the posts. The remaining sides are formed by joining the wall sections with horizontal ties (Figure A).

8 Screw each post to the deck with eight 3-in. galvanized deck screws. Use at least one temporary brace to hold the section straight and leave the braces in place until you frame the roof. Lay out the octagon by placing the end cuts from the posts and the remaining horizontal ties on the deck. Then remove them as you install each wall section.

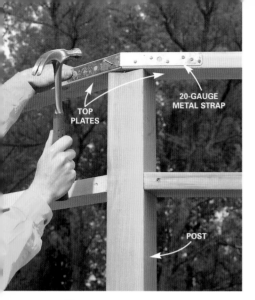

9 Nail the metal straps to the outside of each upper corner after nailing the top plates to the top of the posts. The straps provide a structural ring to support the outward pressure of the rafters.

Labels on photo: TOP PLATES • 20-GAUGE METAL STRAP • POST

FIGURE C
Wall details

22-1/2° BEVEL ON LEFT SIDE (8 REQD.)

22-1/2° BEVEL ON RIGHT SIDE

CUT FROM 5/4 x 8 STOCK (16 REQD.)

4" — 1-1/8"
3-1/2"
5-1/2"
7"
45°
3" DIA. HOLE
1-1/2" DIA. HOLE
SCREW HOLE
6"

DECORATIVE CORNER BRACE

51-1/2"
22-1/2"
22-1/2"
①
2x4 TOP PLATE (8 REQD.)
4x4 POST (8 REQD.)
79"
90"
⑦
⑤
③ PER SIDE
⑦

WALL ASSEMBLY
47"
22-1/2°
⑦
2x4 HORIZONTAL TIE (33 REQD.)
A
34-1/2"
A
23-1/2"
2"
⑦

9-3/8" x 48" PLASTIC LATTICE * (15 REQD.)
3/4" x 3/4" x 48" CLEATS * (88 REQD.)
⑥
HORIZONTAL TIE
CLEAT
⑥
WALL SLAT
* TRIM TO FIT AT ASSEMBLY

SECTION AA

5-1/2" (49 REQD.)
2" (14 REQD.)
3/4"
19-7/8"
1-1/2"
CUT FROM 1x6s

WALL SLATS

Walls: Posts and horizontal ties

Screw the horizontal ties to each of the posts using 3-in. deck screws (Photo 7). This goes faster if you make a small, 22-1/2 degree, pie-shaped block to keep each post positioned as you screw in the horizontal pieces.

After assembling each section, stand it in position (Photo 8). Brace each wall with a 2x6 screwed to the decking and at the top of one post to hold it straight until the gazebo is complete. Use the rest of the horizontal ties and post cut-offs (Photo 8) as spacers to help lay out the exact octagonal shape of the gazebo.

Nail the 2x4 top plates to the posts as shown in Figure A, then nail the metal straps (Photo 9) to the top plates. The metal straps provide a strong ring of support when the weight of the roof pushes out on the top plates later.

Cut and install the decorative corner braces (Photo 10) before beginning work on the roof. The braces provide strength as well as decoration.

Cutting the rafters and side slats

Don't let the roof framing scare you into putting on a flat roof. Cut the rafters to the dimensions given in Figure D, and you should have a close fit. Everyone measures and cuts a bit differently, so you may need to trim a bit here and there for a good fit.

Now's a good time to cut all the rest of the decorative parts like the rafter ends, side slats and cleats for the slats and lattice. Photo 13 shows you an easy method to cut

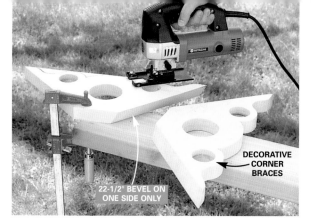

10 Cut the decorative shapes of the corner braces with a jigsaw. Cut the holes with a drill and 3-in. and 1-1/2 in. hole saws. A 22-1/2 degree bevel is cut on one side of each brace with a circular saw, and there are eight left-hand and eight right-hand patterns (Figure C).

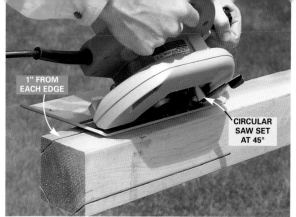

11 Cut the center hub for the rafters from a 4x4 by beveling the edges at 45 degrees, then finish cutting it with a handsaw to 12 in. in length.

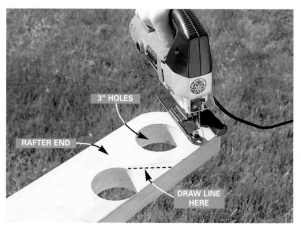

12 Cut the decorative rafter ends with a jigsaw after cutting the holes with a 3-in. hole saw. Sand the sharp edges with 100-grit sandpaper. Next cut the 55-degree angle on the inside end of the rafter and the "bird's-mouth" (notch for the top plate) as shown in Figure D.

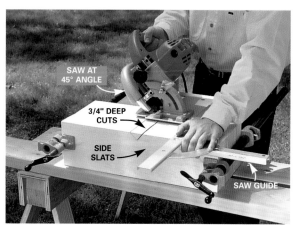

13 Clamp the side slats together and cut the diamond shapes with a circular saw. Set the blade at 45 degrees and just deep enough so the cuts meet at the center.

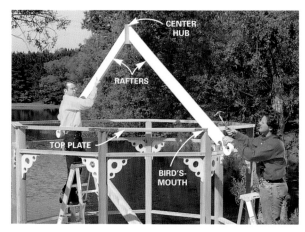

14 Position the "wishbone" (two rafters screwed to opposite ends of the hub) diagonally over the posts and onto the top plate, then toenail each rafter into the top plate. Screw the remaining six rafters to the hub with 3-in. galvanized deck screws, then nail each rafter end to the top plate as shown in Figure A.

15 Position the intermediate rafters to the center of each top plate and header block, then nail the intermediate rafter to the top plate and the header block.

16 Adjust the spacing of the slats with a carpenter's pencil, then nail through the cleat into the slats with No. 4 galvanized casing nails. Predrill the holes into the cleats and plastic lattice for a No. 4 galvanized casing nail. The lattice adds a great deal of rigidity to the structure.

In the photo: SIDE SLATS, CLEATS, LATTICE, CARPENTER'S PENCIL

Work Smart

Staining the rafters, side slats and cleats before you install them saves a lot of tedious cut-in work with a brush later on. We used a white solid color stain.

the side slats in groups to save time.

You can cut the slats and lattice cleats a little long, stain them, then trim them to exact length later.

After the stain is dry, screw two of the main rafters to the center hub (Photo 14), then grab a helper and position this "wishbone" across opposite corners of the top plate as shown. Check for fit and recut the bird's-mouth if necessary. If it's windy, take a break and wait for calm weather. A strong wind can send you and your helper right on Dorothy's heels across Kansas.

Screw the remaining rafters to the hub from a ladder positioned inside the gazebo, then toenail the rafters to the corners of the top plates with 8d galvanized casing nails. After the rafters are in position, nail the header blocks between each rafter (Figure A and Photo 15). Next, nail the intermediate rafters to the headers from

FIGURE D
Roof details

HUB — CUT FROM 4x4 — 45° — 1-1/2" — 1-3/4" — 12" — ⑦ RAFTER

OCTAGONAL CENTER CAP — CUT FROM 2x6 — 5-1/2" — 45°

RIDGE CAP (8 PAIR REQD.) — 15° BEVELS — 3/4" — 2-1/2" — 94-1/4" — 18° — 3/4" — 3/4" — 5-5/8"

RAFTER (8 REQD.) — 79-3/8" — 55° — 6-3/4" — 3-13/16" — CUT FROM 2x6 — 100-1/4" — 4" — 2-3/4" — BIRD'S-MOUTH — 3" DIA. HOLES — 1-1/2" — 2-3/4" — 8" — 90°

INTERMEDIATE RAFTER (8 REQD.) — 2ND CUT 1-1/2" — 3/4" — WASTE — 52-1/4" — 1ST CUT — 2-1/2" — 3-5/8"

HEADER BLOCK (8 REQD.) — 16° — 15" — CUT FROM 2x6 — 12-1/4"

ROOF DECKING — 1/8" PILOT HOLES — 1/2" x 5-1/2" LAP SIDING — ⑧ — 73° — 1" OVERLAP — 59" (FIRST PIECE)

the upper side of the header into the end of the rafter with 16d galvanized box nails. Toenail the intermediate rafters into the center of each top plate.

Installing the lattice, slats and cleats

Before you nail the siding onto the rafters, you'll need to install the cleats and lattice as well as the side slats to give the gazebo its structural strength. We used plastic lattice

6" CEDAR LAP SIDING

TEMPORARY BRACE

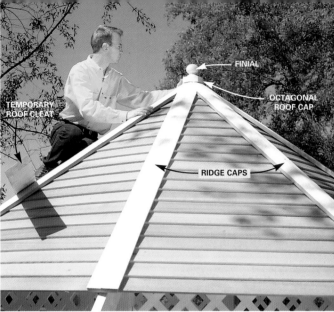

TEMPORARY ROOF CLEAT

FINIAL

OCTAGONAL ROOF CAP

RIDGE CAPS

17 Nail the cedar lap siding to the rafter with "splitless" galvanized siding nails. Place the nails so they're just above the top of each lower course to allow for expansion. This will keep the siding from splitting later.

18 Center the roof cap onto the top of the center hub after the ridge caps are installed and nail it to the hub with 16d galvanized finish nails.

for lateral strength, although wood lattice will work too. The plastic lattice is uniform in thickness and only gives the illusion of overlapping strips. The plastic lattice nails easily, and because it's white, it's one thing you won't have to paint or stain. Be sure to nail the lattice and cleats well and you'll notice the gazebo frame get more solid as each panel is fastened in place.

Finishing the roof

To cut the siding for the roof, start at the bottom of each triangle of the roof and work your way to the top (Photo 17). Your cuts don't have to be exact, because the ridge

caps will cover the joints. You may need to predrill the siding to prevent splitting near the edges. As you work your way to the top, nail a cleat into the rafters so you can climb up and finish the top. When you're finished nailing the siding to the roof, nail the octagonal center cap to the top of the hub.

Now cut and nail the ridge caps to the rafters. Notice that the ridge caps have a 15-degree bevel on each center edge (Figure D). Cut them to fit neatly around the center cap. Use 8d galvanized nails every 8 in. to nail the ridge caps to the rafters.

Work Smart

Compound cuts consist of a miter and a bevel cut. The miter is made across the face of the board, and the bevel is cut through the thickness of the board. Roof framers need to make compound cuts to make rafters fit precisely.

To make compound cuts with a circular saw, set the blade of the saw for the bevel cut, then set the protractor-cutting guide at the miter angle for the miter cut. Then follow the protractor guide with your saw table, and both angles will be cut simultaneously.

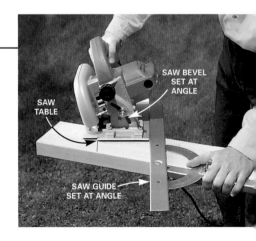

SAW BEVEL SET AT ANGLE

SAW TABLE

SAW GUIDE SET AT ANGLE

Rustic yard shed

Spacious, attractive and lots of natural light.

—*Travis Larson*

W ho doesn't need a better place to stow all that stuff cluttering up the garage? Wheelbarrows, lawn mowers, bikes, fertilizer spreaders and lawn and garden supplies all steal precious garage space. A yard shed will not only free up your garage but also help you organize and neaten your home and let you park the cars inside the garage again.

We've bent over backward to design a shed that's easy to build yet has lots of useful features. We combined standard 2x4 wall construction with prefabricated roof trusses to make roof framing easy, eliminate tricky soffit (eave overhangs) work and simplify trim details. We added an easy-to-build sliding door for wide shed access without the hassles or expense of swinging doors. Additional features include the open portico and wide roof overhangs. They'll shade you from the hot sun and shelter you from the rain so you can work in the open air or just relax.

In this story, we'll show you the step-by-step process of how to frame and finish this shed. While time-consuming, the process doesn't require any advanced carpentry skills. If you've done some framing and siding and a tad of roofing, you're qualified to tackle this

Project at a glance

Skill level
Intermediate to advanced

Special tools
Circular saw
Drill
Scaffolding with wheels

Approximate cost
$3,500 (excluding concrete floor)

FIGURE A
Framing details

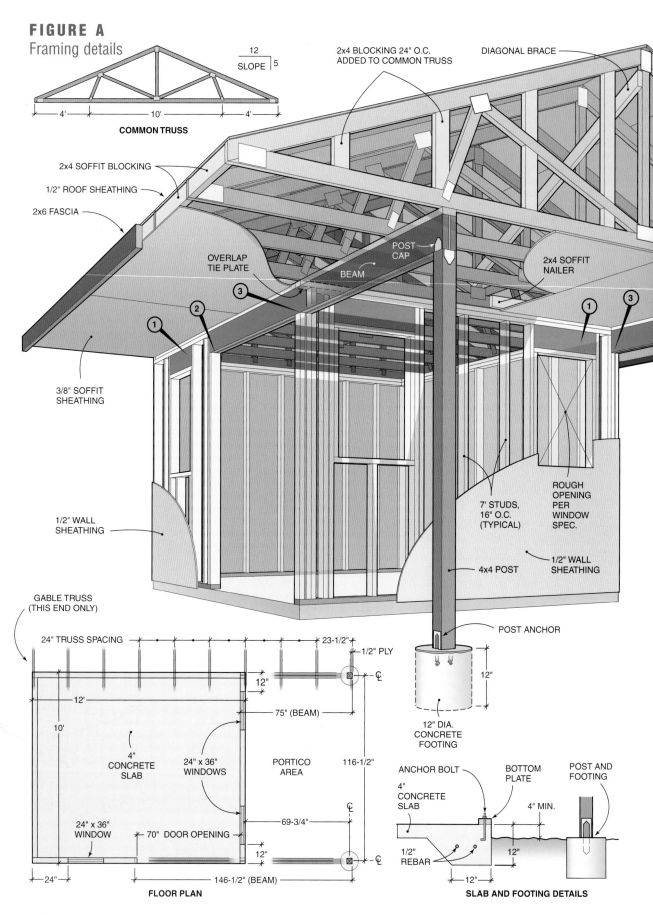

12
SLOPE | 5

COMMON TRUSS

4' 10' 4'

2x4 BLOCKING 24" O.C.
ADDED TO COMMON TRUSS

DIAGONAL BRACE

2x4 SOFFIT BLOCKING

1/2" ROOF SHEATHING

2x6 FASCIA

OVERLAP
TIE PLATE

POST
CAP

BEAM

2x4 SOFFIT
NAILER

③

②

①

③

①

3/8" SOFFIT
SHEATHING

1/2" WALL
SHEATHING

ROUGH
OPENING
PER
WINDOW
SPEC.

7' STUDS,
16" O.C.
(TYPICAL)

4x4 POST

1/2" WALL
SHEATHING

POST ANCHOR

GABLE TRUSS
(THIS END ONLY)

24" TRUSS SPACING

23-1/2"

1/2" PLY

12"

12'

75" (BEAM)

10'

116-1/2"

4"
CONCRETE
SLAB

24" x 36"
WINDOWS

PORTICO
AREA

69-3/4"

24" x 36"
WINDOW

70" DOOR OPENING

12"

24"

146-1/2" (BEAM)

FLOOR PLAN

12" DIA.
CONCRETE
FOOTING

12"

ANCHOR BOLT

BOTTOM
PLATE

POST AND
FOOTING

4"
CONCRETE
SLAB

4" MIN.

1/2"
REBAR

12"

12"

SLAB AND FOOTING DETAILS

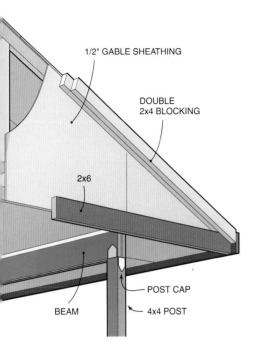

1/2" GABLE SHEATHING

DOUBLE
2x4 BLOCKING

2x6

BEAM

POST CAP

4x4 POST

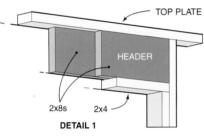

TOP PLATE

HEADER

2x8s   2x4

DETAIL 1

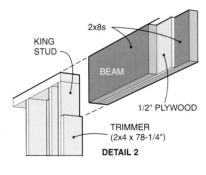

2x8s

KING
STUD

BEAM

1/2" PLYWOOD

TRIMMER
(2x4 x 78-1/4")

DETAIL 2

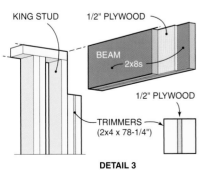

KING STUD   1/2" PLYWOOD

BEAM
2x8s

1/2" PLYWOOD

TRIMMERS
(2x4 x 78-1/4")

DETAIL 3

project. We spent about $3,500 (excluding the concrete work) for top-grade materials. The materials lists tell you what we used, but it's easy to shave off $1,000 or more by excluding some of the cosmetic trim, or substituting a less expensive material for the rough-sawn cedar. If you want to further cut costs, eliminate skylights and use standard shingles in lieu of the architectural-grade shingles.

Size it to suit

Because we're using standard wall construction and roof trusses, you can build virtually any size shed you wish using these basic construction techniques. The trusses we show are designed to handle the 4-ft. wide soffits. You can also order trusses with shorter soffits or a different roof slope. Our trusses have a 5/12 slope, which means they drop 5 inches for every 12 horizontal inches.

Contact your local building department and ask if a building permit is needed. Be ready to supply the exact location of the shed on your property along with dimensions and building details. Make a copy of Figure A and submit that along with a site plan and that'll probably be

ROUGH FRAMING MATERIALS

ITEM	QTY.	ITEM	QTY.
Framing materials		**Roof trusses**	
4x4 x 8' treated (portico posts)	2	Common trusses	9
2x4 x 10' treated (bottom plates)	2	Gable end truss	1
2x4 x 12' treated (bottom plate)	1	**Hardware**	
		16d cement-coated nails (framing nails)	15 lbs.
2x4 x 8' treated (bottom plate)	1	8d cement-coated nails (sheathing nails)	10 lbs.
2x4 x 12' (top and tie plates)	14	1-1/2" joist hanger screws (connector fasteners)	1 lb.
2x4 x 7' (studs)	60	Rafter ties (truss anchors)	16
2x8 x 14' (door/ portico beam)	2	H-clips (plywood joints)	36
2x8 x 8' (portico beam, window headers)	4	Post anchors (post-to-concrete connection)	2
4x8 1/2" plywood sheets (roof and wall sheathing)	25	Post caps (post-to-beam connection)	2

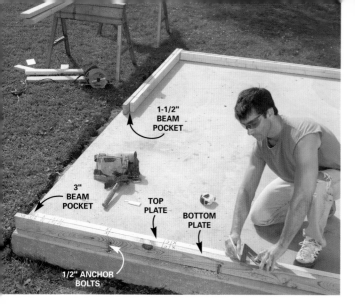

Labels on image: 1-1/2" BEAM POCKET · 3" BEAM POCKET · TOP PLATE · BOTTOM PLATE · 1/2" ANCHOR BOLTS

1 Cut the top and bottom plates to length (see Figure A), then mark and drill 5/8-in. anchor bolt holes in the bottom plates. Tack the pairs together and mark the window, door and stud locations.

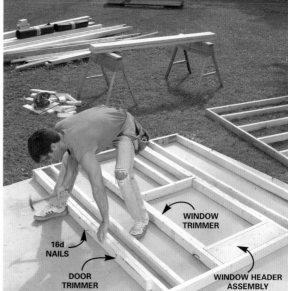

Labels on image: 16d NAILS · DOOR TRIMMER · WINDOW TRIMMER · WINDOW HEADER ASSEMBLY

2 Assemble the headers and nail them to the top plates. Then nail the full-length studs to both plates, and finally add the trimmers and other framing for the doors and windows.

all you'll need. If you want to wire your shed, you'll need an electrical permit as well.

A few rented tools will save gobs of time

You'll need only an apronful of tools, a circular saw and a screw gun to build this shed, but a couple of rental tools will speed construction. A 6-ft. section of scaffolding, complete with wheels and planks, will simplify roof-related construction. Set it up inside the shed and you'll have a safe platform for setting the trusses. Set it up outside and it'll make sheathing the roof and installing the fascia boards and the first few rows of shingles much easier. If you're productive, you'll even have rental time left on Sunday afternoon to side the gable ends.

Work Smart

Lay out the wall plates ahead of time, then mark on the forms where you'd like the anchor bolts placed (two on the short walls, three on the back wall) so they won't end up in the doorway or beneath studs.

To save time when you're nailing, also consider renting a pneumatic sheathing stapler (Photo 11) and a roofing nailer (Photo 14).

Pouring the slab

We hired a concrete contractor to pour our floor: a 4-in. thick slab with edges thickened to 12 in. around the perimeter (Figure A). It cost us about $1,200. But if you've done concrete work before, you can certainly pour this simple slab yourself for $500 or less. Form it so the top is at least 4 in. above the ground to protect the wood trim and siding from water runoff and splashing. Embed two rows of 1/2-in. rebar in the footings during pouring to strengthen the edges. You'll need to order 4.5 yards of concrete plus any concrete you want for walks, patios or footings outside the structure.

Although we put a paver brick patio in front of the shed and under the portico, you can save time and money by pouring a concrete slab in those areas instead. Just make sure that the concrete outside the shed slopes away so water won't seep in under the walls.

Also dig footings to support the portico posts (Figure A). Use string lines to find the post positions, then dig 12-in. diameter, 12-in. deep footings and fill them with concrete to 4 in. below the slab height (to leave room for the finished patio floor). If you extend a concrete patio slab under the posts, increase the thickness of the slab to 8 in. in a 3 x 3-ft. area to support the additional weight.

3 Stand the walls and drop them over the anchor bolts. Nail the corners together and install the anchor bolt washers and nuts. Then plumb and temporarily brace each corner with a long 2x4 on the inside.

4 Set, plumb and brace the posts. Rest a straight 2x4 on the beam trimmers. Level it and mark both posts for height. Cut off the posts with a circular saw.

5 Assemble the beams and set them on the posts and trimmers. Nail them to the stud walls and to the post/beam connector.

6 Nail "tie" plates over the top plates, overlapping the corners. Use 16d nails spaced over the studs below. Then nail plywood sheathing to the walls.

Otherwise, pour 12-in. diameter, 12-in. deep footings and use your string lines to accurately position post brackets in the wet concrete.

Wall and beam construction

Get started on your wall framing by cutting the treated bottom and top plates to length (see Figure A for dimensions and Photo 1). Mark and drill the 5/8-in. diameter anchor bolt holes, then temporarily tack the plates together with 8d nails and lay out the studs and window and door openings. Note that the bottom plates on each side of the door opening and at the back corner of the portico are longer than the top plates. That's where the trimmers (beam supports) rest on the bottom plates (Photo 1) to support the portico and door opening beams.

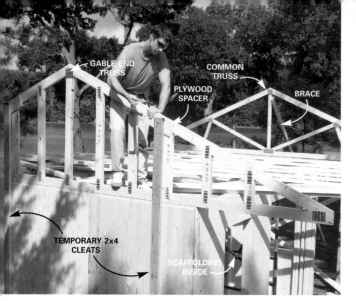

7 Lay out the truss positions on the top plates. Erect trusses at each end of the roof. Center them, brace them plumb and solidly toenail each one to the walls with 16d nails.

8 Stretch a string between the end trusses and align the intermediate truss peaks with the string. Lay out and tack them to a temporary "ribbon" board to keep them in place and aligned.

Assemble each wall and set it aside to use the slab for assembling the other walls (Photo 2). After they're built, slip them over the anchor bolts and nail them together at the corners with five 16d nails. Plumb and brace the walls at the corners with the braces on the inside of the shed so they won't interfere with the wall sheathing (Photo 3).

Now stand, plumb and brace the posts and assemble and set the beams. Brace the posts back to the building, to each other and to stakes pounded into the ground to keep them plumb and solid for setting the beams (Photo 5). Nail the beams, then cap the walls and beams with "tie" plates, overlapping them at the corners (Photo 6) and over the tops of the beams. Drive two 16d nails at each end and at least one 16d nail every 16 in. Then sheathe the walls with plywood, driving nails or staples every 8 in. along edges and every 12 in. otherwise. After you sheathe the walls, you can remove the bracing, but leave on the post braces until the roof trusses are set and sheathed.

Now go ahead and lay out the truss positions on the tie plates using Figure A as a guide. You'll have a fair number of 2x4s left over from the wall construction, but don't worry. You'll need most of them for blocking to support the soffit plywood along the eaves and around

the edges of the portico, for siding backers on the end common truss, and for diagonal bracing for the end trusses. Still have leftovers? Use them to build shelving in your new shed!

Ordering and installing roof trusses

Ordering roof trusses from a lumberyard means that the truss manufacturer will engineer the trusses to safely handle the spans that you specify. So you can order trusses to fit any span or width of shed without worrying about strength issues. To make a longer shed, simply order more trusses, one more for every 2 ft. of building length. Bring Figure A with you when ordering the trusses and the staff will be able to help you with the order. By the way, you can expand the portico, too. Make it as wide as 8 ft. and as deep as 12 ft. simply by using double 2x10s instead of 2x8s for the beams (but make the door height 2 in. shorter).

You'll be ordering two types of trusses: "common" trusses, the ones that can free-span open spaces, and "gable end" trusses. Gable end trusses have vertical 2x3 studs spaced every 16 in. to simplify siding installation (Photo 7). But they aren't designed to span wide-open areas. Since the end truss at the portico doesn't have a wall beneath it, you'll have to install a common truss and

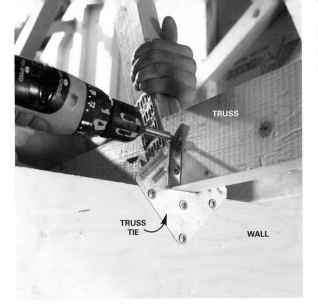

9 Screw truss clips to the tops of the walls and to the trusses with special 1-1/2 in. truss screws.

TRUSS

TRUSS TIE

WALL

10 Cut and nail blocking spaced every 2 ft. on the end common truss. Then scribe, cut and sheathe both end trusses.

TEMPORARY SUPPORT BLOCK

2'

EXTRA BLOCKING

BEAM SHEATHING

11 Snap a chalk line 48-1/4 in. up from the truss ends and nail down the first row of plywood sheathing. Add plywood clips midway between trusses and nail on the second row of sheathing.

PLYWOOD CLIP

CHALK LINE ON TRUSSES

TEMPORARY SAFETY CLEAT

48-1/4"

12 Nail two layers of 2x4s over the gable sheathing flush with the top of the roof to form small over-hangs. If you plan to add skylights to the roof, follow the manufacturer's instructions.

FLUSH WITH PLYWOOD

GABLE VENT OPENING

FLUSH WITH TRUSS END

add blocking for the sheathing as we show in Photo 10 and Figure A.

Lay out the top plates for truss placement (see Figure A), then cluster the trusses toward one end of the building with the tips supported by the scaffolding. That way you'll be able to center, set and brace the end trusses and then stand each truss in sequence without shuffling

trusses around. After standing the gable end trusses, plumb and brace them back to stakes driven into the ground before standing the other trusses. A great way to safely stand the gable end trusses is to use a couple of temporary 2x4 cleats nailed to the wall (Photo 7). They'll give you something to anchor the truss to while toe-nailing and adding bracing.

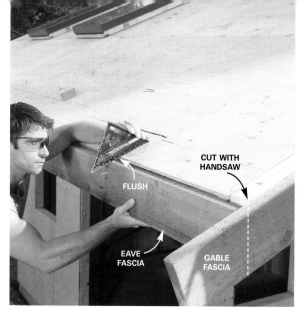

13 Nail the 2x6 gable and eave fascia boards flush with the rooftop. Cut off the gable fascia flush with the eave fascia. Then fit and nail the 1x3 and 1x2 trim in place (Figure B, p. 175).

CUT WITH HANDSAW
FLUSH
EAVE FASCIA
GABLE FASCIA

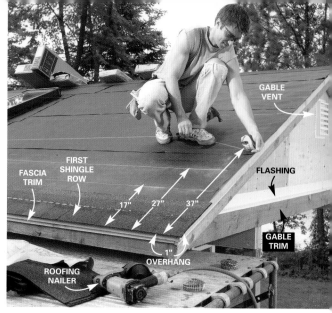

14 Staple No. 15 roof felt to the roof. Snap chalk lines every other shingle row to keep rows straight. Then nail on the shingles, allowing a 1-in. overhang. Staple more roof felt to the walls and install the windows.

GABLE VENT
FASCIA TRIM
FIRST SHINGLE ROW
FLASHING
17" 27" 37"
GABLE TRIM
1" OVERHANG
ROOFING NAILER

15 Nail blocking between the roof trusses (see Figure A), then cut the soffit plywood to fit and nail it to the blocks and trusses.

BLOCKING BEHIND FASCIA
SOFFIT PLYWOOD

16 Install all of the exterior trim as shown in Figure B, following the numbered sequence in the photo.

POST TRIM
FRIEZE BOARDS
BEAM TRIM
OTHER VERTICAL TRIM
DOOR TRIM
WINDOW TRIM
WATER BOARD AND FLASHING

Lay out a nailing 2x4 "ribbon" with the same pattern as with the wall plates (Photo 8). Use the ribbon to place and hold each truss in position until you install the roof sheathing (Photo 11). String a line at the ridge to help center the middle trusses. Tack each truss in order to the ribbon and toenail each one to the plates (Photo 8). The metal clips (truss ties) solidly anchor the trusses to the walls (Photo 9). After the trusses are in place, you may need additional diagonal bracing (see Figure A). The booklet that comes with your trusses will tell you exactly where to put them.

Nail on the plywood following a chalk line as we show in Photo 11. Lay the roof sheathing along the chalk line to keep the first row perfectly straight. We added plywood clips midway between trusses to tie the sheets together. That prevents warping that can show up well after the shingles are on. Offset all plywood butt seams at least one truss space on each row from the one below it.

Siding and trim

Begin the exterior finishing by nailing on the fascia boards. We show a three-part fascia made from a 2x6 and two 1x3 and 1x2 trim boards (Photo 14). You can simplify the fascia details by eliminating one or both trim boards. But whatever style you choose, it's easiest to cut and install the gable fascia first, leaving the eave ends long, and then running the eave fascia into it (Photo 13). Then cut off the overhanging gable fascia in place with a handsaw. We won't show you shingling details here. Use the directions on the shingle packages for installation procedures. Cut and install the 3/8-in. soffit plywood, adding blocking wherever necessary to secure outer edges that won't be supported by siding trim.

Start cladding the walls by stapling up No. 15 felt, starting at the bottom and overlapping each row by 2 in. Then install the corner boards and 2x6 "water boards" at the bottom (Photo 16). Lap the water boards at least 1/2 in. over the edge of the slab to keep water out. Cap the top of the water board with 1-1/2 in. drip cap flashing. Slit the felt and slip the flashing under it. Then cut and

FIGURE B: Exterior cladding details

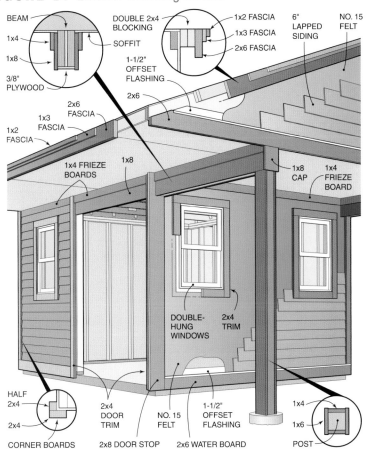

EXTERIOR CLADDING MATERIALS

ITEM	QTY.	ITEM	QTY.
Roofing		1x8 x 12' (beam fascia)	1
Rolls of No. 15 organic felt	2	1x8 x 8' (beam fascia)	3
Squares of shingles (roofing)	4	1x6 x 8' (post casing)	4
Bundle of ridge shingles (ridge cap)	1	1x4 x 8' (post casing)	4
Siding and trim (rough-sawn cedar)		1x4 x 10' (frieze boards)*	1
4x8 x 3/8" (soffit plywood)	8	1x4 x 12' (frieze boards)*	2
2x6 x 14' (water board)*	1	1x4 x 8' (frieze boards)*	4
2x6 x 12' (water board)*	2	3/4 x 8' (cedar lap siding)	32
2x6 x 8' (water board)*	1	3/4 x 12' (cedar lap siding)	42
2x6 x 10' (gable bottom boards)*	4	**Hardware and windows**	
2x6 x 12' (gable fascia)	4	2" siding nails	10 lbs.
2x6 x 10' (eave fascia)	4	3" siding nails (1-1/2" trim)	5 lbs.
1x3 x 12' (gable fascia)*	4	1-1/4" roofing nails (shingles)	10 lbs.
1x3 x 10' (eave fascia)*	4	5/16" staples (roofing felt)	1 box
1x2 x 12' (gable fascia)*	4	4d galv. box nails (soffit plywood)	1 lb.
1x2 x 10' (eave fascia)*	4	1-1/2" x 10' drip cap flashing	8
2x4 x 8' (corner boards)	5	2' x 3' vinyl double-hung windows*	3
2x4 x 12' (window casing)*	3	2' x 4' No. 106 Velux fixed skylights*	2
2x4 x 8' (door trim)	2	No. 106 skylight flashing kits*	2
2x8 x 8' (door stop)	1	*Optional parts	
1x2 x 14' (door track valance)*	1		

LEAVE 1/8" GAPS

SCRIBE CUTS

17 Scribe and cut the siding to fit around openings, then nail it through the sheathing into the studs with siding nails.

DOOR FRONT

BACKSIDE 1x6 DOOR FRAME

CONSTRUCTION ADHESIVE

18 Cut the door parts using Figure C as a guide. Lay out the 1x6 back-side frame and glue and screw the plywood to it using the edges of plywood to square the door.

nail on the corner boards. Note that we made the corners from a full 2x4 and half of another one. Nail them together and put them up as a unit.

Since the windows are well protected from weather, you don't have to flash them to keep water out. Simply trim them with 2x4s. Finish the top of the walls with 1x4 frieze boards, and clad the beams and posts with 3x4-in. thick trim as shown. Side the walls, leaving 1/8-in. gaps at the ends of the siding for caulk.

In the opening photo, you'll see decorative brackets. We cut those out of 2x8s with a jigsaw. Use any curve you wish and cut a 60-degree angle on the top and a 30-degree angle on the bottom. Toenail them to the corner boards and soffit with 8d galvanized finish nails.

Building the sliding door

We chose a sliding door for this shed because it is easy to build, trouble free and best of all, gives a clear 6-ft. opening for wide access. Building a sliding door isn't as tricky as you might think. To build this door, you simply glue, screw and nail the front and back frames to a plywood core. Cut the two sections of plywood to length and width (see Figure C), lay them together and use them as a guide for measuring the lengths of the door frame parts.

Assemble the door on the shed floor to keep everything flat and square, and dry-fit the parts before gluing and fastening them (Photos 18 – 19).

To hang the door, screw the roller tracks to the soffit (Photo 21). You'll need two 6-ft. tracks mounted end to end. You may have to drill additional holes through the track so the screws hit the trusses. Slip the wheel trucks into the track, mount the brackets on the top of the door (Photo 20) and then, with a helper, lift the door onto the tracks. The directions that come with the rollers will give you the details.

Finishing touches

If you choose natural wood siding, it's best to protect it with an exterior finish to keep it from graying over time. We coated our siding with two coats of Penofin clear oil finish. Although it's not visible in the photos, we stained the soffit undersides with a moss green opaque stain for added contrast.

1x4 CENTER TRIM

FRONT SIDE 1x4 DOOR FRAME

ALTERNATE DOOR FRAME JOINTS

1x3 EDGE TRIM

ROLLERS

ROLLER BRACKET

CENTER LINE

19 Glue and nail the front side frame through the plywood and into the back-side frame with 2-in. nails. Space the center trim boards 3/16 in. (a carpenter pencil's width) apart.

20 Cut the 1x3 trim and glue and screw it to the edge of the door. Position and screw the door roller brackets to the top edge.

FIGURE C
Sliding door details

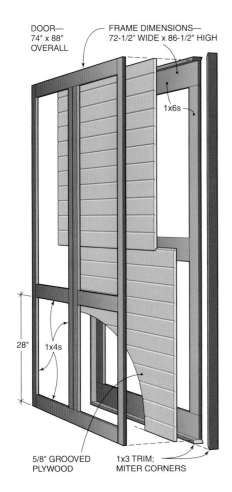

DOOR— 74" x 88" OVERALL

FRAME DIMENSIONS— 72-1/2" WIDE x 86-1/2" HIGH

1x6s

1x4s

28"

5/8" GROOVED PLYWOOD

1x3 TRIM; MITER CORNERS

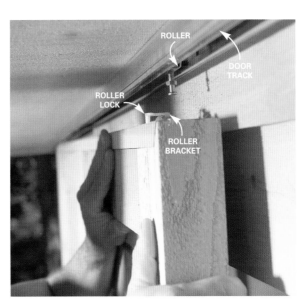

ROLLER

DOOR TRACK

ROLLER LOCK

ROLLER BRACKET

21 Screw the track to the soffit framing (drill new holes as necessary). Slide the rollers into the track, then slip the rollers into the brackets and lock them into place.

SLIDING DOOR MATERIALS

ITEM	QTY.	ITEM	QTY.
4x8 x 5/8" (grooved fir plywood siding)	2	National V13B Gate Latch	1
1x4 x 8' (front door frame)	4	Johnson 1120 series pocket door hangers	1 set
1x4 x 6' (front door frame)	3	Johnson 100 series 6' pocket door track	2
1x6 x 8' (back door frame)	2	Door handles	2
1x6 x 6' (back door frame)	3		

Gallery of ideas

A shed has to hold lots of stuff—but it doesn't have to look plain and boring. These sheds offer plenty of storage and great looks.

For information on obtaining plans for building the sheds and other structures shown here, see Resources, p. 252.

Schoolhouse storage shed

This 10 x 12-ft. shed has a spacious open-air entry, 6-ft. wide double doors and a single service door for convenience. The louvered cupola lends a touch of charm while providing plenty of natural ventilation. Fiber-cement siding, a concrete floor, and composite trim and columns mean lower maintenance.

Craftsman screenhouse

This craftsman-style screenhouse is large enough for dining and entertaining, yet small enough for a cozy feel. The floor is constructed on a foundation of pressure-treated 6x6s leveled into a gravel base. The rafters, shingles, roof boards, screen panels and trim are all constructed using attractive, rot-resistant cedar.

Cottage-style shed

This 10 x 12-ft. shed offers plenty of storage, light and charm. The large, carriage-style doors are actually an 8-ft. overhead door in disguise. Framing the hip roof and dormer will bring your carpentry skills up a notch.

Craftsman storage shed

With 100 sq. ft. of floor space, a 17 x 4-ft. attic storage area and an open-air porch, this may well be the ultimate shed. Double doors and gable-end attic door provide great access, while the covered porch provides space for working or relaxing. It's all topped off with a zero-maintenance metal roof.

Gallery of ideas

> **Stone-and-timber yard shed**

Stone knee walls, solid 6x6 posts and cedar shingles define this garden cottage, storage shed. Not for the faint of heart, building this shed will muster all of your do-it-yourself talents (and consume most of your summer as well).

∧ **Outdoor living room**

This attached open-air pavilion uses a unique "sandwich-style" system for creating the posts, beams and rafters. Post bases sided with cedar shingles help ground this light, airy summer hangout.

Ultimate garden shed

This 8 ft. x 9-1/2 ft. storage area has loads of room for your lawn and garden equipment, while the smaller front room makes the ideal potting shed. The floor is built using heavy timbers and large cement pavers. The structure also uses cost-effective barn sash windows, board-and-batten siding and metal roofing.

6

CHAPTER

Dream furniture & planters

3-hour cedar bench

Build it in one afternoon!

—Travis Larson

The beauty of this cedar bench isn't just that it's easy to assemble and inexpensive—it's that it's so doggone comfortable. You can comfortably sit on your custom-fit bench for hours, even without cushions. In this story, we'll show you how to build the bench and how to adjust it for maximum comfort.

Sloping the back and the seat is the secret to pain-free perching on unpadded flat boards. But not all bodies are the same, and it's a rare piece of furniture that everyone agrees is seatworthy. This bench has a bolted pivot point where the back and seat meet that lets you alter the backrest and seat slopes to fit your build during one of the final assembly steps (Photo 10). The materials will cost about $85, and cutting and assembly will only take about

Project at a glance

Skill level
Beginner

Special tools
Circular saw
Screw gun
Drill

Approximate cost
$85

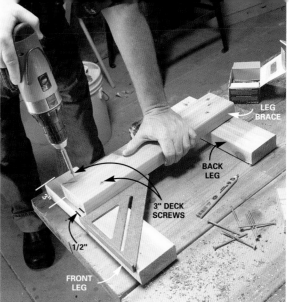

LEG BRACE

BACK LEG

3" DECK SCREWS

GUIDE SQUARE

1/2"

FRONT LEG

1 Cut out the bench parts following the measurements in Figure A. Use a square to guide the circular saw for accurate, square cuts. Cut 45-degree angles on the ends of the seat and back supports 1 in. down from the ends as shown (also see Photos 4 and 5).

2 Fasten the leg brace to the legs 3 in. above the bottom ends. Angle the 3-in. screws slightly to prevent the screw tips from protruding through the other side. Hold the brace 1/2 in. back from the front edge of the front leg. Use a square to make sure the brace and legs are at exact right angles.

SHOPPING LIST

ITEM	QTY.	ITEM	QTY.
1x3 x 8' cedar	2	3" deck screws	1 lb.
2x10 x 8' cedar	1	6d galv. casing nails	1/4 lb.
2x4 x 8' cedar	5	3/8" x 5" bolts with nuts and washers	2

FIGURE A
Bench parts

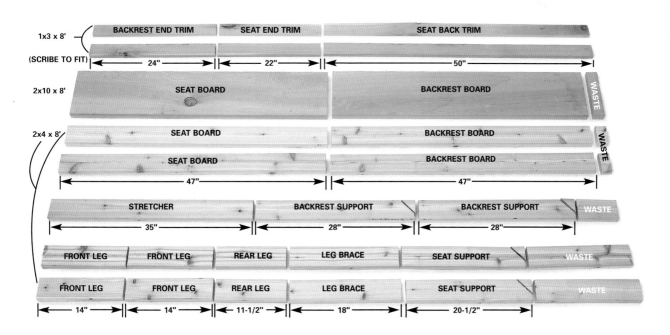

1x3 x 8'
BACKREST END TRIM | SEAT END TRIM | SEAT BACK TRIM

(SCRIBE TO FIT) ← 24" → ← 22" → ← 50" →

2x10 x 8'
SEAT BOARD | BACKREST BOARD | WASTE

2x4 x 8'
SEAT BOARD | BACKREST BOARD | WASTE
SEAT BOARD | BACKREST BOARD | WASTE
← 47" → ← 47" →

STRETCHER | BACKREST SUPPORT | BACKREST SUPPORT | WASTE
← 35" → ← 28" → ← 28" →

FRONT LEG | FRONT LEG | REAR LEG | LEG BRACE | SEAT SUPPORT | WASTE
FRONT LEG | FRONT LEG | REAR LEG | LEG BRACE | SEAT SUPPORT | WASTE
← 14" → ← 14" → ← 11-1/2" → ← 18" → ← 20-1/2" →

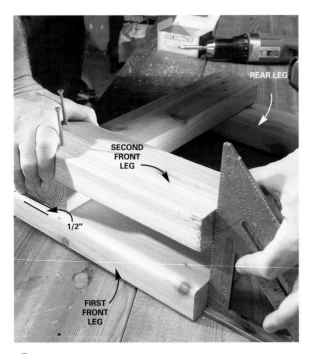

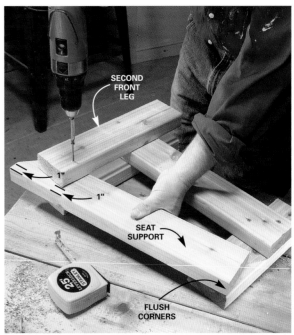

3 Align the second part of the front leg with the first one using a square and screw it to the leg brace as shown.

4 Slip the seat support between the two front legs, positioning it as shown. Drive a single 3-in. screw through the front leg into the seat support.

three hours. Follow the step-by-step photo series for details on the simple construction.

Build it from eight 8-ft. long boards

A circular saw and a screw gun are the only power tools you really need for construction, although a power miter saw will speed things up and give you cleaner cuts. Begin by cutting the boards to length. Figure A shows you how to cut up the eight boards efficiently, leaving little waste.

After cutting the pieces to length, screw together the leg assemblies (Photos 2 – 6). Be sure to use a square to keep the leg braces square to the legs (Photo 2).

Buy Smart

When you're picking out the wood at the lumberyard, choose boards that above all are flat, not twisted. That's especially important for the seat and back parts. Don't worry so much about the leg assembly 2x4s, because you cut them into such short pieces that warps and twists aren't much of a concern.

That way both leg assemblies will be identical and the bench won't wobble if it's put on a hard, flat surface. We spaced the leg brace 1/2 in. back from the front of the legs to create a more attractive shadow line. Then it's just a matter of connecting the leg assemblies with the stretcher (Photo 7), screwing down the seat and backrest boards and adjusting the slopes to fit your body.

The easiest way to adjust the slope is to hold the four locking points in place with clamps and then back out the temporary screws (Photo 10). To customize the slopes, you just loosen the clamps, make the adjustments, retighten and test the fit. When you're satisfied, run a couple of permanent screws into each joint. If you don't have clamps, don't worry—you'll just have to back out the screws, adjust the slopes, reset the screws and test the bench. Clamps just speed up the process.

Round over the edges

We show an option of rounding over the sharp edge of the 1x3 trim, which is best done with a router and a 1/2-in. round-over bit (Photo 12). Rounding over the

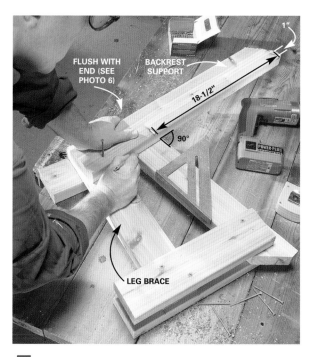

5 Position the backrest support on the leg assembly as shown, making sure it's at a right angle with the seat support, and mark the position on the seat support. Then drive a 3-in. screw through the middle of the backrest support into the leg brace.

6 Clamp the backrest support, seat support and rear leg as shown using the line as a guide. Drill a 3/8-in. hole through the center of the assembly. Drive a 3/8-in. x 5-in. bolt fitted with a washer through the hole and slightly tighten the nut against a washer on the other side.

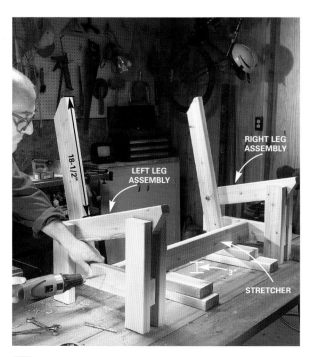

7 Assemble the other leg assembly to mirror the first as shown. (The back support and rear leg switch sides.) Prop the stretcher 3 in. above the workbench, center it between the front and rear bench legs and screw the leg braces into the ends with two 3-in. deck screws.

8 Center the first 2x4 seat board over the leg assemblies and flush with the front ends of the seat supports. Screw it to the seat supports with two 3-in. deck screws spaced about 1 in. away from the edges. Line up the 2x10 with the first 2x4, space it about 5/16 in. away (the thickness of a carpenter's pencil) and screw it to the seat supports with two 3-in. deck screws. Repeat with the rear 2x4.

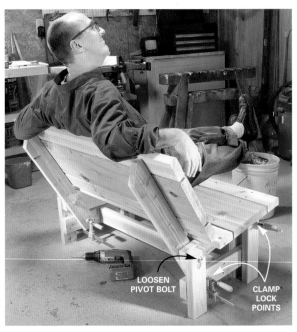

9 Rest the bottom backrest 2x4 on carpenter's pencils, holding the end flush with the seat boards and screw it to the seat back braces. Then space and screw on the center 2x10 and the top 2x4 backrest boards.

10 Sit on the bench and decide if you'd like to tilt the seat or the backrest or both to make the bench more comfortable. To make seat or back adjustments, loosen the bolts and clamp the bottoms of the seat back supports and the fronts of the seat supports. Then back out the four screws at those points. Loosen the clamps, make adjustments, then retighten and retest for comfort. When you're satisfied with the fit, drive in the four original screws plus another at each point. Retighten the pivot bolts.

edges can protect shins and the backs of thighs and leave teetering toddlers with goose eggs on their melons instead of gashes. So the step is highly recommended. If you don't have a router, round over the edge either by hand-sanding or with an orbital or belt sander. In any event, keep the casing nails 1 in. away from the edge to prevent hitting the nailheads with the router bit or sandpaper (Photo 12).

Building a longer bench

We demonstrate how to build a 4-ft. long bench, plenty of space for two. But you can use the same design and techniques for building 6- or 8-ft. long benches too. You'll just have to buy longer boards for the seat, back, stretcher and the trim boards. While you're at it, you can use the same design for matching end or coffee tables. Just match the double front leg design for the rear legs, and build flat-topped leg assemblies with an overall depth of 16-3/4 in.

Seal the legs to make it last

If you want to stain your bench, use a latex exterior stain on the parts after cutting them to length. After assembly, you won't be able to get good penetration at the cracks and crevices. Avoid clear exterior sealers, which will irritate bare skin. But the bench will last outside for more than 20 years without any stain or special care even if you decide to let it weather to a natural gray. However, the legs won't last that long, because the end grain at the bottom will wick up moisture from the ground, making the legs rot long before the bench does. To make sure the legs last as long as the bench, seal the ends with epoxy, urethane or exterior woodworker's glue when you're through with the assembly.

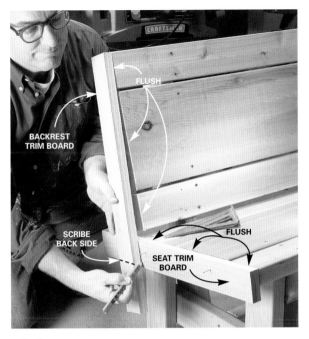

11 Tack the seat trim boards to the seat with the ends flush with the front and top. Scribe and cut the trim boards to fit. Nail the boards to the seat and backrest boards with 6d galvanized casing nails, keeping the nails 1 in. back from the seat edges.

12 Ease the edges of the trim boards with a router and a 1/2-in. round-over bit. Hold the router sideways to get at the seat/back corner.

A bench with a past

About 15 years ago, I decided to throw together some simple outdoor benches so my growing family could relax outside and enjoy the yard. But they had to be better looking and more comfortable than the flat benches they were replacing. I wanted them to feel more like a chair, be light enough to move around easily and stand up to the elements. After much experimentation, I came up with a version of this design and used it to make three benches. At times they'll be arranged around the fire ring, or for larger social gatherings, placed on the patio or deck. Most often, however, all three encircle the herb garden, our favorite outdoor hangout.

After all those years without any shelter or finish, the benches are showing their age. The crisp, new look has long passed, now replaced with puppy teeth marks, a few cracks, a deep gray hue and even some rot at the bottom of the feet. But they're still as sturdy and comfortable as the day they were made. This new version has a few improved features. I wanted to make it easier to build (no fancy angles and fewer parts), even more comfortable (adjustable to fit), and even more durable (the feet bottoms are sealed).   — Travis

Yard & garden trio

A chair, love seat and table for your outdoor living room.

—Bruce Kieffer and David Radtke

At first glance, this trio of handcrafted outdoor furniture looks as if it's been part of the family for generations. The structure is solid and traditional, and the wood is stained a rich, weathered gray.

The carefully fitted joints give this chair, love seat and table the true look of furniture and not a stapled-together crate. Despite the refined look, they're not difficult to build. The construction-grade cedar parts are joined with dowels, glue, and screws hidden by wood plugs.

The knots and imperfections characteristic of lower grade cedar add to the furniture's charm. When you select your wood, however, be sure the knots are tight, the boards are straight, and there are no cracks to weaken the furniture.

To achieve the aged appearance, we brushed on a liberal coat of thinned-down gray deck stain (one part stain to two parts mineral spirits). We continued brush-

Project at a glance

Skill level
Intermediate

Special tools
Dowel hole drilling jig
Router
Flush-trimming saw

Approximate cost
$250 for all three

BACK-LEG TEMPLATE

1" x 1" GRID

1 Make full-size templates for the shaped pieces. Transfer the intersecting points from our grid drawings to your full-size grids, then connect the points.

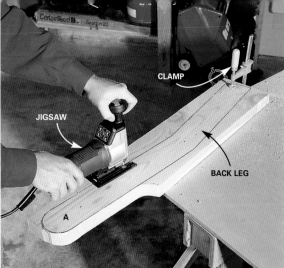

CLAMP

JIGSAW

BACK LEG

A

2 Cut out the shaped pieces using a jigsaw. Use a fine-tooth blade and carefully follow the drawn lines to reduce the amount of sanding needed to smooth the sawn edges.

ing with the grain until the stain saturated the wood. To simulate wear, we brushed some areas even more to lighten the stain.

The three pieces should take you about two weekends to build. To simplify and speed up the cutting, we've provided templates for the shaped pieces that you can transfer to thin plywood.

Project background

The construction of all three pieces is very similar. We'll show you step-by-step how to build the chair; then you'll be able to build the love seat, which is essentially a longer version of the chair. One difference is the layout of the love seat's back top; see (B) in Figure A. Also, the love seat has an added center seat support (K) that's cut to fit between the back bottom and front seat supports (D). Glue and screw this extra piece in place just before attaching the seat slats (G). After making the chair and love seats, you'll find the table a snap (Figure B).

Make the chair templates

Gather all the tools plus your standard layout and carpentry tools. Using scrap 1/4-in. thick plywood, make full-size templates of the shapes for the back legs (A), chair back top (B), arms (E), and side seat supports (F). Start by cutting your template stock to the rectangular

sizes shown in the grid drawings in Figure A. Draw a 1 x 1-in. grid on your template pieces, then transfer and enlarge the shapes from our drawings to your templates (Photo 1). Mark the screw locations too. Cut out the template shapes and sand the sawn edges smooth.

Cutting the parts

Cut all the pieces A through J to the dimensions given in the Cutting List. Trace the shapes from your completed templates onto the back legs, chair back top, and side seat supports (A, B and F). Cut out the shapes using a jigsaw or band saw, then sand the sawn edges smooth (Photo 2). You'll shape the arms after you assemble the chair by cutting and fitting the notches at the rear of the arms around the back legs.

Drilling screw and dowel holes

Lay out and drill the screw plug holes and screw clearance holes in the legs (A and C). Lay out and drill the dowel holes on the edges of the back top and back bottom (B and D), and in the ends of the side seat supports, side stretchers and back slats (F, H and J); see Photo 3.

Laying out the back slat dowel holes in the back top (B) and back bottom (D) can be a little tricky, so be careful. Don't measure from one mark to the next. Instead, add the dowel hole spread distances together, and measure and mark from one end with your tape measure. When you're done marking, double-check everything. Remember, you'll be using 5/16-in. dia. dowels for these holes. To correctly mark these back-slat dowel hole locations, assume a spread of 3/4 in. between the dowel hole centers. The first hole center for the first slat is 1-1/4 in. from the end of B and D. The next hole center is another 3/4 in. from the first. The first hole center for the second slat is an additional 1-5/8 in. plus 3/4 in. for the next hole. For the first hole center for the third slat, measure an additional 1-5/8 in., then another 3/4 in. Continue this method until the last slat.

Routing and sanding

Now's the time to round some sharp edges and do some sanding before assembly. Mount a 3/8-in. radius round-over bit in a router to rout the edges on the pieces (Photo 4). See Figure A for which edges to round. Leave the router set up this way to do the edges of the arms after the shapes are cut.

Using a belt sander first, then an orbital sander, finish-sand all the pieces. You'll still have a bit more to do later after the chair's assembled.

Assemble the sides and back

Glue, dowel and clamp the side assemblies (A, C, F and H) together (Photo 5). Use a thin dowel or stick to spread the glue in the dowel holes. We found it was better to gently

SHOPPING LIST

ITEM	QTY.
Chair	
2x8 x 8' cedar	1 pc.
2x4 x 8' cedar	2 pcs.
1x4 x 8' cedar	4 pcs.
3/8" dia. x 2" dowel pins	16
5/16" dia. x 1-1/2" dowel pins	36
3" galvanized deck screws	12
1-5/8" galvanized deck screws	21
Love Seat	
2x8 x 8' cedar	1 pc.
2x6 x 8' cedar	1 pc.
2x4 x 8' cedar	2 pcs.
1x4 x 8' cedar	6 pcs.
3/8" dia. x 2" dowel pins	16
5/16" dia. x 1-1/2" dowel pins	72
3" galvanized deck screws	15
1-5/8" galvanized deck screws	28
Table	
2x4 x 8' cedar	1 pc.
1x6 x 8' cedar	1 pc.
1x4 x 8' cedar	2 pcs.
3/8" dia. x 2" dowel pins	16
3" galvanized deck screws	8
1-5/8" galvanized deck screws	12
Glue and Finish for all Three	
Weatherproof or waterproof glue	16 ozs.
Exterior deck stain	1 qt.
Mineral spirits to thin stain	2 qts.

CUTTING LIST

KEY	QTY.	SIZE & DESCRIPTION
Chair		
A	2	1-1/2" x 7-1/4" x 35" cedar (back legs)
B	1	1-1/2" x 5-1/2" x 22-1/4" cedar (back top)
C	2	1-1/2" x 3-1/2" x 25-1/4" cedar (front legs)
D	2	1-1/2" x 3-1/2" x 22-1/4" cedar (back bottom and front seat support)
E	2	3/4" x 3-1/2" x 23-1/2" cedar (arms)
F	2	3/4" x 3-1/2" x 14" cedar (side seat supports)
G	6	3/4" x 2-3/4" x 25-1/4" cedar (seat slats)
H	2	3/4" x 2" x 14" cedar (side stretchers)
J	9	3/4" x 1-1/2" x 13-1/2" cedar (back slats)
Love Seat		
A	2	1-1/2" x 7-1/4" x 34" cedar (back legs)
B	1	1-1/2" x 5-1/2" x 43-5/8" cedar (back top)
C	2	1-1/2" x 3-1/2" x 25-1/4" cedar (front legs)
D	2	1-1/2" x 3-1/2" x 43-5/8" cedar (back bottom and front seat support)
E	2	3/4" x 3-1/2" x 23-1/2" cedar (arms)
F	2	3/4" x 3-1/2" x 14" cedar (side seat supports)
G	6	3/4" x 2-3/4" x 46-5/8" cedar (seat slats)
H	2	3/4" x 2" x 14" cedar (side stretchers)
J	18	3/4" x 1-1/2" x 13-1/2" cedar (back slats)
K	1	1-1/2" x 3-1/2" x 16-1/4" cedar (center seat support)
Table		
A	4	1-1/2" x 2-1/2" x 19-1/4" cedar (legs)
B	4	3/4" x 4-1/2" x 13" cedar (aprons)
C	6	3/4" x 2-7/8" x 16-3/4" cedar (top slats)
D	2	3/4" x 2" x 13" cedar (side stretchers)

FIGURE A
Chair and love seat

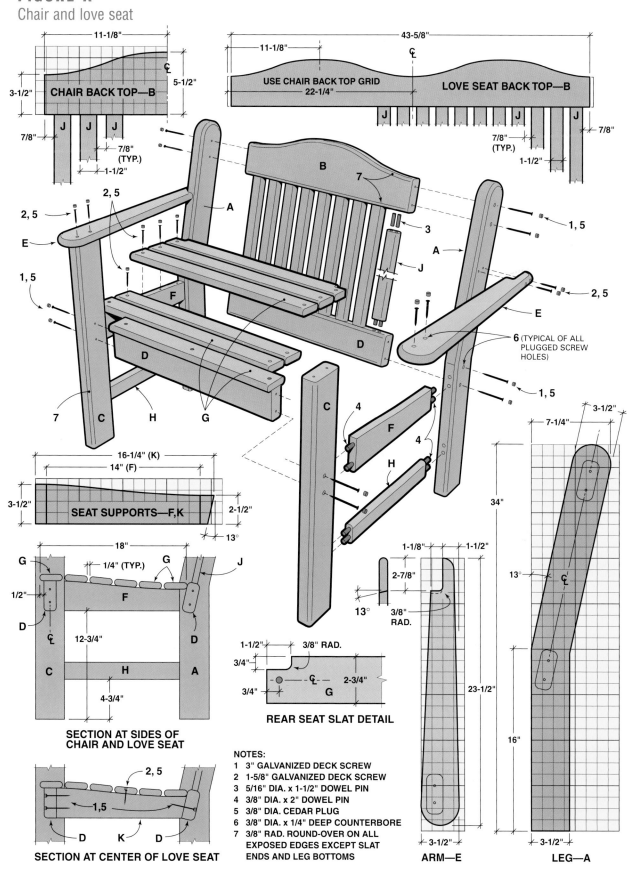

CHAIR BACK TOP—B — 11-1/8", 5-1/2", 3-1/2", J, J, J, 7/8", 7/8" (TYP.), 1-1/2"

43-5/8", 11-1/8", USE CHAIR BACK TOP GRID, 22-1/4", LOVE SEAT BACK TOP—B, J, J, J, J, 7/8" (TYP.), 7/8", 1-1/2"

2, 5, E, 1, 5, B, 7, 3, J, A, 1, 5, 2, 5, E, 6 (TYPICAL OF ALL PLUGGED SCREW HOLES), 1, 5

7, C, H, G, D, A, F, D, C, 4, F, 4, H

SEAT SUPPORTS—F,K — 16-1/4" (K), 14" (F), 3-1/2", 2-1/2", 13°

18", G, 1/4" (TYP.), G, J, 1/2", F, D, D, C, H, A, 12-3/4", 4-3/4"

SECTION AT SIDES OF CHAIR AND LOVE SEAT

2, 5, 1,5, D, K, D

SECTION AT CENTER OF LOVE SEAT

REAR SEAT SLAT DETAIL — 1-1/2", 3/8" RAD., 3/4", 3/4", 3/4", 2-3/4", G

1-1/8", 1-1/2", 2-7/8", 13°, 3/8" RAD., 34", 23-1/2", 16", 3-1/2"

ARM—E

3-1/2", 7-1/4", 13°, 13°, 16"

LEG—A

NOTES:
1. 3" GALVANIZED DECK SCREW
2. 1-5/8" GALVANIZED DECK SCREW
3. 5/16" DIA. x 1-1/2" DOWEL PIN
4. 3/8" DIA. x 2" DOWEL PIN
5. 3/8" DIA. CEDAR PLUG
6. 3/8" DIA. x 1/4" DEEP COUNTERBORE
7. 3/8" RAD. ROUND-OVER ON ALL EXPOSED EDGES EXCEPT SLAT ENDS AND LEG BOTTOMS

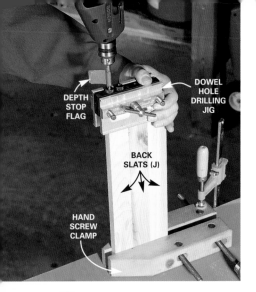

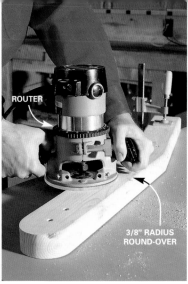

3 Drill the dowel holes in the ends of the back slats. Clamping the slats side by side like this gives the dowel-drilling jig more surface area to clamp onto.

4 Rout the edges of all the pieces (except the end cuts). Clamp the pieces to your work table, or use a router pad to hold the pieces as you rout them.

5 Glue, dowel and clamp the side pieces together. Be careful not to apply too much glue and create a mess.

hammer the dowels in the ends of pieces F and H first. Putting dowels in the legs first may cause some of the ends of these pieces to split when all the pieces are assembled.

Glue, dowel and clamp the back pieces together (B, D and J). Start by inserting two dowels in one end of every back slat (J). Glue and clamp the back slats to the back top (B), one at a time. Insert the dowels in the other ends of the back slats. Then, with the help of a friend, align and attach the back bottom (D). Start at one end and work to the other end.

Align, glue and screw the sides to the assembled back and the front seat support (D). Once again, an extra set of hands is helpful here.

Attach the seat slats

Trim the length of the front seat slat (G) so it fits between the front legs. Cut the notched ends of the back seat slat as shown in Figure A and see that it fits between the back legs. Lay out and drill the screw plug and clearance holes (for the wood plugs) in the seat slats, then glue and screw the front and back seat slats in place. Attach the rest of the seat slats so the gaps between them are equal.

To make wood plugs to cover the recessed screws, use a 3/8-in. dia. plug cutter. Glue and insert the plugs in the

holes to cover the screws. Drill a shallow 3/4-in. dia. hole in a piece of scrap wood. Fill the hole with glue and use it as a reservoir to dip the plugs in and apply the glue. When the glue is dry, trim off the tops of the plugs (Photo 6).

Attaching the arms

Trace the back leg notches from your arm template to the arm pieces (E). Then cut out the notches using a jigsaw or band saw (see Figure A for the dimension and angle details). Make the final fit of the angled inside radiused corners using a round file (Photo 7). When that's done, trace and cut out the shapes of the arms and rout the rounded-over edges. Predrill the plug and screw holes, then finish-sand and attach the arms (Photo 8) with galvanized deck screws.

Apply the finish

You can protect your furniture with the finish we described on pp. 190 and 191. (Also see the end of the Shopping List for the stain we used.) A clear exterior finish is another option, but it will slow down the aging process. It depends on the look you want. However, be sure you choose some type of waterproof finish to keep the pieces from drying out and splitting.

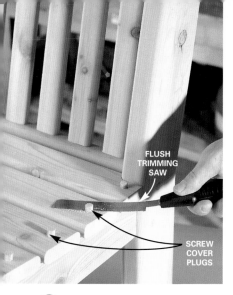

ROUND FILE

ARM PRIOR
TO SHAPING

E

ARM
OVERHANGS
FRONT LEG
3/8" ON
INSIDE

FLUSH
TRIMMING
SAW

SCREW
COVER
PLUGS

6 Use a flush-trimming saw or sharp chisel to trim off the heads of the screw cover plugs. Finish-sand them with a sanding block, then an orbital sander.

7 Using the partially finished chair as a convenient support, file the angled radiused corner of the arm notch so it fits around the back leg.

8 Align and clamp the arms to the front legs. Insert the screws that go into the back legs, remove the clamps and then screw the arms to the front legs.

FIGURE B
Table

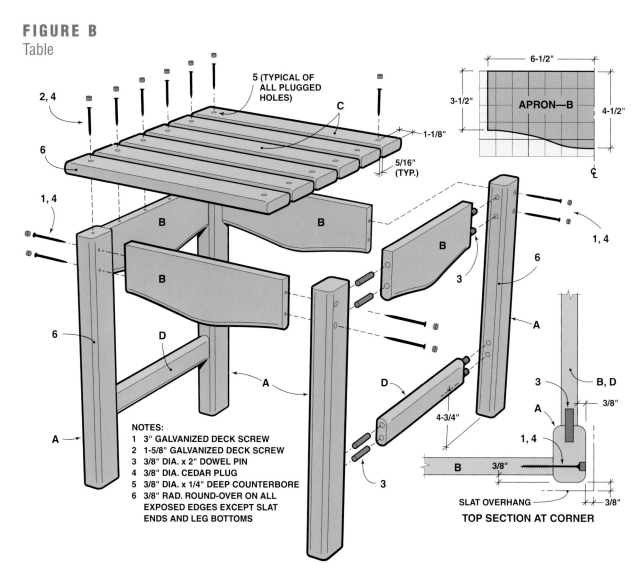

2, 4

6

1, 4

6

6

A

5 (TYPICAL OF
ALL PLUGGED
HOLES)

C

1-1/8"

5/16"
(TYP.)

B

B

B

B

D

1, 4

3

6

A

D

3

3

6-1/2"

3-1/2"

APRON—B

4-1/2"

1, 4

4-3/4"

B, D

3/8"

3

A

1, 4

B

3/8"

SLAT OVERHANG

3/8"

TOP SECTION AT CORNER

NOTES:
1 3" GALVANIZED DECK SCREW
2 1-5/8" GALVANIZED DECK SCREW
3 3/8" DIA. x 2" DOWEL PIN
4 3/8" DIA. CEDAR PLUG
5 3/8" DIA. x 1/4" DEEP COUNTERBORE
6 3/8" RAD. ROUND-OVER ON ALL
   EXPOSED EDGES EXCEPT SLAT
   ENDS AND LEG BOTTOMS

Folding grill table

A fold-up companion for your barbecue.

—Bruce Wiebe

After this collapsible cedar table was built, our family wondered how we ever grilled without it. The legs nest under the top for quick storage or easy carrying. All you need to build it is a drill, a saw, basic hand tools, a short stack of cedar boards and half an afternoon.

The table is made entirely from 1x4 cedar boards. You can make the table from eight 6-foot boards, but buy 10 to allow for possible miscuts and to give you more choice for the top slats.

Cut the parts

You can use a handsaw to cut the parts, but an electric jigsaw speeds up the job significantly. Use a square to help make straight cuts (Photo 1). To ensure matching legs and frame parts, clamp two boards together and mark and cut them at the same time (Photo 2). Cut slats one or two at a time. You'll cut the stretchers after bolting on the legs.

Project at a glance

Skill level
Beginner

Special tools
Jigsaw
Speed square
Drill

Approximate cost
$35

EASY FOR EVERYONE

1 Cut the boards for the top and the frame that supports it using a jigsaw or handsaw and a square. (See the exploded view diagram below.)

2 Clamp the leg boards together (rough side in) and cut both of them at once to create identical leg pairs. Drill the 3/8-in. bolt hole in the upper end before unclamping.

SHOPPING LIST

QTY.	DESCRIPTION
2	2-1/2" x 3/8" carriage bolts
2	3-1/2" x 3/8" carriage bolts
4	3/8" wing nuts and flat washers
1	Box 1-5/8" deck screws
10	1x4 x 6' cedar boards
1	Pint Penofin wood finish
1	Drill with countersink

CUTTING LIST

KEY	NAME	QTY.	DIMENSIONS IN INCHES
A	Top slat	12	1x4 x 19
B	Long side piece	2	1x4 x 41-1/2
C	Short side piece	2	1x4 x 15-3/4
D	Leg	4	1x4 x 28-3/4 (15° angled end cut)
E	Leg stretchers	2	1x4 x 15-3/4 (Cut to fit)
F	Leg spacers	2	1x4 x 6-3/4
G	Leg stop blocks	4	1x4 x 4-3/8 (15° angled end cut)

(Note: All parts cut from "1x4 S3S" cedar, so each board is a "fat" 3/4 thick and 3-1/2 wide, with two smooth edges, one smooth side and one rough side.)

FIGURE A
Grill table

APPROX. 42-3/4"

19"

Ⓐ

41-1/2"

Ⓑ

Ⓖ

Ⓒ

1-5/8" DECK SCREWS

1-3/4" RADIUS

3/8" DIAMETER

Ⓕ

Ⓒ

Ⓑ

Ⓓ

3-1/2" x 3/8" CARRIAGE BOLT

CUT TO FIT

2-1/2" x 3/8" CARRIAGE BOLT

28-3/4"

Ⓔ

15-3/4"

3 Lay the frame on the top boards and lightly trace the frame shape so it's easy to see where to drill holes. Space the top boards with about 1/16-in. gaps between them.

8d NAIL

DRILL BIT WITH COUNTERSINK

4 Drill two holes on each top board end with a countersink bit and screw them to the frame. A nail is handy for creating even spacing.

To assemble the frame, drill two holes in the ends of the longer frame boards and add a countersink hole for the screwheads to nestle into. Cut the slats and place them top-side up on a flat surface (Photo 3). Center the frame on the slats to create a 3/4-in. overhang on all four sides. Then lightly trace the frame shape on the slats with a pencil.

Lift off the frame, and drill and countersink screw holes in the slats using the traced lines as a guide. Then screw the slats to the frame (Photo 4). Lightly tap a couple nails between the slats while screwing them to the frame to create the approximate 1/16-in. spacing between the slats. The end slats will overhang the frame approximately 3/4 in. to match the slat overhang along the frame sides.

Attach the legs

Flip the tabletop upside down and screw the pair of angled blocks to the corners of one end (Photo 5). Butt the rounded leg ends against the spacer blocks, then drill and bolt on the outer leg pair with the shorter 2-1/2-in. carriage bolts, washers and wing nuts. Now attach the inner leg pair to the other frame, first screwing in the spacer blocks to allow the legs to nest inside the other pair (Photo 6).

Add the angled blocks, then drill and bolt on the second leg pair with the longer 3-1/2-in. carriage bolts.

With the legs flat on the underside of the table, measure for the stretchers, cut, drill and fasten them to the legs (Photo 7). To pull out the legs, lift the more widely spaced pair first so the second pair can be raised without catching on the first pair's stretcher (Photo 8).

Sand, finish, then grill

Sand the table with 100-grit paper and, with a sanding block or rasp, slightly round the top edges of the slats. Put on your favorite finish; we used two coats of Penofin penetrating oil finish (cedar color). Pull out the legs, tighten the wing nuts and grill away.

Buy Smart

Wood quality varies, so pick over the lumber for flat, straight boards that are free of large or loose knots.

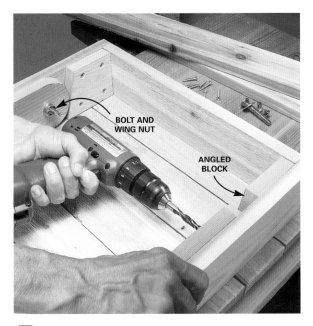

5 Screw a pair of angled blocks in one end of the frame, then butt the rounded ends of the legs against the blocks. Drill through the frame and bolt on the legs.

BOLT AND WING NUT

ANGLED BLOCK

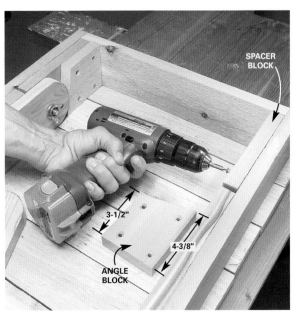

6 Screw the spacer blocks in the other frame end. These allow the other pair of legs to nest inside the first pair. Then drill and bolt on the second pair of legs.

SPACER BLOCK

3-1/2"

4-3/8"

ANGLE BLOCK

7 Screw stretchers across each pair of legs. For best fit and overall results, mark and cut the stretchers based on the actual spacing between the legs.

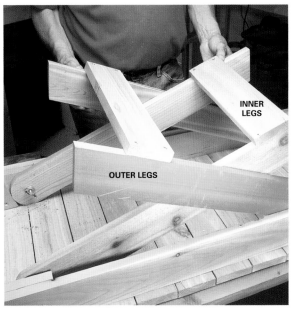

8 Test the fit of the legs in the frame by pulling the legs up from the frame. If they bind and scrape, sand the sides for a smoother fit.

INNER LEGS

OUTER LEGS

Patio planters

Give your potted plants a simple, stylish home—outdoors or in.

—David Radtke

This planter is designed to make your patio or deck gardening much easier. Instead of filling it with dirt and planting each flower or plant individually, you simply set prepotted plants right into the planter. You can conveniently switch plants as the season changes or unload the planter and move it to a new location.

We designed this project to fit any pot with an 11-in. diameter or less and a maximum height of 10-1/2 in. To create the illusion of a fully planted box, you just fill in around the pots with wood chips, bark or other mulch covering. The base or bottom of the planter has 7/8-in. holes drilled every 6 in. to drain away any excess water. The side boards have a 1/4-in. space between them to ventilate the mulch and keep it from getting soggy.

Buying the right lumber

You'll notice the legs are treated pine and not cedar like the sides and top apron. Treated pine is less likely to split along the grain (a nasty problem with cedar). Pick treated 2x12 material for the legs with as few large knots as possible. You'll be able to cut around knots on a single board, so bring a tape measure when you select the lumber. Choose straight cedar for the sides and

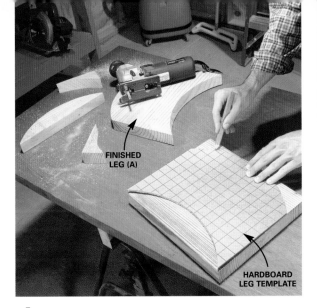

1 Using a full-size template made from Figure A, trace the outline of the planter legs onto pressure-treated 2x12 pine boards. Sand the edges with a finish or belt sander followed by 100-grit hand-sanding to gently ease the edges.

2 Make straight cuts using a 12-in. Speed square held firmly against the back of the 2x6.

FIGURE A
Leg template (enlarge 400% or until overall leg height equals 13 in.)

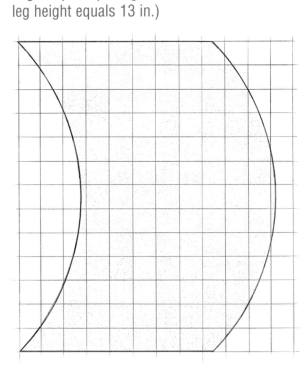

CUTTING LIST

KEY	QTY.	SIZE & DESCRIPTION
Large planter		
A	4	1-1/2" x 11-1/4" x 13" treated pine legs
B	1	1-1/2" x 11-1/4" x 48" treated pine base
C	4	1-1/2" x 5-1/2" x 48" cedar side panels
D	4	1-1/2" x 5-1/2" x 14-1/4" cedar end panels*
E	2	1-1/16" x 4-1/2" x 57" cedar side aprons
F	2	1-1/16" x 4-1/2" x 20-1/4" cedar side aprons*
Small planter		
A	4	1-1/2" x 11-1/4" x 13" treated pine legs
B	1	1-1/2" x 11-1/4" x 36" treated pine base
C	4	1-1/2" x 5-1/2" x 36" cedar side panels
D	4	1-1/2" x 5-1/2" x 14-1/4" cedar end panels*
E	2	1-1/16" x 4-1/2" x 45" cedar side aprons
F	2	1-1/16" x 4-1/2" x 20-1/4" cedar side aprons*

*Cut to fit

3 Plane only the edges where the side boards C and D meet. This chamfered edge should be about 3/8 in. wide when completed. Clamp a board to the edge of your workbench to stop the workpiece from drifting while you stroke the edge of the board with the plane.

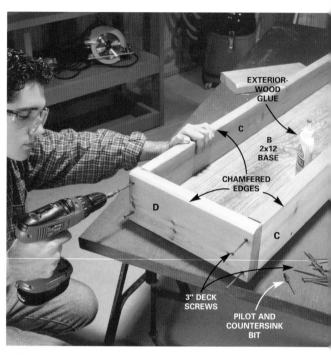

4 Cut your 2x12 base to length, then screw the lower sides (C) to the base. Align the base and sides so they're flush on the bottom sides. Predrill for each screw using a pilot/countersink combination bit. Then screw the ends to the sides.

Plan Smart

We've shown you two planters of different lengths, but you can adapt them to fit your unique space. You can even change the width by nailing a treated 2x2 to the side of the 2x12 base piece and lengthening other parts accordingly to accommodate a slightly wider pot. To build either the small or large planter shown, follow our clear step-by-step photos and refer to the Cutting List for lumber lengths.

remember that some knots here can add to the overall beauty.

Feel free to use other species of wood such as redwood, cypress or even a plantation-grown tropical wood like ipe (available at some lumberyards).

Use paint, stain or a combination of both

We chose an exterior enamel paint for the legs and apron pieces to accent the deck oil stain/sealer on the base and sides. Stain is a better choice than paint for the base and sides because they'll be exposed to more moisture than the legs and top. The photo shows the excellent results you can get by staining the entire project with an exterior oil deck stain.

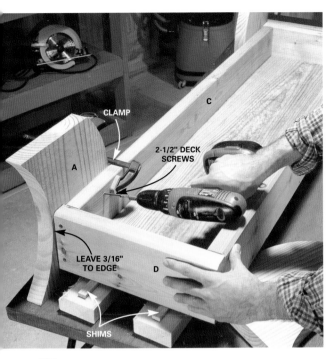

5 Shim the base up 1-3/4 in. on each side using scrap pieces of wood, then clamp the legs one at a time to the sides (C). Screw the sides to the legs with 2-1/2 in. deck screws. Use three screws per leg.

6 Clamp the upper sides flush to the tops of the legs. Be sure to align the upper and lower side ends before drilling and screwing this piece in place. Again, use three 2-1/2 in. deck screws per leg. Next, screw the upper end panels (D) to the upper sides. Make sure the chamfers face each other on each side.

7 Rip the 5/4 x 6 in. deck boards to 4-1/2 in. to make the top apron frame. Use a rip guide on your circular saw or a table saw if you have one. Plane and sand the cut edge to match the factory-machined edge of the deck board.

8 Glue and nail the side apron pieces (E) flush with parts C below. Next, nail the apron end pieces to the end panels (D). You'll notice the inside edge of F will be about 1/4 in. out from the inside of the planter to adequately cover the tops of the legs.

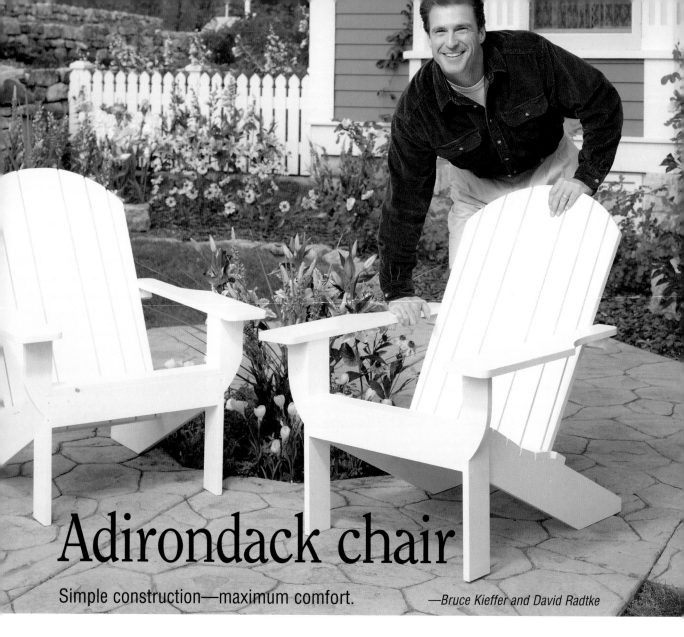

Adirondack chair

Simple construction—maximum comfort. —*Bruce Kieffer and David Radtke*

P lop down in one of these solid wood chairs and you'll appreciate the comfort of this traditional design. You don't have to be an expert to build it either. All the parts can be cut with a circular saw and jigsaw, then assembled with a drill with a Phillips-tip bit, a few clamps and glue. Even if you're a novice, you'll be able to follow our plan drawing and clear step-by-step photos. And the Shopping List and Cutting List will help you spend less time head-scratching and more time building.

We made our chair from yellow poplar. Poplar is lightweight, strong, inexpensive and easy to work with, plus it takes paint beautifully. If you have trouble finding it, almost any other wood will do: Alder, aspen, maple and white oak are excellent hardwood choices, and cedar, cypress, fir and pine are good softwood choices. Keep in mind that hardwood will be more durable, but softwood is certainly strong enough for this project.

Traditional Adirondack chairs are painted, but you can choose a clear outdoor deck finish if you prefer. If you do opt for paint, check out the painting tips on p. 208 to help achieve a tough, long-lasting and good-looking painted finish.

Project at a glance

Skill level
Beginner

Special tools
Jigsaw
Drill
Bar clamps

Approximate cost
$80 per chair

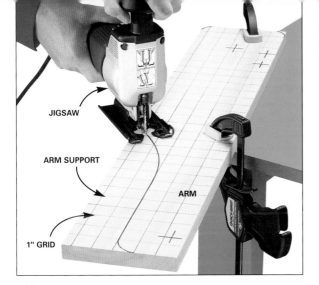

JIGSAW

ARM SUPPORT

ARM

1" GRID

1 Draw full-size grids onto the arm and back leg pieces and follow the curves with a jigsaw.

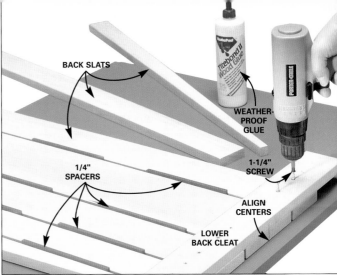

BACK SLATS

WEATHER-PROOF GLUE

1/4" SPACERS

1-1/4" SCREW

ALIGN CENTERS

LOWER BACK CLEAT

2 Slip 1/4-in. spacers between the back slats as you screw the horizontal back supports (G, L and N) to the slats. Predrill and countersink each hole and apply weatherproof glue to each joint.

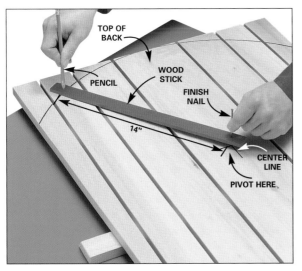

TOP OF BACK

WOOD STICK

PENCIL

FINISH NAIL

14"

CENTER LINE

PIVOT HERE

3 Make a compass from a scrap of wood by drilling a hole near each end. Put a nail in one end and use a pencil in the other hole to draw the 14-in. radius to form the curved top.

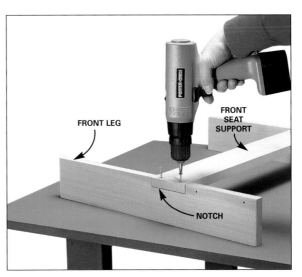

FRONT LEG

FRONT SEAT SUPPORT

NOTCH

4 Cut and notch the front legs (E) with a jigsaw. Then glue and screw the front seat support into the notches.

Transfer the grid patterns

Enlarge the grids directly onto the board, or make a full-size pattern and transfer the shape to the board.

Once the shape is drawn, follow the lines with a jigsaw (Photo 1). Write "pattern" on the first leg and arm pieces and use them to make the others. If you're making more than one chair, now's the time to trace all the arm and leg pieces for each chair. The left arms and legs are mirror images of the right. Also, trim the small cutout piece of each arm (C) to make the arm support (K) for each side.

Cut the tapered back pieces

The two tapered back pieces are tricky to cut, and the safest way to do it is to cut them from a wider board. Draw the tapers shown in Figure A onto a 1x6 cut to length. Nail each end of the board to the tops of a sawhorse, placing the nails where they'll be out of the saw's path. Use a No. 4 finish nail on each end and hammer it in flush with the surface. Set the depth of your circular saw 1/8 in. deeper than the thickness of the board, and cut the taper from the wide end to the narrow end. Next,

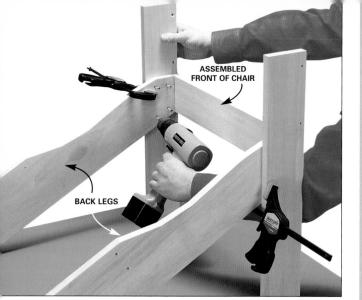

5 Clamp the back legs (B) to the front assembly to accurately position them. Work on a flat workbench surface so the chair won't wobble. Apply glue, drill pilot holes and drive 1-1/4 in. deck screws.

draw a straight line on the remaining part to define the second piece and cut it. Note: Before you begin assembly, sand all the pieces and ease the edges with 100-grit sandpaper, followed by 150-grit.

Assemble the back first

Lay the back pieces face down on your workbench (Photo 2). Line up the bottoms and insert 1/4-in. spacers between the slats. Cut your 1/4-in. spacers from scrap boards or scrap 1/4-in. plywood. Screw each of the horizontal back supports G, L and N to the slats with 1-1/4 in. exterior deck screws. Predrill and countersink each screw hole.

You'll need to cut a bevel on the top side of the center horizontal back support (L). A table saw works best, but you could use the same circular saw method you used earlier to cut the tapered side back slats (H). Just set the bevel on your circular saw to 33 degrees, nail the 1x6 board to the sawhorses, mark the width and make the cut.

Work Smart

When you're building more than one chair, set up an assembly line and cut the building time per chair by 40 percent.

With a framing square, check that the back slats and horizontal supports are positioned 90 degrees to each other as you glue and screw the assembly (Photo 2). Once the back is fastened, turn the back assembly over, mark the top radius and trim it with a jigsaw (Photo 3).

Screw the chair frame together

Using your jigsaw, cut the notches on parts E as shown in Figure A. Glue and screw the front seat support (D) to the front legs (Photo 4). Next set the front assembly vertically on your workbench and glue and screw the back legs B to the front legs (Photo 5). Again, drill pilot and countersink holes for each screw. Then glue and screw the arm supports to the outer sides of the front legs (E).

FIGURE A
Adirondack chair

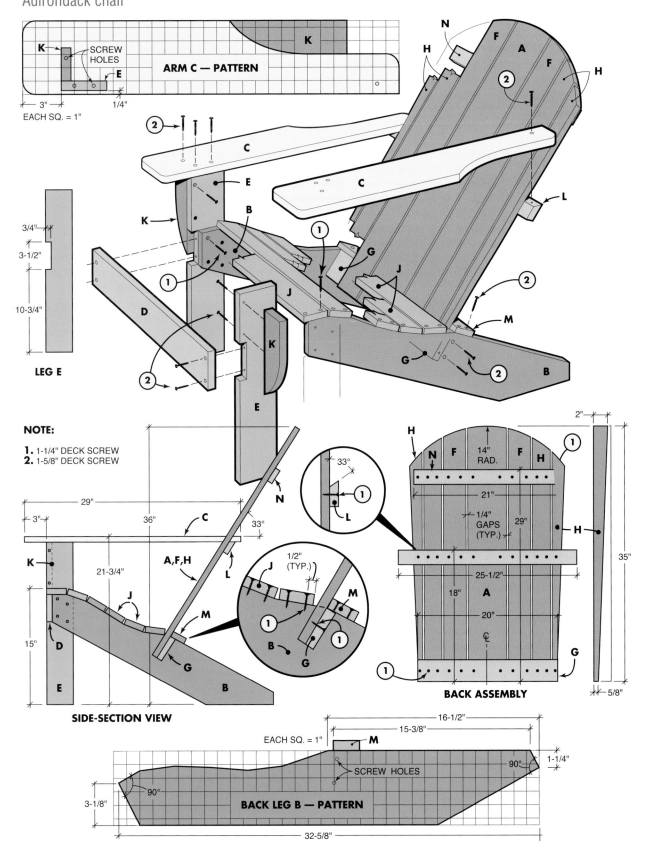

ARM C — PATTERN

3"

1/4"

EACH SQ. = 1"

K

SCREW HOLES

E

K

2

C

E

K

B

3/4"

3-1/2"

10-3/4"

LEG E

D

1

2

K

E

NOTE:

1. 1-1/4" DECK SCREW
2. 1-5/8" DECK SCREW

N

2

A

F

F

H

H

2

C

L

1

G

J

J

2

M

G

2

B

29"

3"

36"

C

33°

A,F,H

L

K

21-3/4"

J

M

15"

D

E

G

B

SIDE-SECTION VIEW

33°

1

L

1/2"
(TYP.)

J

M

1

B

G

1

H

N

F

14"
RAD.

F

H

1

21"

1/4"
GAPS
(TYP.)

29"

H

25-1/2"

18"

A

20"

C

G

1

BACK ASSEMBLY

2"

H

35"

5/8"

16-1/2"

15-3/8"

M

EACH SQ. = 1"

90°

1-1/4"

90°

3-1/8"

BACK LEG B — PATTERN

32-5/8"

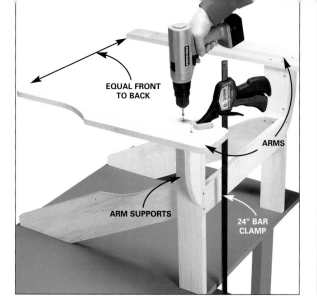

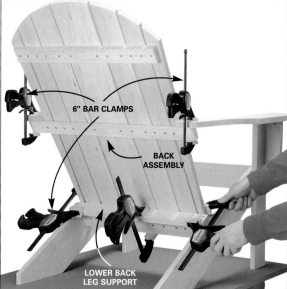

6 Glue and screw on the arm supports (K). Then glue and screw the arms to the front legs and arm supports. Use clamps to position the arms so they overhang the insides of the front legs by 1/4 in.

7 Glue, clamp and screw the lower back leg support (M) to the back legs first. Then glue and clamp the back assembly, first to the back legs, then to the arm supports. Drill pilot and countersink holes for the screws.

Position the arms on the tops of the front legs and the arm supports (K). Make sure the arms hang 3 in. over the front leg and 1/4 in. over the inside edge of each leg. Before fastening the arms, make sure they're parallel (Photo 6).

Screw the back leg support (M) to each leg (see Figure A) and then set the back assembly into the frame and clamp it in place (Photo 7). Make sure the back of each arm projects 3/4 in. past the center back support (L). Glue and predrill each joint, screw the assembly together and then remove the clamps.

To finish the assembly, predrill and countersink holes in the ends of the seat slats. Position them approximately 1/4 in. apart and screw them to the back legs as shown. Use a power screwdriver where possible, and a hand screwdriver in tight places.

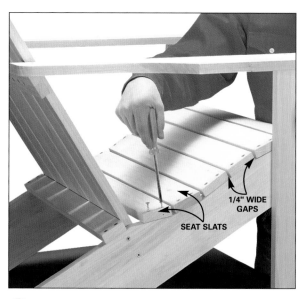

8 Predrill all the pilot and countersink holes in the seat slats before you position them. Screw the seat slats (J) to the back legs with 1-1/4 in. deck screws (use 1-5/8 in. screws in softwood), spacing them 1/4 in. apart.

Painting tips

You can use either a water-based or oil-based exterior primer and enamel topcoat.

Start applying the primer with the chair upside down. Use a 1-in. wide sash brush for coating the edges of the seat slats, and then use a 3-in. wide roller to apply primer to the flat surfaces and a 2-in brush to smooth out the primer. Prime the back, then turn the chair over and

prime the other surfaces in the same manner.

Let the primer dry over night, then use a paint scraper to remove any runs and 120-grit sandpaper to lightly sand the entire surface. Apply the topcoat in the same order you applied the primer, then let the paint dry for at least three days before use.

Pedestal picnic table

An elegant design for relaxed outdoor dining.

—Ken Collier and Travis Larson

I f you're looking for a more refined picnic table, one that will fit right in at a dinner party for adults as well as at an afternoon barbecue with the kids, here's the design for you.

Its pedestal support ensures that no one can complain about "having the leg." The round top is made from 1-in. thick "five-quarter" deck boards (abbreviated as "5/4"). This means it has a stronger top than one made of 1x6s and a less chunky look than one made of 2x6s. Unlike many other tables, this one has no screws or nails visible on the top.

You'll appreciate the strong and simple way this table is assembled. Rather than using elaborate dowel or mortise-and-tenon joints to hold the base together, we've used a long threaded rod that goes right through the pedestal legs from top to bottom (Figure A). It gives enormous strength and rigidity to the table. The only drawback is that you need to buy an extra-long bit to drill the extra-long hole.

The 48-in. dia. top will easily seat six or seven people.

Project at a glance

Skill level
Intermediate

Special tools
Bellhangers bit
Circular saw
Drill

Approximate cost
$400 for clear redwood
$250 for cedar
$150 for treated lumber

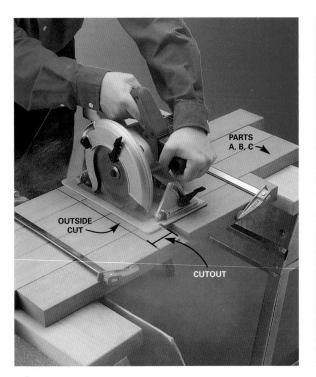

PARTS
A, B, C →

OUTSIDE
CUT →

CUTOUT

1 Make a wide cutout in the base pieces so they can overlap in an "X" shape. First make the two outside cuts, then numerous cuts in between.

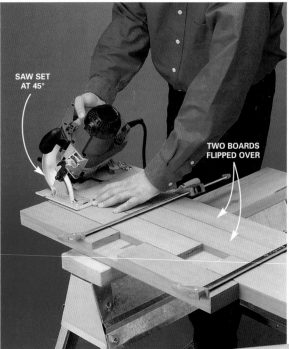

SAW SET
AT 45°

TWO BOARDS
FLIPPED OVER

2 Cut beveled ends on the same pieces, cutting them all at once. Note that two of the boards have to be flipped over before you cut.

What it takes to build

Although this project isn't difficult, it is more complicated than the typical A-frame picnic table. You need a jigsaw to cut out the round top, and you have to be a bit more precise with your circular saw. A power sander will help you clean up the edges. You'll need a hacksaw to cut the threaded rod to length, a socket wrench to tighten the nuts, and a couple of 14-in. capacity clamps. To drill the long holes for the threaded rod, you need to buy a 12-in. long x 1/2-in. dia. "bellhangers" bit (Photo 3).

We used clear, vertical-grain redwood for our table just because of its wonderful appearance. You can use pressure-treated wood for the base, but we recommend that you stay with redwood or cedar for the top to avoid potential food contamination. If you choose pressure-treated wood for your table, be sure to use plates and cutting boards so that food doesn't come into direct contact with the wood.

Build the base and top support

Cut the four parts that form the X-shaped feet and top support (parts A, B and C) to the lengths given in the Cutting List. A blade designed for trim work will give you the smoothest cuts. Draw a line across each board in the middle.

Lay the four boards on a pair of sawhorses and clamp them edge to edge so the lines you drew earlier all line up. Draw where the half-lap cutout (see Figure A) will be across all four boards. This cutout is what allows the boards to overlap to make an "X."

Adjust your circular saw (use scraps for testing) so it cuts exactly half the thickness of your boards, then saw a series of cuts to remove the wood in the half-lap cutouts (Photo 1). Use a square to guide the saw on the outside edges for more accuracy. Use a piece of scrap 2x4 to check that the cutout is wide enough before removing the clamps. Clean up the cutout with a Surform file or rasp.

FIGURE A
Pedestal picnic table

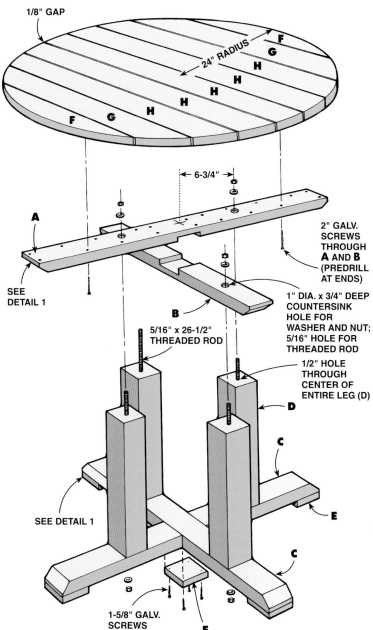

1/8" GAP

24" RADIUS

F
G
H
H
H
H
G
F

6-3/4"

A

2" GALV. SCREWS THROUGH **A** AND **B** (PREDRILL AT ENDS)

1" DIA. x 3/4" DEEP COUNTERSINK HOLE FOR WASHER AND NUT; 5/16" HOLE FOR THREADED ROD

B

SEE DETAIL 1

5/16" x 26-1/2" THREADED ROD

1/2" HOLE THROUGH CENTER OF ENTIRE LEG (D)

D

C

SEE DETAIL 1

E

C

1-5/8" GALV. SCREWS

E

Detail 1

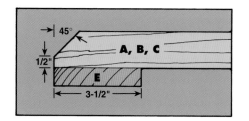

45°

A, B, C

1/2"

E

3-1/2"

SHOPPING LIST

ITEM	QTY.
2x4 x 8'	2
4x4 x 8'	1
1x4 x 12'	1
5/4 x 6" x 12'	3
1x8 x 8' (for clamping jig)	1
1/2" dia. x 12" drill bit	1
2" galv. deck screws	22
1-5/8" galv. deck screws	70
5/16" x 26-1/2" threaded rod	4
5/16" nuts and washers	8
Brown caulk	1 tube
Water-repellent preservative	1 qt.

CUTTING LIST

KEY	PCS.	SIZE & DESCRIPTION
A	1	2x4 x 46"
B	1	2x4 x 26"
C	2	2x4 x 41"
D	4	4x4 x 23-7/8"
E	5	1x4 x 3-1/2"
F	2	5/4 x 6" x 30"
G	2	5/4 x 6" x 42"
H	5	5/4 x 6" x 50"
J	2	1x4 x 24"
K	4	1x4 x 18"

FIGURE B

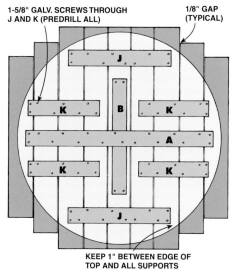

1-5/8" GALV. SCREWS THROUGH J AND K (PREDRILL ALL)

1/8" GAP (TYPICAL)

J

K

B

K

A

K

K

J

KEEP 1" BETWEEN EDGE OF TOP AND ALL SUPPORTS

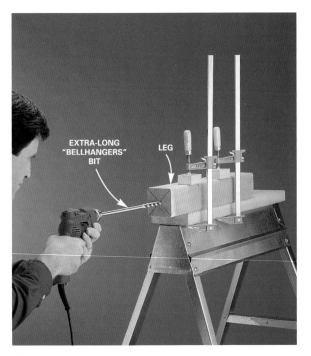

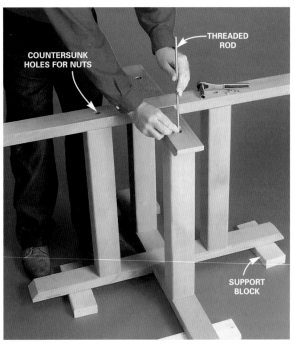

3 Drill long holes through the legs using an extra-long bit. Sight carefully to keep the bit straight, and drill in from both ends.

4 Assemble the base using threaded rod to hold it all together. Putting the base up on blocks lets you attach the nuts and washers underneath.

Now get ready to cut the beveled ends on the four boards (Photo 2). Because each half-lap joint is assembled with one piece upside down, you need to flip either part A or part B over (not both), and flip over one part C, before you can cut the beveled ends. Line up the ends of the boards, clamp them together, and cut the angled ends (Photo 2). It works better if you mark your cutting line on the ends of the boards so that when you cut, the wide part of the saw base is supported by the boards. After the cut, flip the boards over and sand all the cut surfaces at once. Then remove the clamps and repeat the process at the other end.

Mark and drill the 1-in. holes in parts A, B and C (see Figure A). Be sure that you drill them on the sides of the boards that don't have the beveled cuts. Then drill the 5/16-in. holes.

Cut and drill the legs

Cut the four pieces of 4x4 that make the pedestal legs (part D). If you're cutting them with a circular saw, mark a line on all four sides and then cut from opposite sides.

It's more important to have the ends flat and square, and all four pieces the same length, than to make them exactly the length given in the Cutting List. So if you need to trim them a bit, go ahead.

Drill a 1/2-in. or slightly larger hole through the center of each pedestal part, going in halfway from each end (Photo 3). Sight carefully to be sure the bit is going in parallel to the leg. By the way, don't try to substitute a spade bit in an extension—it'll cut so badly that it'll burn out both your arms and your drill.

Sand all the parts you've worked on so far. Screw a nut onto the threaded rod, then cut your threaded rod to length with a hacksaw. File the cut end smooth and screw the nut off the cut end to machine the threads. Assemble the two base pieces (C) to make an "X," and support it on sawhorses or blocks. Stand the 4x4 legs on the base, put pieces A and B on top of them and fit the threaded rods to hold the unit together (Photo 4). Tighten the nuts from both ends using a ratchet wrench and deep socket. Screw on the feet (E). Fill the holes where the nuts are with brown caulk.

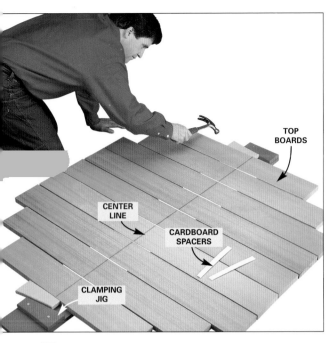

5 Hold the top boards with a wooden clamp made from a 1x8 and a couple of wedges. Cardboard spacers keep the gaps uniform, and a line in the middle of each board helps you position them.

6 Draw a circle using a nail in the middle for a pivot and a piece of wire as a compass. Then remove the boards and cut the shapes with a jigsaw.

Build and connect the top

Begin making the top by cutting the boards F, G and H to the lengths given in the Cutting List. Cut the longest pieces (H) first, then cut parts F and G. Draw a line across the back of each board in the middle. Then assemble a clamping jig out of 1x8, as shown in Photo 5. Lay the boards on it upside down, with their center lines aligned and 1/8-in. cardboard spacers between them (Photo 5). Tighten the wedges on the jig just enough to hold the boards in position.

Put a nail in the middle of the middle board, and draw a circle on the boards (Photo 6). Use a wire for a compass. Take the boards out of the jig, cut out the arcs with a jigsaw, and reassemble the top on the clamping jig, including the spacers. You will need to reposition a wedge block.

Set the upside-down pedestal assembly onto the boards (Photo 7) and screw it down. Cut the cleat boards (J and K), and screw them down as well. Flip the table over, remove the spacer and sand the top. Apply an exterior finish, and you're done.

7 Attach the base to the top with screws, and add the 1x4 cleats. Sand the edge of the top and apply a water-repellent finish.

Cedar potting bench

Build this handy potting bench in a weekend.

—Jeff Gorton

Whether you're a spare-time gardener or a hard-core enthusiast, this bench is for you. It has plenty of storage to keep all your plant supplies in one convenient location, and it features a built-in potting soil container and a grate-covered dirt catcher to make messy potting and cleanup a snap.

We designed this bench to be strong without complex joints. An experienced woodworker can complete this potting bench in a day. If you're a beginner, allow two or three days.

You'll need basic carpentry tools like a tape measure, large and small squares, and a chisel. You could make most of the cuts for this potting bench with a circular saw. However, a power miter box will ensure perfectly square end cuts, and a table saw is almost essential for

cutting the grate slats. If you don't have a table saw, ask a friend, neighbor or the staff at the lumberyard to cut the pieces for you. You'll also need a drill with the bits mentioned in the story and a jigsaw.

Choose straight, nice-looking lumber

We used cedar for our bench, but pine is cheaper. Consider using pressure-treated pine if you'll be leaving the bench outside. All of these are available at home centers and lumberyards. But make sure to pick straight boards

Project at a glance

Skill level
Intermediate

Special tools
Table saw
Power miter box
Jigsaw
Wood rasp

Approximate cost
$200

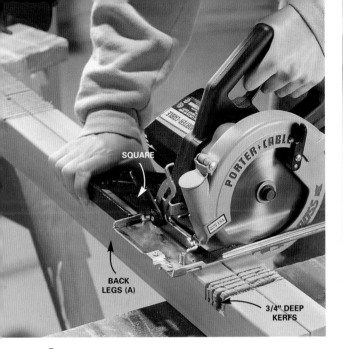

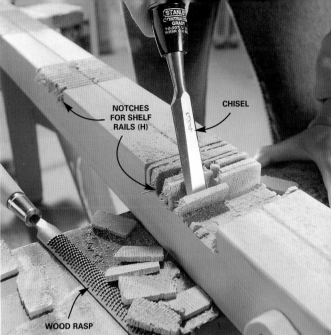

1 Mark the notch locations on the legs (A and B) using the dimensions in Figure A. Make a series of 3/4-in. deep saw kerfs about 1/4 in. apart to create the notches.

2 Chisel out the waste wood from the notches and smooth the bottom with a wood rasp.

with at least one nice-looking side. You can hide a few minor defects on the back or underside of the bench. Also, avoid boards with large knots, which will weaken key parts and make it harder to cut the notches.

When you get your materials home, cut the pieces to size using the Cutting List. Many of the parts, like the 1 x 1-in. slats for the grate and the 2-1/2 in. wide legs, have to be cut the length of the board. This operation, called ripping, is possible with a circular saw, but it's much quicker, easier and more accurate with a table saw.

Make tight-fitting joints for a strong bench

Photos 1 and 2 show how to notch the legs for the horizontal cross members. Notching looks tricky, but it's simple if you follow these key steps: First clamp each pair of legs together, and using dimensions from Figure A, mark the lower edge of each notch. Use a square to draw lines across the boards at these marks. Then align the corresponding horizontal board with this line and mark along the opposite edge to get an exact width. Using the boards in this manner to mark the width of the notch is more accurate than measuring. When you saw the notch, cut to the waste side of the pencil line, leaving the line on

3 Spread a small bead of construction adhesive in each notch and lay the horizontal pieces in place. Use a framing square to make sure the cross members are at right angles to the legs, then drive a pair of 2-in. screws at each joint.

the board. You can always enlarge the notch or plane the board to fit a notch that's too tight, but you can't shrink a notch that's too wide. Tight-fitting joints strengthen the bench and look better too.

Assembly is quick once the parts are cut

Photos 3 and 4 show how to assemble the leg sections and connect them to form the bench frame. Before you screw the horizontal pieces to the legs, pick the best-looking side of the boards and make sure it's facing the front of the bench. (The best sides are facing down in Photo 3.) Drill 5/32-in. clearance holes through the cross members to avoid splitting them and to allow the screws to draw the boards tight to the legs.

Use only one 1-1/4 in. screw to attach parts F and G to the front legs. Center the screw so it doesn't interfere with the 3-in. screws you'll be installing to secure the leg assembly (Photo 4). Use a 3/4-in. spacer block (Photo 4) to align the cross members (E) before you drive in the 3-in. screws.

If you'll be leaving your bench outdoors, use stainless steel screws or corrosion-resistant deck screws. For extra strength and durability, put a small dab of construction adhesive on each joint before you screw the pieces together. To hide the 3-in. screws that secure the front legs, use a 3/8-in. brad point drill bit to drill 1/4-in. deep recesses before you drill the 5/32-in. clearance holes. Then glue 3/8-in. wood buttons into the recesses after you screw the parts together.

Keep a framing square handy as you assemble the leg sections and bench frame and use it to make sure the

SHOPPING LIST

ITEM	QTY.
2x6 x 8' cedar (rip to 2-1/2" for legs)	1
2x4 x 6' cedar (rip to 2-1/2" for lower cross members)	1
2x4 x 4' cedar	1
1x2 x 4' cedar	3
1x3 x 8' cedar	1
1x4 x 8' cedar	2
1x8 x 4' cedar	3
5/4 x 6 x 4' bullnose cedar	9
2' x 2' 3/4" plywood	1
Hardware	
1-1/4" stainless steel screws	80
2" stainless steel screws	50
3" stainless steel screws	10
1-1/4" finish nails	1 lb.
3/8" wood screw plugs	30
3/8" wood button plugs	10
10-oz. tube of construction adhesive	1
Water-resistant wood glue	1
6"x 8" decorative shelf brackets	4
10"x 14" x 18" deep wastebasket	1
14" x 20" x 4" deep litter pan	1
100-grit sandpaper sheets	2

CUTTING LIST

KEY	PCS.	SIZE & DESCRIPTION
A	2	1-1/2" x 2-1/2" x 62" (back legs)
B	2	1-1/2" x 2-1/2" x 33" (front legs)
C	2	1-1/2" x 2-1/2" x 21" (lower cross members)
D	1	1-1/2" x 2-1/2" x 21" (middle cross member)
E	2	1-1/2" x 3-1/2" x 21" (upper cross members)
F	2	3/4" x 2-1/2" x 47" (lower rails)
G	1	3/4" x 3-1/2" x 47" (upper rail)
H	2	3/4" x 3-1/2" x 47" (shelf rails)
J	1	3/4" x 7-1/4" x 47" (backsplash)
K	2	3/4" x 7-1/4" x 47" (shelves)
L	1	3/4" x 3-1/2" x 42-1/2" (bench-top support)
M	2	3/4" x 1-1/2" x 10-1/2" (cover cleats)
N	2	3/4" x 1-1/2" x 12-1/2" (grate cleats)
P	2	1" x 5-1/2" x 23" (bench-top ends; cut to fit)
Q	5	1" x 5-1/2" x 23" (bench top)
R	7	1" x 1" x 23-1/2" (slats)
S	12	1" x 1" x 4" (spacers)
T	2	3/4" x 1-1/2" x 25-1/2" (container cleats)
U	2	3/4" x 1-1/2" x 16-3/4" (bench-top cleats)
V	4	1" x 5-1/2" x 47" (lower shelf)
W	1	12-3/4" x 20-1/4" x 3/4" plywood (container support)

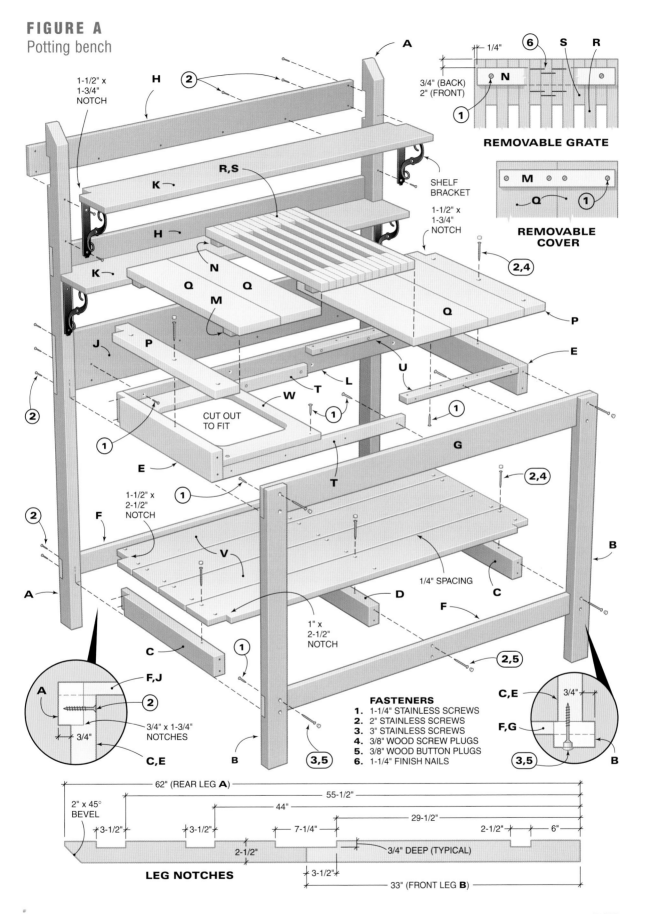

FIGURE A
Potting bench

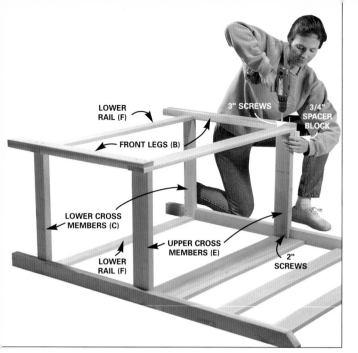

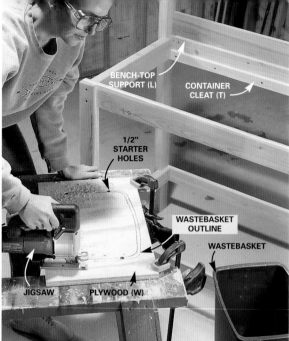

4 Screw the horizontal cross members (C and E) to the back leg assembly. Drill and countersink the front leg assembly and attach it to members C and E with 3-in. screws. Cover the screws with decorative wood plugs.

5 Trace the wastebasket onto the 3/4-in. plywood (W). Draw a second line about 1/2 in. inside the traced outline. Drill a 1/2-in. starter hole and cut along the inside line with a jigsaw. Screw the bench-top support (L) and container cleats (T) to the bench and screw the plywood (W) into place.

assemblies are square before you tighten the screws.

Photo 5 shows how to mark and cut the plywood that supports the potting soil container. We used a plastic wastebasket, but any container with a lip will work. Trace the shape on a piece of plywood and then cut the hole a little smaller so the plywood supports the lip.

The bench top is made of 1-in. thick bullnose cedar decking. Join two pieces with cleats to make a removable cover for the dirt container (Photo 7). Glue 1 x 1-in. slats together with water-resistant wood glue to form the grate (Photo 6). Scrape off excess glue before it dries. Then allow the glue to dry overnight before you sand the grate and trim the ends flush. Screw cleats to the bottom of the grate to keep it positioned and allow easy removal.

The width of the end pieces (P) varies, depending on the dimensions of your decking. To determine the width, first center the grate, removable cover and three more boards on the bench top, leaving an equal space on each end. Then measure the distance from the last board to the outside edge of the back leg and cut and notch the end pieces to fit.

Glue 3/8-in. wood plugs into 3/8-in. by 1/4-in. deep recesses to hide the screws that hold the two end pieces (P) and lower shelf boards in place. Sand them flush after the glue dries.

Complete the potting bench by notching the 1x8 shelves (Photo 9) and securing them with 2-in. screws through the horizontal 1x4 shelf rails (H). We used black metal shelf brackets to support the ends.

Protect your bench with a good finish

Unfinished cedar has some resistance to decay, but the best strategy is to apply a top-quality exterior finish to keep the wood from cracking, splitting and rotting. Penetrating oil–type finishes with a small amount of pigment provide a natural look and reduce fading. Finishes that leave a film provide the best protection. Take extra precautions to seal the bottom of the legs to keep them from absorbing moisture from the damp ground. For interior use, any good-quality varnish will work.

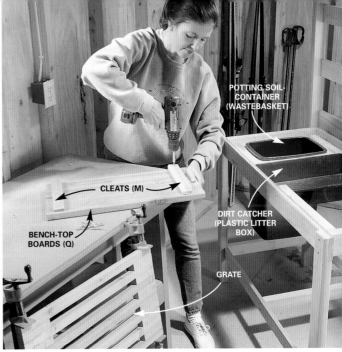

6 Glue and nail the slats and spacers together to make the grate. Drill 1/16-in. pilot holes for the nails to prevent splitting the wood. Spread water-resistant glue on both surfaces and nail the slats and spacers together with 1-1/4 in. finish nails. Clamp the completed assembly with bar clamps and allow it to dry overnight. Trim the 23-1/2 in. grate to 23 in. with your circular saw or table saw and sand the edge smooth.

7 Assemble the cover for the dirt container by screwing cleats (M) to the bottom of the 5/4 x 6-in. decking (Q). Screw cleats (N) to the bottom of the completed grate.

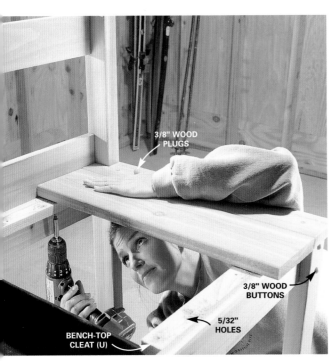

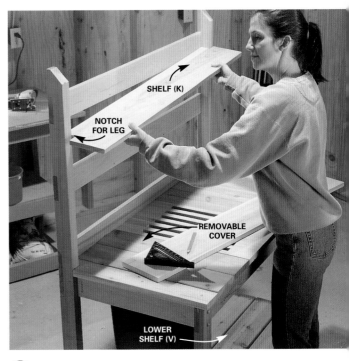

8 Attach the fixed benchtop pieces (Q) with 1-1/4 in. screws driven up through the bench-top cleats (U). Secure the bench-top ends (P) and bottom shelf boards (V) by driving 1-1/4 in. screws through predrilled and countersunk holes. Conceal these screws with wood plugs glued into the recesses. Sand the plugs flush when the glue dries.

9 Notch the shelves (K) and slide them into place. Screw through the shelf rails (H) into the shelves. Support the front of the shelves with metal brackets.

Dream fences, walls & lighting

Modular concrete retaining wall

Get an attractive, hardworking wall with this DIY-friendly project.

—Spike Carlsen

Until concrete retaining wall systems muscled their way onto the scene 20 years ago, there were few do-it-yourself-friendly materials to choose from. Rock and stone were labor intensive to gather (or expensive to buy) and tricky to install. Treated timbers, despite claims to the contrary, often rotted within 15 years. Railroad ties looked like, well, railroad ties, and other options, like poured concrete or mortared brick, were best left to the pros. But concrete retaining wall systems—easy to install, widely available, reasonably priced, long-lasting and available in a wide selection of colors and patterns—changed all that.

A retaining wall can solve many problems. It can convert steep, hard-to-mow hills into terraced, usable planting beds. It

Project at a glance

Skill level
Beginner to intermediate

Special tools
Transit
Hand tamper

Approximate cost
$10–$12 per sq. ft. of retaining wall face

EASY FOR EVERYONE

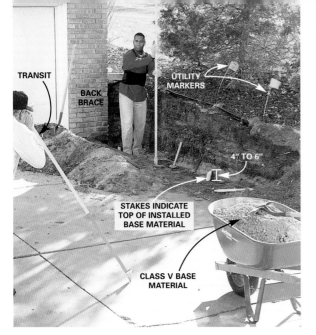

1 Excavate and level the area where you'll be installing the wall. Use a transit or a 4-ft. level taped to a straight 2x4 to establish a common stake height, indicating the top of your sand leveling bed (see Figure A). Create a flat area at least 4 to 6 in. deep and 24 to 28 in. wide for installing compactable base material. Provide a clear area of at least 12 in. behind the wall for installing the crushed rock as shown in Photo 7.

2 Install 4 to 6 in. of base material level to the tops of the stakes, then compact it until it's about 1 in. below the tops. Rent a hand tamper (about $5 a day) for small projects, or a gas-powered tamper (about $50 for a half day) for walls more than 30 ft. long.

can prevent erosion, help level a patio area, create tree borders or simply add visual interest to a rolling yard.

The retaining wall system we installed uses nylon pins to align and secure horizontal rows of 80-lb. blocks. (See Resources, p. 252.) Other block systems use lips, gravity and filled cores to connect rows and increase strength. Your system may differ, but most of the preparation and installation steps remain the same. Here's how to install your wall.

Don't skimp on time, tools or materials

The wall we built was a weekend-long project, and an exhausting one at that. It took a day to rip out the old, collapsing retaining wall, to dig farther into the hill to provide room for the backfill gravel and to help unload materials. It took another day to install the base, blocks and backfill.

Before launching into this project, contact your local building code official. Depending on the height and location of your wall, there may be structural, drainage and setback (the distance from wall to property line)

considerations. A permit may be required.

Unless you own a heavy-duty truck (and back!), have your blocks, compactable base, sand and backfill gravel delivered. Blocks may cost slightly more at specialty landscaping stores than at home centers, but landscaping stores are often better equipped to deliver the small batches of base, sand and gravel that you'll need for installing the blocks.

We used a transit level (Photo 1) to establish a flat base. But unless you own or rent one and know

Plan Smart

For safety's sake, call your utility companies and have them mark the location of underground wires and pipes; the service is usually free. For more information, call the North American One-Call Referral System at 888-258-0808.

how to use it properly, just use a 4-ft. level taped to a long, straight 2x4, especially for short walls. The tamper, brick tongs and block chisel are available at rental yards.

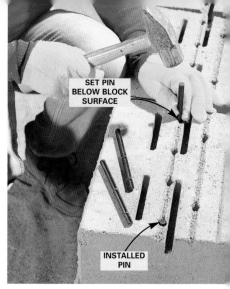

3 Provide a flat-as-a-pancake sand base for installing the first course of blocks. With the tops of the stakes as guides, use a long, straight screed board to level the sand. A hand trowel is good for fine-tuning small dips and humps.

4 Install the first course of blocks, using a taut string line to establish a straight row. Use a 4-ft. level to level blocks lengthwise and a torpedo level to level them front to back. Once the first row is installed, pack native soil to grade level on both sides to anchor the wall in place. The brick tong makes handling and positioning the 80-lb. blocks easier and safer.

5 Drive in the pins to lock courses to one another and help establish the 3/4-in. backset for each row. Use an extra pin to set the installed pins below the surface of the blocks so they don't interfere with blocks on the next row. To maintain wall strength, offset the vertical joints of the row you're installing at least 4 in. from those of the row below.

FIGURE A
Anatomy of a retaining wall

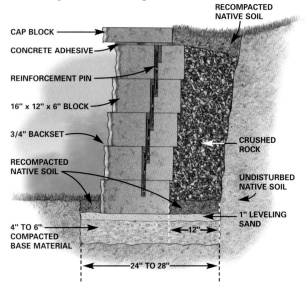

A retaining wall is only as straight and solid as the base it's built on. For a 4-ft. tall wall, excavate a trench deep enough to accommodate 4 to 6 in. of compacted base, 1 in. of leveling sand and half the height of the first course of blocks. Step succeeding courses back 3/4 in., overlap vertical joints at least 4 in. and secure one row to the next with pins. Backfill with crushed rock, except for the top, where you should install a 6-in. "cap" of native soil to help keep surface water from entering the rock-filled trench. Use concrete adhesive to secure the cap blocks.

Build straight and solid from start to finish

Starting with a solid, level and well-compacted base is an absolute necessity. Failure to do this will result in a weak, wavy wall. Bear in mind:

■ If your wall is higher than 4 ft., most concrete block manufacturers require extra engineering and installation steps not shown here. These steps range from using special reinforcement fabric to installing a series of terraces rather than one tall wall. Most manufacturers provide good printed installation guidelines. If you purchase your blocks from a specialty landscape center, there may be an on-site designer or engineer to help you.

■ Contact local utility companies to mark the location of underground wires and pipes. Telephone and cable TV wires are often buried just beneath the surface.

Plan Smart

If your wall borders a sidewalk or deck, you may need a code-compliant rail. Contact your local building code department.

HAND-PROTECTING BLOCK CHISEL

V-GROOVE

6 Cut blocks to size by first scoring the top and bottom with a block chisel, then turning the block on its side and finishing the task with a series of solid blows.

CRUSHED ROCK

7 Backfill behind the retaining wall with crushed gravel. Crushed, rather than smooth, gravel locks together and helps direct backfill pressure downward (rather than outward). The backfill also provides a fast path for water drainage and acts as a tree root barrier.

■ In the Midwest, the compactable base material shown in Photo 2 is often referred to as "Class V" (as in the Roman numeral for five). In other regions, the rock may vary and the material may go by a different name. The important quality of the material is its different-sized rock and sand particles that interlock and compact to create a solid base. It's the same material used beneath roadbeds and paver patios. Make sure you use the right stuff. It's NOT the same as the crushed gravel you use for backfill.

■ The 16-in. wide x 12-in. deep x 6-in. high blocks we installed weigh 80 lbs. each. A brick tong (Photo 4) doesn't make them lighter, but it does make them less clumsy to handle, easier to position and less likely to crush fingers.

Work Smart

Install that first row of blocks dead level. Otherwise those dips and humps will haunt you with each succeeding course.

CONCRETE ADHESIVE

CAP BLOCKS

8 Install the cap blocks using two 1/4-in. beads of concrete adhesive to secure them in place. Cap blocks can be positioned with a slight overhang or back-set, or set flush with the wall face.

Decorative privacy fence

Design and build a great-looking fence in just two weekends.

—*Duane Johnson*

L ooking for more privacy, a corral for the kids and pets or an attractive border on the edge of your yard? Consider building your own fence— it's the ideal project for weekend carpenters of every ability level. You can build a simple fence with as few tools as a posthole digger, hammer, power saw and tape measure and little if any woodworking experience. On the other hand, you could pick a design that's so challenging only a skilled builder should attempt it.

The design we show here falls somewhere in the novice-to-intermediate difficulty range. It's primarily a privacy fence intended to enclose a backyard and garden in the middle of a busy neighborhood. However, we added lattice and a gate to make it more friendly and inviting. While these features complicate the project a bit, don't let them put you off. The basic design and assembly procedures that we'll demonstrate work well for both simple and complex fences. Once you master these basics, you'll be able to design and build a fence that fits your home, the surrounding landscape and your ability level.

Wood fences aren't cheap

Even the simplest hand-crafted wood fence costs more than your garden-variety chain-link fencing. A wood fence will be even more expensive in the long run if you include the cost of periodic staining or painting. So for both economy and convenience, chain-link fencing is usually your best bet. But for beauty and versatility, wood wins hands down.

Neighborhood concerns

Most communities have ordinances that regulate fences, because they visually affect your neighbors' property as well as your own. So before you get too far into the plan-

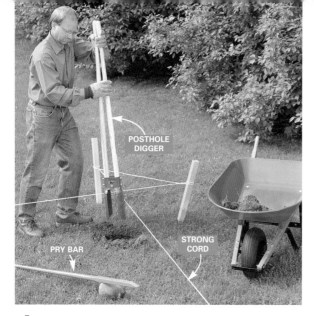

1 Stretch lines to mark the fence location, then dig holes 8 in. in diameter for the corner posts using a posthole digger. Use a steel pry bar to knock rocks loose and break through tree roots. Remember to call your utility company to check for buried lines before digging.

POSTHOLE DIGGER

PRY BAR

STRONG CORD

2 Plumb the corner posts with a level and tamp 6 in. of soil around their bottoms to anchor them. Trim the tops to the exact height later (Photo 7).

LEVEL

4x4 CORNER POST

TAMPING STICK

ning process, call your local building inspector and ask about local codes. Many locales limit fence height to 4 or 5 ft. (Our design is 6 ft. high, which isn't acceptable in some areas.) Many have "setback" requirements; that is, the fence has to be a certain distance from the property line. And the fence has to look at least as attractive from the outside as it does on the inside. (You can't face the least attractive side toward your neighbors.) Check whether a building inspector has to approve your plan and issue a building permit before you can start work.

And let your neighbors know what you're up to before you begin. Otherwise the sudden change may shock them, and you'll have to smooth some ruffled feathers!

Allow two weekends to complete an average fence: one weekend to lay out and set the posts, and the second to assemble the fencing.

Fence-planning basics

Our fence design, like most, consists of repeating sec-

Plan Smart

Look through the design books of local fence-building companies to find creative ideas. Many companies will also sell you materials and offer free advice. And keep a sharp eye out for attractive designs in your own neighborhood.

tions supported on both ends by 4x4 posts, spaced from 6 to 8 ft. apart. Two 2x4s span the distance between the posts, which, when fastened "on edge" (1-1/2 in. side facing down), are strong enough to support the fence boards without sagging (Figure A). The third (top) 2x4 primarily supports the lattice. When you use 2x4s to span more than 8 ft., they usually sag within a few years. The same thing will happen if you fasten the 2x4s "flat" (with the 3-1/2 in. side down).

Since the 4x4 posts and 2x4 framework provide the strength, you can add just about any pattern of fence boards and trim to finish the fence.

It's best to use a rot-resistant wood, either cedar, redwood, or pressure-treated lumber. Expect both redwood and cedar fences to last 15 to 20 years, or longer where weathering from sun and rain is less severe. Pressure-treated wood will last even longer. However, most treated species, when left unfinished, tend to warp, crack and split more readily than cedar and redwood. You'll have to apply paint, stain or another water repellent to keep a treated wood fence looking good. By the same token, both redwood and cedar will last longer and look better if you apply a water-repelling finish to them too.

Rough-surfaced boards absorb stain better than smooth, while smooth wood accepts paint better. Two other factors can complicate your plans:

One. A design that requires exact post spacing. The 6-in. square lattice in our design meant that we had to accurately space our posts an exact multiple of 6 in. apart (6 ft. 6 in., 7 ft., etc.). Sure, we could fudge an inch or so either way, but not much more if we were to keep the lattice looking symmetrical.

Unless you're lucky, you'll end up with an odd-sized fence section or two. Put that section at the most obscure corner of your yard!

Two. A sloped landscape. Lattice also limits your options when it comes to following the sloped contours of the yard. The lattice looks best if it's level, so you'll have to "step" it up and down slopes (Figure B). The bottom of the fence doesn't matter as much; you can either follow the contour of the ground or step it as well (Figure B).

Without lattice or other details that require a level approach, a fence can simply follow the contours of the lot. To help choose the best option for your fence, sketch your fence design and try out the slope options on paper first.

Finally, keep in mind that your fence should look attractive on both sides. The sides of our fence are virtually identical.

The layout and corner posts

To look good, a fence has to be straight. So the first task is to find the fence corners and stretch tight string lines between them. If you're working near the property line, you'll have to find the official boundary markers or hire surveyors to reestablish them.

With the fence lines clearly marked, dig holes for the

Buy Smart

When buying fence boards, look for wood specifically labeled as such. They're usually rough-surfaced and slightly thinner than regular 1x4s and 1x6s, but they cost less. Quality varies widely, so check the stacks at several lumberyards or local fence companies.

FIGURE A
Fence details

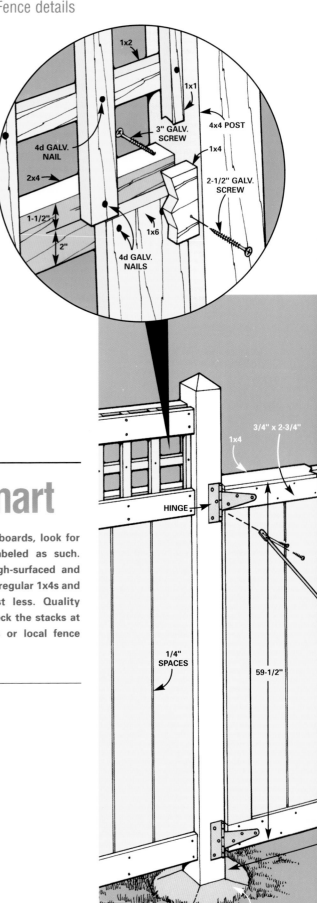

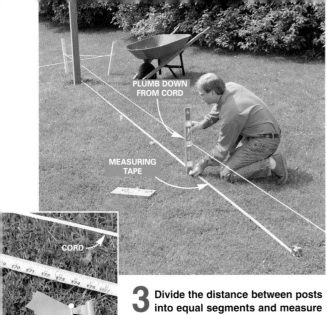

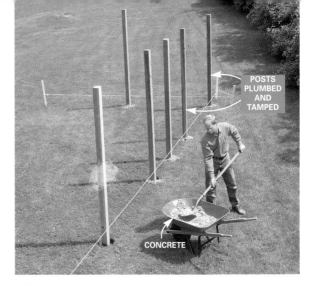

3 Divide the distance between posts into equal segments and measure and mark the exact location of each post along the string line. A nail with a ribbon makes highly visible markers.

4 Dig the holes, plumb and anchor the posts, then fill the holes with concrete to about 1 in. above ground level.

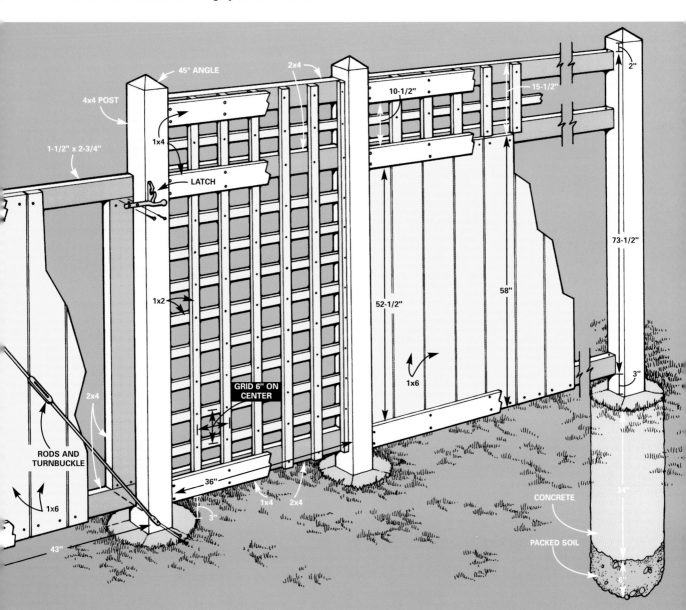

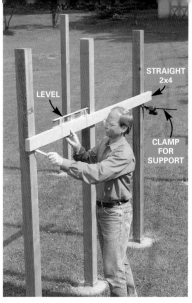

5 Smooth the concrete with a wood or metal float, angling the top away from the post for better drainage.

6 Mark the locations of the 2x4 framework on each post with a straight 2x4 and level. Then mark the finished height of each post.

7 Cut the post tops to height with a circular saw. Clamp a jig to the post to guide the saw.

FIGURE B
Options for slopes

Stepped top, angled bottom

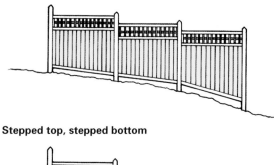

Stepped top, stepped bottom

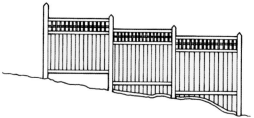

Angled top and bottom

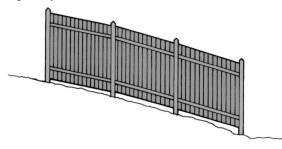

corner posts (Photo 1). Call your local utility before you dig so they can come out and mark buried gas, electrical, water and telephone lines.

You'll work up a sweat hand-digging with a post hole digger, but it's our favorite tool for fence work. Renting a gas-driven post hole auger might save you a little time, but it'll still give you a workout.

You have to bury posts deep enough so that the steady force of the wind doesn't gradually tip them over. Bury 1 ft. of post for every 2 ft. it extends above ground. Our posts extended about 80 in. above ground and 40 in. below. Finally, drop in the corner posts and tamp 6 in. of soil around them to keep them plumb (Photo 2).

Now measure the distance between corner posts (a 50-ft. tape comes in handy here) and divide the distance into equal segments (Photo 3). Remember to allow 3-1/2 in. for each 4x4 post. Also allow space for special sections in your plan, like the gate and lattice adjacent to it.

Handy Hints®

As the concrete hardens, it'll shrink, opening a narrow gap between the post and concrete. Fill this crack with a bead of acrylic caulk to keep out water.

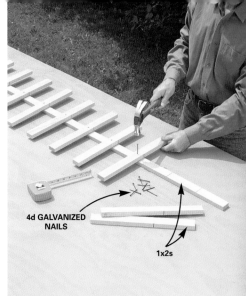

8 Clamp a jig to the post to cradle the 2x4 framework, and screw the 2x4s to the posts with 3-in. galvanized decking screws.

9 Cut the fencing boards to length and fasten them to the 2x4s with 6d galvanized nails. Space the boards 1/4 in. apart to allow for normal expansion.

10 Lay out the 1x2 lattice on 6-in. centers. Then fasten it with 4d galvanized nails.

11 Nail the lattice in place with 6d galvanized nails. Use a framing square to align the vertical pieces and keep them straight.

12 Screw 1x4s over the board and lattice ends using 2-1/2 in. galvanized decking screws.

Dig all the post holes and plumb the posts with your level, again tamping 6 in. of soil around each to hold them in place (Photo 4). After you fill the holes with concrete, check each of them again for plumb. It's tough to move them once the concrete sets! Give the concrete two days to harden.

Assembling the framework

Layout work was painstaking, but now you move into the fun part where your fence comes together quickly. The framework for our fence consists of three 2x4s in each section (Figure A). Start from the highest point in your yard and mark the height of the middle 2x4 on each post, keeping the 2x4 level from post to post (Photo 6).

13 Assemble the gate on a flat surface. We used screws to strengthen it and keep it perfectly square.

1x6s

2" GALVANIZED SCREWS

2x4s

14 Shim the gate to center it in the opening, and screw heavy-duty hinges to both the gate and post. Then add a turn-buckle to reinforce the gate, and a latch.

HINGE

SHIMS

Step it up or down 6 in. (to be consistent with the lattice) on slopes. Then measure up from the line to locate the top 2x4 and down to locate the lower. (The height of the lower will vary if you angle it to follow the contours of the ground.)

Cut the post tops. Use a circular saw set at a 45-degree angle (Photo 7). Warning: Sawing from a ladder is difficult and can be dangerous. The guide (ours is painted yellow in Photo 7), made from four 4-1/4 in. long 1x4s nailed together and clamped to the post, made the cutting easier and safer.

Measure the 2x4s for each section, and cut them to length so they fit snugly between the posts (Figure A, inset). Although the sections are supposed to be equal, expect small variations. Predrill the 2x4s with a 5/32-in. bit before fastening them, so the 3-in. galvanized deck screws draw the 2x4s tight to the posts.

Fasten the fencing boards. Two 6d nails driven at the top and bottom are strong enough to hold each fencing board (Photo 9), particularly since a 1x4 covers them. Use *hot-dipped* galvanized nails for the best corrosion resistance.

We prestained the fence boards and lattice to save time. Stain won't last as long as paint, but it's easier to

renew. We expect our stain to last about five years before it fades and cries out for another coat.

We made our lattice from 1x2s that we ripped from wider boards on a table saw. However, you can usually buy both the square and angled types of lattice preassembled at lumberyards, although in a much smaller grid. Preassemble it on a flat surface (Photo 10) before nailing it in place (Photo 11).

Finish the fence by covering the joints with 1x4s to match the 2x4s on the other side. Cut them accurately so they won't leave unsightly gaps at the ends (Figure A, inset).

Building the gate

Our gate is virtually identical to the fence, except we continued the 2x4s and 1x4s completely around the perimeter (Figure A). And we capped the top with a 1x3. For additional strength, we fastened the boards to the 2x4s with 2-in. galvanized decking screws and the 1x4s with 2-1/2 in. galvanized decking screws (Photo 13). But gates have a tendency to sag anyway, especially if the kids swing on them! So we screwed two threaded rods connected by a turnbuckle diagonally across the gate to reinforce it (Figure A).

Boulder wall

You don't have to be a stonemason to build a great-looking wall.

—*Gary Wentz*

Building a dry stone retaining wall is hard work, but it's also fun. Maybe it's the low-tech appeal of doing what humans have done for thousands of years. Maybe it's the satisfaction of turning a pile of rocks into something beautiful and useful that will last for centuries. Maybe it's the challenge of fitting together a giant, three-dimensional puzzle. Whatever the reasons, many people find working with stone enjoyable and satisfying.

You can, of course, turn any pleasant project into drudgery by overdoing it. Two hours of wall-building is enjoyable exercise; six hours is an ordeal. To keep it fun, think of your wall as a summer hobby, to be plugged away at on Sunday afternoons, not a project to be completed in a weekend.

Why dry?

"Dry" simply means that mortar isn't used to cement the structure together. Rather, the stones are carefully fit into place and held there by gravity.

Mixing up and slopping on mortar are, of course, a nuisance. But that's not why we leave it out of our wall recipe. A dry stone wall, put together well, will actually outlast a mortared wall for two reasons: It can flex slightly, moving with the ground beneath it instead of cracking like a stiff mortared wall would; and since it doesn't rely on mortar, it won't fall apart as mortar wears away, as all mortar eventually does.

Project at a glance

Skill level
Beginner to intermediate

Special tools
Hand sledgehammer
Sturdy wheelbarrow

Approximate cost
Varies greatly

Do it right

Some dry stone retaining walls have stood for hundreds of years, even though they were thrown up carelessly. But building this way is a gamble. A poorly built wall may stand for decades. Then again, it may topple over next spring. Worse, it could come apart as kids play on it, resulting in broken bones. The method we show isn't the only way to build a dry stone wall, and it certainly isn't the easiest. But the extra effort pays off with safety and longevity.

Finding rocks

Gravel pits, quarries, farms and construction sites are good sources of low-cost or no-cost rock. But always ask before you take.

Getting rocks home is the hard part. Building a wall takes a lot of rock. (We used 10 tons to build our 35-ft. long, 3-ft. high wall.) So even if you have a full-size pickup truck, you'll need to make lots of trips.

For the backyard builder, rocks fall into two categories: angular (like shale, sandstone, marble or slate) and rounded (usually granite). Angular rocks have a definite grain, sort of like wood. So the forces of geology

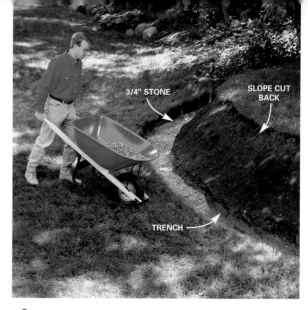

1 Cut back the slope and dig a 1-ft. deep, 2-ft. wide trench at its base. Keep the topsoil and subsoil separate and pile both nearby; you'll need them for backfill. Fill the trench with a 6-in. bed of 3/4-in. stone.

break them into irregular blocks with flat sides and sharp, squarish edges. These flat surfaces make the rocks easier to fit together. They're also easier to split because they usually break along predictable lines.

Rounded rocks (like the ones we used) are much harder and have a less definite grain. They come in all shapes, but they tend to have humped surfaces. Fitting them together takes a lot more trial and error; you set one in place, find it's too wobbly and try another.

In most regions, Mother Nature has made choosing a rock-type simple; you just take what you can get. Still, there are a few things to keep in mind while filling your truck or trailer:

- You'll need a mix of sizes; everything from baseball-size on up. But don't play Hercules. If it's too big, leave it alone.

- The flatter a rock's surfaces are, the better. Block-shaped rocks are valuable; round rocks are almost worthless.

- Long rocks, which are used as "tiestones" (Photo 4), are treasures. The more you have, the stronger your wall.

- Wedge-shaped rocks are handy for "chinking" (Photo 5).

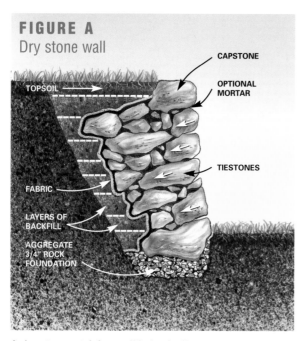

FIGURE A
Dry stone wall

A dry stone retaining wall is basically an organized pile of rocks that leans against an embankment and is held together by its own weight.

2 Lay your first course along the outer edge of the trench. Now's the time to roll into place any rocks that are too big to lift onto upper courses.

3 Tuck landscape fabric in behind the first course, fold it over the rocks, shovel in backfill and tamp the soil down by pounding it with a post. You'll need to repeat this entire process after each course.

Rock shopping

If rocks are scarce in your area, or if you have no way to transport them, you can buy a load and have it dumped in your yard. Begin by looking in the Yellow Pages under "Stone" or by calling a landscaping supplier. But don't just phone in an order. One advantage of buying stone is that it usually gives you a choice of types and colors. So go and browse before you buy.

Prices vary widely, depending on what you get and whom you get it from. A farmer may deliver a load of fieldstone for little more than the cost of transportation. A few tons of richly colored granite from a landscaping supplier may cost you $1,000.

Planning your wall

Establish the course of your wall by laying out a garden hose and adjusting it until you establish the path you want the wall to follow. Then cut back the slope and dig the foundation trench.

Here are a few things to keep in mind as you plan your layout:

- If you have dirt hauled in (check the Yellow Pages under "Landscape") to create or enlarge a slope, it should be thoroughly soaked a couple of times—by a garden hose or rain—so it settles before you build against it.

- Big tree roots can slowly tear a wall apart, so you'll need to cut back any that threaten to reach your wall.

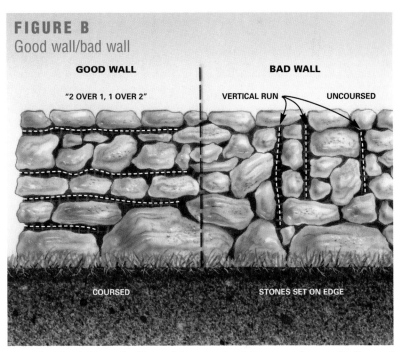

FIGURE B
Good wall/bad wall

GOOD WALL — "2 OVER 1, 1 OVER 2" — COURSED

BAD WALL — VERTICAL RUN — UNCOURSED — STONES SET ON EDGE

The left side of this wall will stand forever; the right may collapse with the next heavy rain.

4 Lay the fabric back against the slope and set the next course. Each course should be wider than the previous. Note: For clarity, we show three courses exposed here. You're better off completing an entire course before moving on to the next.

5 Drive chinking stones into the wall's face to fill gaps or secure loose rocks. Wear safety glasses to protect your eyes from shards of stone.

Foundation first

Soil moves as it gets soaked and dries, freezes and thaws. A dry stone wall is flexible and will survive centuries of minor shifting. But big shifts can make it crumble in just a few years.

That's why a simple foundation and landscape fabric are good ideas. A trench lined with 3/4-in. stone provides drainage and absorbs some movement of the soil below (Photo 1). Landscape fabric (available from landscape suppliers), placed against the back side of the wall (Photo 3), keeps soil from working its way into the wall and gradually forcing stones apart.

Smart stone-setting

You build a dry stone wall by repeating three steps over and over again: Lay a "course" (a horizontal row of rocks); backfill with subsoil you removed when you cut back the slope; and "tamp" or pack down the backfill. Then on to the next course. Pretty simple, but not necessarily easy. Here are some time- and labor-saving tips:

Work Smart

Carefully choose rocks for the face of the wall. If you have different colors, mix them into a patchwork. For a neat, geometric look, lay stones with their flat sides facing out; for a rustic look, leave rounded, irregular sides exposed.

- Building with stone is like putting together a jigsaw puzzle. So begin by spreading out the rocks just as you would the pieces of a puzzle.

- Put your best, wide, flat stones aside to be used as capstones (Photo 6).

- Use your biggest stones for the first course. That way you won't have to heave them up into place later.

- If, after the first course, you have a few biggies to raise onto the wall, use a wood plank to roll them up into place.

- Fitting stones together is mostly trial and error. Cut down on both by mentally measuring the shape and size of the stone you need first. Then go hunt for the perfect fit. You may even want to use a tape measure.

- Stone cutting is no fun. And doing it well is difficult. So we recommend you don't. But if you must, you can knock off troublesome crags or knobs with a hammer and cold chisel. *If you do, wear eye protection and keep others out of the flying-stone zone!*

6 Lay capstones, checking them with a level as you go. Capstones should bring the wall to a height roughly level with the embankment. Then tuck the fabric in behind the capstones, backfill and add topsoil.

Ten commandments of stonebuilding

1. Make "one over two, two over one" your wall-building motto. Lay the stones of one course over the vertical gaps between stones of the previous course; just like a bricklayer lays bricks. If you don't do this, you get "vertical run" and a weaker wall (Figure B).

2. Use tiestones, long rocks laid perpendicular to the face of the wall (Photo 4). You'll need one tiestone at least every 4 ft. on each course. But you can't have too many; the more tiestones, the stronger the wall.

3. All rocks on the face of the wall must slant down toward the inside of the wall. Those that don't will eventually fall out (Figure A).

4. Keep it roughly coursed. If you're working with very irregular stone, you're likely to build jagged, uneven courses. This makes the next course harder to fit together. Soon you have no courses at all and lots of vertical run. Try instead for roughly even courses, by avoiding peaks and filling in valleys with smaller stones (Figure B).

5. Lay rocks flat, not on edge (Figure B).

6. Use chinking, small stone wedges driven between larger rocks, to tighten up loose-fitting rocks and fill gaps in the wall's face (Figure A).

A freestanding wall

A freestanding dry stone wall is similar to a retaining wall, but with a few variations. You have to be more fussy about the fit of the stones. A retaining wall leans against a solid mound of earth. A freestanding wall leans in on itself, so the two faces must slant into each other and lock together. The key to a strong freestanding wall is "V-slant." Each course must be highest at the faces, with a gradual depression in the middle. With each stone tilting down toward the middle, gravity holds each in place and the entire wall together.

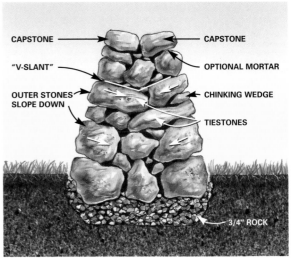

A freestanding dry stone wall should be as wide at its base as it is tall. Both faces should lean inward at least 2 in. for each foot of height. Amateurs shouldn't build more than 3 ft. tall.

7. Make it as thick as it is high. If your wall will rise 3 ft. above the ground at its base, the course under the capstones should be 3 ft. thick.

8. Don't build it more than 4 ft. high. The higher the wall, the more potential for injury should it collapse.

9. Don't make the face of the wall perfectly vertical. To hold back all that earth, it must lean into the slope. A minimum of 2 in. of backward tilt for each foot of height is a good rule of thumb.

10. Mortar if you must. You should have large, tight-fitting capstones that will stay solidly in place by themselves. If not, cement them with a mortar mix like Quikrete or Sakrete (Figure A).

Low-voltage yard lights

Enjoy the beauty of your landscape (and sure footing) after sunset.

—Sam Satterwhite and Spike Carlsen

The outdoor lighting at my first house consisted of two 100-watt floodlights screwed into a pair of sockets by the back door. Let there be no doubt; they cast plenty of light. But they also attracted bugs and moths by the hundreds, cast bizarre shadows, blinded you if you looked at them and—as for ambiance—well, forget about that.

Low-voltage outdoor lights provide a pleasant alternative to this glaring example. They can be strategically positioned to highlight the plants and features you want to highlight. They can be used for safety—to illuminate paths, steps and dark zones. When artfully placed, they can be as beautiful and natural looking as the landscape itself. And since they're low voltage (you can literally add wires and lights to the system while it's operating), they're safe to use and install.

Here we'll show you the special tips and tricks the pros use to install these lights.

Selecting the right design and components

Walk into any home center or garden center and you're guaranteed to run into a towering display of low-voltage lighting. You'll find prepackaged sets and individual lights; plastic fixtures and metal ones; lights you can shine down from trees and up from ponds. The bottom line is, you'll get what you pay for. We decided to pay for metal "architectural grade," low-voltage halogen lights. The halogen bulbs cast a whiter, more focused beam than standard lights—almost like natural sunlight. And the bulbs last longer, some up to 10,000 hours. The metal construction of the fixtures means greater longevity for them too, and we loved the natural burnished look.

As you design and shop for your lighting system, keep in mind:

- Buy a larger transformer than you'll initially need so you can add lights later as your landscape

1 Lay out your light fixtures and wire. Use 10-gauge wire for the main lines from the transformer to where the lights begin, then switch to 12-gauge wire between the lights. To bury the wires where they cross the lawn, use a flat-nosed shovel to cut a slot and fold back the sod. Bury these wires at least 6 in. deep so they won't be damaged if the lawn is aerated. In protected planting beds, the low-voltage wire can simply be covered by mulch or soil.

2 Install the transformer in a central location near an outdoor GFCI outlet. Mounting it on a post allows you to easily change the photocell's orientation. Connect the 10-gauge main wires to the transformer by stripping off 3/4 in. of insulation, twisting the small strands together, then attaching them to the terminals. The 600-watt transformer shown (about $300) has a built-in timer and photocell, two circuits, and a switch and terminals for setting voltage output to 12, 13 or 14 volts. Since the transformer will always be plugged in, you must replace the standard outlet cover shown with an in-use weatherproof cover, available at home centers and hardware stores.

(and imagination) expands. If you'll be installing 400 watts of lights, buy a 600-watt transformer.

- Avoid overlighting. Outdoor lights look best as accents, broadcasting pools of light. Flooding sitting or planting areas with too much "stadium lighting" can make them look washed out.

- When lighting a path, decide whether you want to light only the path or both the path and the features around it. As a rule, the broader the field you want to light, the higher the light pole you'll need. Path lights with a 20-watt halogen bulb at a 24-in. height should be spaced every 10 ft.

- Consider seasonal factors. Install lights where they won't be easily damaged by plows or shovels. And bear in mind that some plants, like hydrangea bushes, sumac and dogwoods with colorful stems, look cool lit up, even when they're leafless.

Work Smart

For safety's sake, call your utility companies and have them mark the location of underground wires and pipes before you dig. For more information, call the North American One-Call Referral System at 888-258-0808.

Pro tips for better design, layout and installation

Take the time to install your lights correctly and they'll last longer, cast more light where you want it and require less maintenance. Get a first-class installation using these tips:

- If your lights come with press-on fittings—the type that bite through the insulation and into the wire to make their connection—cut them off and use the wire connectors shown in Photo 4. Your connections will be more solid and longer lasting.

- The farther a light is from the transformer (and the more lights installed between it and the transformer), the less light it will put out. Avoid this "voltage drop" by creating a tee (Figure A) and running two short lines rather than one long one. A good rule of thumb is to put no more than 100 watts of lighting on one line. If you want to put 10 20-watt lights on a circuit, make a tee connection with

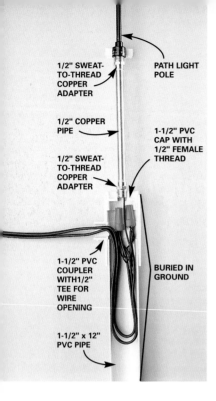

1/2" SWEAT-TO-THREAD COPPER ADAPTER

PATH LIGHT POLE

1/2" COPPER PIPE

1-1/2" PVC CAP WITH 1/2" FEMALE THREAD

1/2" SWEAT-TO-THREAD COPPER ADAPTER

1-1/2" PVC COUPLER WITH1/2" TEE FOR WIRE OPENING

BURIED IN GROUND

1-1/2" x 12" PVC PIPE

3 Construct rock-steady bases for top-heavy path and cone lights from plastic pipe. (The short ground stakes that come with most path lights don't have enough "burying depth" to hold them vertical over time.) This base gives the light an indestructible, sturdy footing; provides a housing for your wire connections; and allows you to make pole extensions of any length, from 1/2-in. copper pipe. If you glue the plastic pipe parts together you won't be able to make the connections shown in Photo 4.

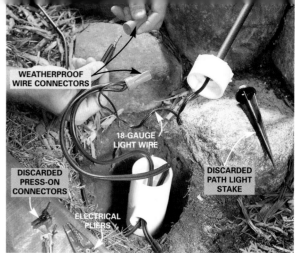

WEATHERPROOF WIRE CONNECTORS

18-GAUGE LIGHT WIRE

DISCARDED PRESS-ON CONNECTORS

DISCARDED PATH LIGHT STAKE

ELECTRICAL PLIERS

4 Connect the wires with weatherproof wire connectors. These wire connectors have a shield on the bottom and a blob of sealant inside that make them weatherproof. If your lights came with press-on connections, cut them off, strip off 1/2 in. of insulation, and install connectors.

CONNECTOR

SHIELD

SEALANT

five lights on one line and five on the other. You can also minimize voltage drop by using a thicker gauge wire.

■ Always leave a little extra wire as you hook up the lights. This will give you the freedom to move a light after you've hooked it up for testing or after you've installed it.

■ Burying the wires should be your last step. Lay everything out, hook up your lights, test your voltage, and look at your results at night before burying the lines.

■ Purchase a transformer with a built-in photocell and timer. Orient the photocell with some western (sunset) orientation so it doesn't turn lights on too early.

Special lights for special effects

A moon light should be installed 15 to 30 ft. high and have one or more branches between it and the ground to simulate moon shadows. Provide at least 24 in. between the light and branches to prevent "hot spots." Make a 4 x 5-in. base from treated lumber or cedar, mount the light base to it and insert your wire connectors into the hollow light base. Attach the assembly to the tree with galvanized or stainless steel screws. Use plastic wire clips with stainless steel nails to secure the wire to the tree every 3 ft.

2-1/4" GALVANIZED SCREW

4" x 5" CEDAR BASE

MOON LIGHT

HOLLOW METAL LIGHT BASE

WEATHER-PROOF WIRE CONNECTOR

WIRE CLIP

POND LIGHT

WEIGHTED BASE

LONG LIGHT CORD

Pond lights are watertight and held in place on the pond bottom by a weighted base. They also have a long cord so you can bury your wire connections in the drier dirt at the pond's edge. To get an idea of the pond light effect, see the opening photo on p. 238.

TARP TO KEEP GROUND CLEAN

MAGNETIC TORPEDO LEVEL

ROCK-STEADY BASE

ALUMINUM STAKES ANCHOR WIRE IN PLACE

HOLE DEPTH MARKER TAPED TO HANDLE

5 Install the path light by digging a hole deep enough so the top of the PVC footing is level with the ground surface. Use a torpedo level to level the light pole and pack soil around the base. Use aluminum tent stakes to secure the unburied wire in the bedding areas, then cover it with mulch.

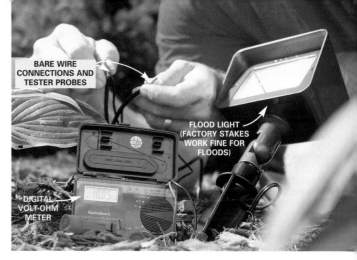

BARE WIRE CONNECTIONS AND TESTER PROBES

FLOOD LIGHT (FACTORY STAKES WORK FINE FOR FLOODS)

DIGITAL VOLT-OHM METER

6 Test each light fixture for its voltage level with a digital voltage meter (about $25 at Radio Shack). Each halogen light should be receiving 10.5 to 12 volts for a consistent look and to avoid premature burnout. Extremely low readings indicate a bad connection somewhere in the system or too many lights on a circuit. Minor voltage adjustments can be made using the voltage controls on the transformer (Photo 2).

FIGURE A
Low-voltage lighting plan

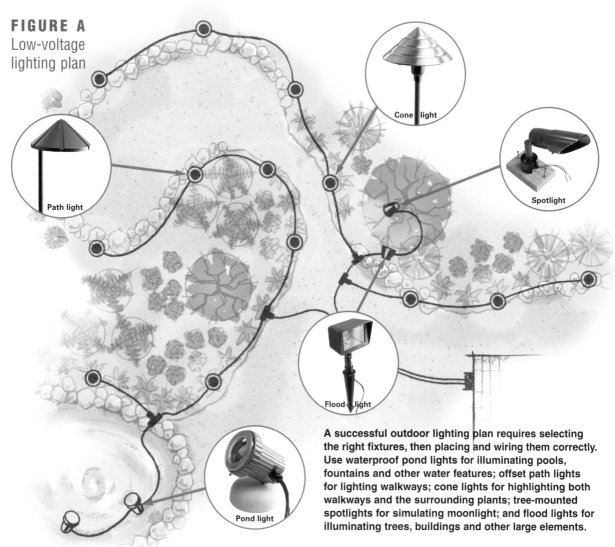

Cone light

Path light

Spotlight

Flood light

Pond light

A successful outdoor lighting plan requires selecting the right fixtures, then placing and wiring them correctly. Use waterproof pond lights for illuminating pools, fountains and other water features; offset path lights for lighting walkways; cone lights for highlighting both walkways and the surrounding plants; tree-mounted spotlights for simulating moonlight; and flood lights for illuminating trees, buildings and other large elements.

Low-voltage deck lighting

Low-voltage systems make deck lighting fast and safer.

—Carl Hines

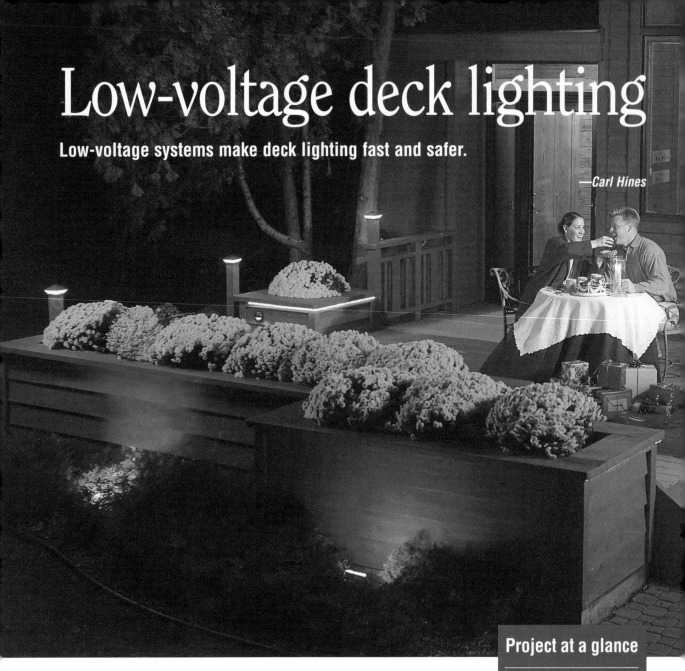

Project at a glance

Skill level
Beginner

Special tools
Drill
Drill bit extension
Electrical pliers

Approximate cost
Varies greatly

I f the night is calling you, pull up a lounge chair and enjoy it from your backyard. Your deck can be the setting for many relaxing evenings. The key is to add lighting that casts a nice glow over sitting areas, highlights features and illuminates steps and walks.

Low-voltage systems do this well, and they're safe and easy to work with. Unlike with standard household voltage, the transformer that powers them simply plugs into a receptacle. In this article, we'll show you how to plan a system for your deck and how to install the transformer and fixtures.

Draw your deck and plan the light positions

There are several types of low-voltage fixtures, each designed for special uses. To decide on which light fixtures to use where, first draw a rough plan of your deck (Figure A). On the plan, note at least the following key features: stairs, sitting and congregating areas, nice features such as railings and plantings and traffic paths. Also note the

The right stuff

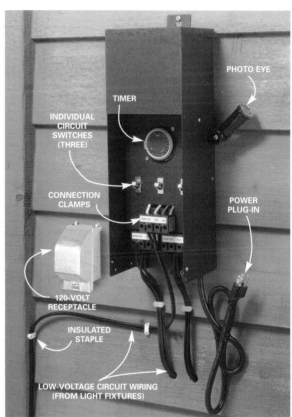

PHOTO EYE

TIMER

INDIVIDUAL
CIRCUIT
SWITCHES
(THREE)

CONNECTION
CLAMPS

POWER
PLUG-IN

120-VOLT
RECEPTACLE

INSULATED
STAPLE

LOW-VOLTAGE CIRCUIT WIRING
(FROM LIGHT FIXTURES)

Sizing the transformer

Add the wattage of each fixture to determine the total load. Our deck:

4 step lights	x 12 watts	48 watts
3 post lights	x 20 watts	60 watts
60 ft. of rope light	x 5.45 watts per foot	327 watts
2 floodlights	x 20 watts	40 watts
Total		**475 watts**
Add 25 percent excess: 475 x 1.25		594 watts
Transformer size: at least 594 watts		

The power center Optional features:

■ **Timer switch, which automatically turns the lights on and off at preset times.**
■ **Photo eye, which turns the lights on at dusk and off at dawn.**
■ **Individually switched circuits, which allow different groups of lights (scenes) to be independently controlled.**

Sizing circuit cables

(Allows for connecting fixtures with a maximum total of 150 watts)

Length of Cable	Wire Size
0 to 50 ft.	Use 12-gauge
50 to 100 ft.	Use 10-gauge
100-plus ft.	Use 8-gauge

location of nearby receptacles that can be used to plug in your transformer.

Take your deck plan to a lighting showroom to select specific fixtures to light each feature. Ask a salesperson to help. Mark the selected fixtures on the plan. Note that a single fixture can sometimes handle several tasks. Next position the transformer on the drawing next to an existing receptacle. If no receptacle is nearby, you'll have to install one. A receptacle controlled by an inside switch is the most convenient setup.

Draw lines to connect the fixtures to the transformer. Minimize the amount of wire you'll need by connecting

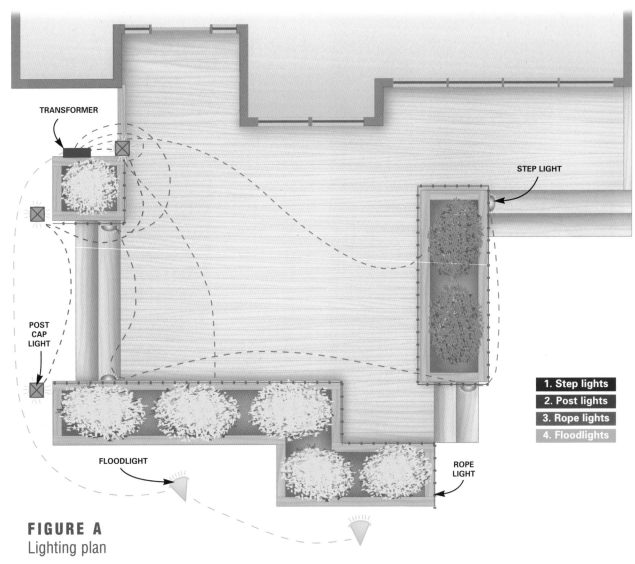

TRANSFORMER

STEP LIGHT

POST CAP LIGHT

1. Step lights
2. Post lights
3. Rope lights
4. Floodlights

FLOODLIGHT

ROPE LIGHT

FIGURE A
Lighting plan

Mark the light fixture locations on your deck plan. Locate the transformer next to an electrical receptacle (if necessary, add one). Draw routing lines for the wiring circuits. For our deck, the post lights (green) highlight the main entrance to the house and light the path to the driveway.

The step lights (blue) add safety by lighting stairways. The rope lights (red) highlight the planter boxes and add ambient light. The floodlights (orange) highlight the plants and add to the look from the street.

multiple fixtures to a single circuit wire. (This may affect the size wire you need. See "Sizing Circuit Cables," p. 243.)

Next, add up the total wattage for all the fixtures (see "Sizing the Transformer," p. 243). Select a transformer size that provides at least 25 percent excess capacity. Also decide what features you want with the transformer.

Running the wiring

Each circuit requires a cable that is made up of a pair of wires. Calculate the total length of cable needed and buy it as one piece. Plan on cutting specific lengths on the job.

Always try to route wires out of sight. You don't have to worry about safety. Low-voltage wiring isn't dangerous. Run the cables under the decking. If a cable must be visible, staple it into a corner or on the least conspicuous surface.

Use insulated staples to fasten the cables to wood members at 2-ft. intervals. The low-voltage wire and the waterproof wire connectors must be buried 6 in. deep into the ground.

Step lighting

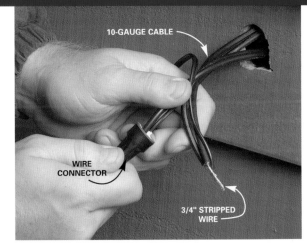

10-GAUGE CABLE

WIRE CONNECTOR

3/4" STRIPPED WIRE

1 Bore a 1-1/2 in. hole from the front side and pull a loop of the cable through. Cut the cable and rejoin the ends along with the light fixture leads with waterproof wire connectors.

Most **step lights** have to be connected through the back. Drill a hole through the planter wall behind the fixture and feed the wires through (Photo 1). Connect the wires with waterproof wire connectors and push the wires back into the hole. Fasten the back plate to the siding (Photo 2) and then install the cover (Photo 3).

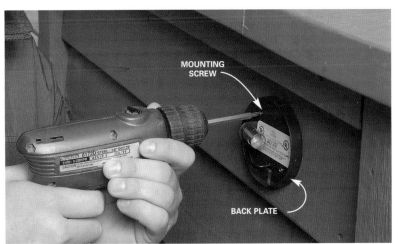

MOUNTING SCREW

BACK PLATE

2 Push the wires back through the hole and screw the back plate to the planter siding.

3 Install the cover plate and tighten the set screws. Staple the wires somewhere on the back side to anchor them.

Wiring a post light

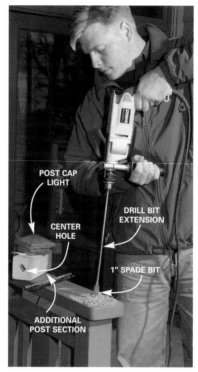

The wires for the **post cap lights** come from below. Again, try to find a hidden route. In our case, we drilled partially through the length of the existing rail post (Photos 4 – 6). After feeding the wire through the rail post, we drilled through the center of an additional post section (Photo 4) and screwed it to the top rail (Photo 7).

4 Bore a 1-in. hole down the center of the rail post. Drill deep enough to get below the second horizontal rail.

5 Drill a 1/2-in. hole from below the rail. Angle up to intercept the 1-in. hole bored in Photo 4.

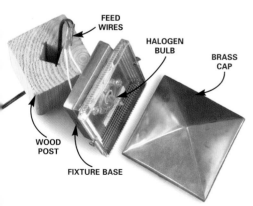

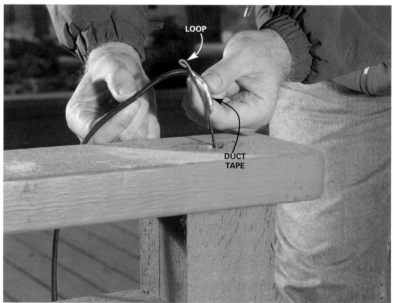

6 Feed a heavy wire or electrician's fish tape through the holes in the post. Tape the circuit cable to the wire and pull it back through the holes. Connect the cable to the post cap light's feed wires with twist connectors.

New-post technique

For the **new posts**, we first cut them in half lengthwise with a circular saw, then cut a groove for the wire and reglued the halves together with urethane glue. Feed the circuit wires through the post before connecting the fixture (Photo 8). Dig a hole 18 to 24 in. deep with a posthole digger to set the post. Adjust the length of the post to the hole's depth.

POST CAP LIGHT

HOLLOWED-OUT POST

CIRCUIT CABLE

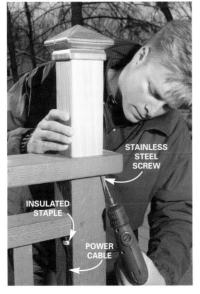

STAINLESS STEEL SCREW

INSULATED STAPLE

POWER CABLE

7 Screw the post light assembly to the rail. Use four corrosion-resistant wood screws, one near each corner.

8 Feed the circuit wires through the post, connect them to the fixture wires with the wire connectors, and push the wire back into the post. Screw the post light to the top of the post, and drop the post into the hole. Partially fill the hole with dirt, plumb the post with a carpenter's level and tamp the dirt around the post. Continue adding dirt, checking for plumb and tamping until the hole is completely filled. Cover the circuit wires with 6 in. of dirt.

Waterproof wire connectors

These are ideal for exterior low-voltage wiring. Strip 3/4 in. of insulation from each wire end. Hold all the ends flush together and twist on a connector. You can get waterproof connectors at home centers, electrical supply stores and irrigation supply stores. If you need help finding a local dealer, call King Innovation at (800) 633-0232, or visit its Web site at www.kingsafety.com.

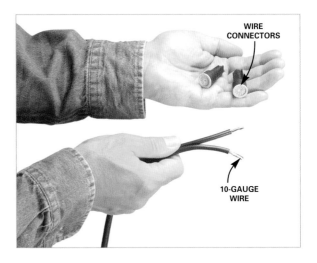

WIRE CONNECTORS

10-GAUGE WIRE

Rope lighting

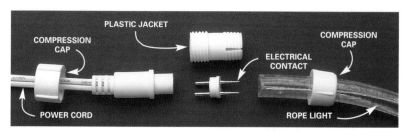

PLASTIC JACKET
COMPRESSION CAP
COMPRESSION CAP
ELECTRICAL CONTACT
POWER CORD
ROPE LIGHT

Rope lighting is unique. It's a flexible, solid-plastic rod with a series of tiny bulbs embedded in it. Calculate the total length needed, add 10 percent and buy one long piece (it's available in 250-ft. rolls) and cut it on the job.

Attach a power connector to one end of the rope lighting (Photo 9). The cord on the power connector then attaches to the circuit wire with twist connectors. You can connect multiple pieces of rope light with straight and 90-degree connectors, but it's quite flexible and we were able to bend it around 90-degree corners without the 90-degree connector.

You can install the rope with clips, but the best system is a plastic rope light track. Cut the track to length and mount it with nails or screws. Predrilling the back of the track and fastening with 3/4-in. corrosion-resistant screws worked best (Photo 10).

Round up a helper and stretch the rope light along the installed track, then cut it to length (Photo 11) at one of the cutting marks. Start with the end with the connected power cord and push it into the track, working to the other end (Photo 12).

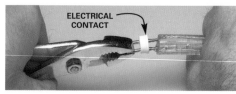

ELECTRICAL CONTACT

9 Connect the power cord to the end of the rope light by inserting the contact pins with pliers. Then assemble the rest of the connector.

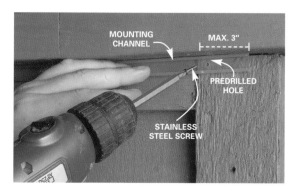

MOUNTING CHANNEL
MAX. 3"
PREDRILLED HOLE
STAINLESS STEEL SCREW

10 Drive 3/4-in. No. 4 stainless steel screws through predrilled holes in the mounting track. Space the screws 2 ft. apart. Fasten the track within 3 in. of its ends.

MOUNTING CHANNEL
WASTE PIECE

11 Cut the rope light to length with a scissors at a marked cutting point; these are spaced every 6 inches.

12 Push the rope light into the channel. A hammer handle or a piece of wood works well as a push tool and is easier on the fingers. Slide on an end cap.

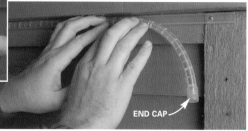

END CAP

Floodlights provide a wash of light that highlights features. Be careful not to direct the light into people's eyes when they're on the deck. Some floodlights come with a hood to reduce glare. A ground stake attached to the bottom of the fixture makes installation a snap (Photo 13). Bury the wire 6 in. deep.

10-GAUGE POWER WIRE

WATERPROOF WIRE CONNECTOR

13 Install the floodlight by pushing the stake into the ground. Cover the wire and waterproof connectors with 6 in. of dirt.

Am I likely to get shocked?

A GFCI (the outlet with test and reset buttons) is specifically designed to prevent lethal shocks and is required by code in exterior situations.

With low-voltage lighting systems, you must install an in-use cover like the one shown to keep the cord end and the outlet dry. The National Electrical Code now requires these covers to be installed on new exterior receptacle boxes. We recommend a sturdy all-metal cover. These covers are available at home centers, hardware stores and electrical wholesalers.

GFCI OUTLET

CORD RUNS THROUGH THIS NOTCH WHEN COVER IS CLOSED

Gallery of ideas

Some outdoor projects are more for function than fun; they create privacy, more usable space or better lighting. But even these projects can be done beautifully. For information on obtaining plans for building the projects shown here, see Resources, p. 252.

∨ Privacy fence

Here's a sturdy fence that's easy to build and looks great on both sides. The posts are cedar-clad, pressure-treated 4x4 posts, and the panels are built using durable "sandwich" construction. Expect to spend $25 to $30 per running foot of fence.

> Terraced window well

Sometimes interior remodeling and exterior landscaping go hand-in-hand. In this case a terraced window well is created to bring in light and provide an easier emergency escape for a basement. As a bonus, you can use the terraces for planting flowers.

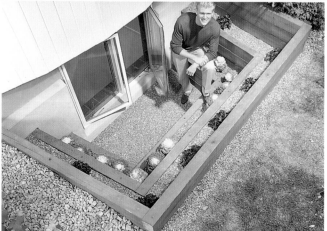

Install a lamppost

A lamppost makes your home more inviting, your sidewalk safer and helps discourage burglars who like to work in the dark. But best of all, it adds curb appeal—both day and night.

Treated lumber retaining wall

Here's a heavy-duty wood retaining wall built from dimensional lumber rather than heavy timbers. The design uses vertical stanchions spaced every 4 ft., with 2x6 treated planks spanning the space in between. One unique feature of this wall is that many of the components can be pre-built in your garage or workshop.

Resources

Pages 10–19: **EPDM rubber liner and black expanding foam** available through Aquascape Designs, www.aquascapedesigns.com.

Pages 20–28: **210-gallon Butterfly pond** available through Atlantic Water Gardens, www.atlanticwatergardens.com. **165-gallon St. Lawrence pond shell with spillway** available through MacCourt, www.maccourt.com. **Pump and filter** available through Beckett Corp, www.beckettpumps.com.

Pages 30–35: **Materials and supplies** available through Aquascape Designs, www.aquascapedesigns.com and Beckett Corp, www.beckettpumps.com.

Pages 36–39: **Water garden pumps, liners and accessories** available through Laguna, www.lagunapondproducts.com; Little Giant Pump Co., www.littlegiant.com; MacArthur Water Gardens, www.macarthurwatergardens.com.

Pages 40–43: **Pond Care 95 Fountain Water Pump Kit** (part #705G) available at www.renapump.com. **Spouting wren ornament** available through www.marylandaquatic.com.

Pages 44–45: **Complete plans** for building the fountains and water gardens shown can be found in these issues of *The Family Handyman* magazine:* Fountain of Stone, April 2005, p. 70; Bamboo Water Garden, April 2002, p. 50; Millstone Fountain, April 2003, p. 31.

Pages 80–81: **Complete plans** for building the decks shown can be found in these issues of *The Family Handyman* magazine:* Wood and Stone Deck, July/Aug. 2001, p. 38; Garden Pond and Deck, May 2003, p. 36; Dream Deck, May 2004, p. 38; Easy-Care Deck, May 2005, p. 36.

Pages 107–109: **Complete plans** for building the arbors, trellises and garden accents shown can be found in these past issues of *The Family Handyman* magazine:* Porch Privacy Trellis, July/Aug 1997, p. 54; Arched Lattice Porch Trellis, Sept. 1999, p. 30; Classic Columned Pergola, June 2002, p. 70; Mix 'n' Match Planters, April 2005, p. 39; All-Weather Table, June 2005, p. 65.

    Complete plans for the arched bridge can be found in this past issue of *Backyard Living* magazine:* Arched Bridge, May/June 2005, p. 38.

Pages 112–123: **Manufacturers and distributors of concrete pavers** can be found at the Interlocking Concrete Pavement Institute website; www.icpi.org. **Additional information on retaining-wall blocks** can be found on the National Concrete Masonry Association website at www.ncma.org/use/srw.html. **Additional information on edgings** can be found at www.snapedgeusa.com and www.pavetech.com.

140–141: **Complete plans** for building the paths and patios shown can be found in these past issues of *The Family Handyman* magazine:* Stone Path, March 2001, p. 38; Perfect Stone Patio and Wall, June 2005, p. 84; Brick & Stone Patio, March 2004, p. 56.

Pages 144–157: **The metal fasteners** used in the story are manufactured by Simpson, www.strongtie.com, and are available through most home centers and hardware stores. **The steel straps** at the top plate and on the roofing are Simpson No. LSTA12. The angles for the rafter hold-downs are Simpson No. A23. The standoffs are Simpson No. APS4.

The Carriage House Shangles are made by CertainTeed, www.certainteed.com.

Pages 178–181: **Complete plans** for building the sheds and gazebos shown can be found in these past issues of *The Family Handyman* magazine:* School-house Storage Shed, July/Aug 2005, p. 36; Craftsman Screenhouse, September 1998, p. 32; Cottage-Style Shed, Sept. 2002, p. 44; Craftsman Storage Shed, June 2001, p. 32; Stone-and-Timber Yard Shed, March 1996, p. 30; Outdoor Living Room, June 2002, p. 34; Screened Patio, July/Aug, 1998, p. 32; Ultimate Garden Shed, July/Aug 2003, p. 26.

Page 223: **The blocks used in this project** are manufactured by Versa-Lok; www.versalok.com.

Pages 250–251: **Complete plans** for building the fences, walls and lighting structures shown can be found in these past issues of *The Family Handyman* magazine:* Privacy Fence, May 2005, p. 70; Treated-Lumber Retaining Wall, Sept. 2000, p. 42; Terraced Window Well, March 2001, p. 80; Lamppost, October 1998, p. 66.

*Back issues are available at most public libraries.

Index

Nails

Nail lengths are identified by numbers from 4 to 60 followed by the letter "d" which stands for "penny." The imperial and metric equivalents are listed here.

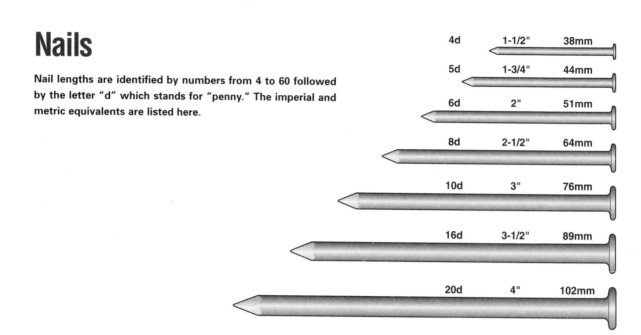

Penny	Inches	Millimeters
4d	1-1/2"	38mm
5d	1-3/4"	44mm
6d	2"	51mm
8d	2-1/2"	64mm
10d	3"	76mm
16d	3-1/2"	89mm
20d	4"	102mm

Fractions and metric equivalents

Fractional inches

Inches (in.)	1/64	1/32	1/25	1/16	1/8	1/4	3/8	2/5	1/2	5/8	3/4	7/8
Millimeters (mm)*	0.40	0.79	1.0	1.59	3.18	6.35	9.53	10	12.7	15.9	19.1	22.2
Centimeters (cm)*							0.95	1	1.27	1.59	1.91	2.22

Whole inches (1–12)

Inches (in.)	1	2	3	4	5	6	7	8	9	10	11	12
Feet (ft.)												1
Millimeters (mm)*	25.4	50.8	76.2	101.6	127	152	178	203	229	254	279	305
Centimeters (cm)*	2.54	5.08	7.62	10.16	12.7	15.2	17.8	20.3	22.9	25.4	27.9	30.5
Meters (m)*												.30

Selected large measurements

Inches (in.)	36	39.4
Feet (ft.)	3	3-1/4†
Yards (yd.)	1	1-1/12†
Millimeters (mm)*	914	1,000
Centimeters (cm)*	91.4	100
Meters (m)*	.91	1.00

*Metric values are rounded off. †Approximate fractions.